Literature into Film

Literature into Film

Theory and Practical Approaches

LINDA COSTANZO CAHIR

FOREWORD BY JAMES M. WELSH

McFarland & Company, Inc., Publishers
Jefferson, North Carolina, and London

Library of Congress Cataloguing-in-Publication Data

Cahir, Linda Costanzo.
    Literature into film : theory and practical approaches /
Linda Costanzo Cahir ; foreword by James M. Welsh.
        p.   cm.
    Includes bibliographical references and index.

    ISBN-13: 978-0-7864-2597-6
    softcover : 50# alkaline paper ∞

    1. Film adaptations — History and criticism.
    2. Film adaptations — Catalogs.   I. Title.
    PN1997.85.C25   2006
    791.43'6 — dc22   2006003234

British Library cataloguing data are available

Cover Photograph: Elijah Wood as Frodo Baggins in *Lord of the Rings:
The Fellowship of the Ring* (2001); Newline Cinema/Photofest

Manufactured in the United States of America

*McFarland & Company, Inc., Publishers
    Box 611, Jefferson, North Carolina 28640
    www.mcfarlandpub.com*

To Stephen and Clare,
on every page and in every frame

Table of Contents

Foreword

by James M. Welsh

"What is truth?" said jesting Pilate, and would not stay for an answer.
— Sir Francis Bacon, "Of Truth"

In reviewing Edward Champlin's biography of Nero (Harvard University Press, 2003) for the *Washington Post*'s "Book World" supplement (30 November 2003), Jonathan Yardley was moved to consider "the elusiveness of historical truth" in a book devoted to an emperor who has been badly misrepresented as an "unbalanced, egomaniacal monster." The "truth" was far more complex, the biographer suggested, if in fact even knowable, since sources are subject to "distortion, selectivity, inaccuracy and just plain bias." But to quote Champlin accurately, not the "truth" but the "reality was more complex." Of course, in a postmodern world, many would not worry obsessively about truth, since they would prefer to think that "truth" is a figment of the imagination, and postmodern sophisticates would not care a fig for a figment. For many contemporary "critics" there simply are no absolutes. Moreover, the "truth" is spun daily by the Orwellian handlers of the president of the United States, who are experts at mass hysteria and deception. Of course, such people would be cynical and suspicious about notions of truth.

Perhaps, therefore, it is bootless to seek historical, biographical, or even fictive "truths" or to worry about the issue of "fidelity" when historical events or personages or fictional narratives are adapted to the screen. Granted, but should not one question the accuracy of such stories or histories? Can there — or *should* there — be any more central issue in the field of adaptation studies? Even for non-believers and infidels?

Some would assert that film is about manipulation and illusion, not

1

truth or reality. Others of us would like to believe that the possibility of Truth in the abstract may still exist, and that Fidelity is both admirable and desirable. Even that icon from the enemy camp, Christian Metz, believed that "'cinematographic language' is first of all [concerned with] the literalness of a plot" (Eberwein 192). Theorists cannot stand to be limited by "literal" constraints, however, and would therefore not admit to being impressed by a merely "literal" adaptation.

The issue can easily be framed in an *auteur* context if one looks to the example of *Rebecca*, adapted for the screen by Robert E. Sherwood and Joan Harrison from the novel by Daphne du Maurier. *Rebecca* was the first film Alfred Hitchcock directed in America for producer David O. Selznick. Du Maurier was not at all pleased to have the project in Hitchcock's hands because she did not believe the developing *auteur* had been properly respectful in filming her first novel, *Jamaica Inn* (1939), adapted by Joan Harrison and Sidney Gilliat, with additional dialogue provided by novelist J.B. Priestley. She expected better treatment with *Rebecca*, and Selznick was determined to protect her future interests and integrity. Selznick assigned the Pulitzer Prize–winning playwright Robert Sherwood as the lead screenwriter over Hitchcock regular Joan Harrison; no doubt Sherwood's contribution (and prestige) helped to earn Selznick the Academy Award nomination.

At any rate, Selznick was determined to harness Hitchcock's tendency to manipulate the source novel, as he had done with *Jamaica Inn*. Selznick made his position perfectly clear in a memo dated June 12, 1939: "We bought *Rebecca*, and we intend to make *Rebecca*." And the battle was joined, with both Hitchcock and Selznick seeking *auteur* status. As Tom Leitch has described the conflict in *The Encyclopedia of Alfred Hitchcock*, the producer and the director had distinctly different notions about how to proceed: "Selznick's allegiance [was] to an American tradition of quality based on fidelity to acknowledged literary classics and popular successes, Hitchcock's to the generic formulas that subordinated character to situation and the flair for witty visual exposition that had served him so well in England." Selznick apparently won the battle (the film was nominated for eleven Academy Awards, after all, and then won Best Picture); but Hitchcock ultimately won the war, when the *auteur* theory emerged in France in the late 1950s and in America a few years later. Old Hollywood was changing; the studio era with its all-powerful producers, like Selznick and Thalberg, was drawing to a close.

As an *auteur* director, Hitchcock was not overly concerned about being faithful to his sources. Consider, for example, the changes he made to Joseph Conrad's *The Secret Agent* as he turned it into *Sabotage* (1936), a film that would teach him the consequences of sacrificing an endearing character in order to maintain suspense. Christopher Hampton remade the film decades later in an adaptation carefully guided by notions of fidelity, but this "faithful" treatment hardly replaced the Hitchcock classic.

One tends not to think of Hitchcock as an adaptor, however, since usually he did not assail the work of writers of the magnitude of Joseph Conrad, or the popularity of Dame Daphne du Maurier. But Hitchcock did adapt drama as well as fiction. *Rope* (1948), for example, was adapted for Hitchcock by Hume Cronyn and Arthur Laurents from the play by Patrick Hamilton; the film is famous more for its dramatic irony, style and technique (most notably for its inventive long takes) than for its box-office success. A second dramatic adaptation, *Dial M for Murder* (1954), adapted by Frederick Knott from his own play, proved more popular, but was famous mainly for its gimmickry. Its 3-D cinematography (courtesy of Robert Burks) was a potentially interesting departure, none the less, for its attempt to place viewers more convincingly within the mise-en-scène. These were interesting experiments, but Hitchcock's best work was still to come. His films stood apart from their sources.

Old Hollywood, then, cared about the issue of fidelity, not especially out of respect for literature or those who created it, but in order to avoid disappointing readers who knew what they wanted and expected. This concern, for example, might explain the uninspired literalness of the Harry Potter movies. Selznick's own *Gone with the Wind*, on the other hand, might be called an example of *inspired* literalness. The more purely "literary" the achievement of the source novel, the less likely it is to be effectively or "faithfully" adapted to the screen.

Jack Clayton's *The Great Gatsby* (1973), adapted to the screen by no less a talent than Francis Ford Coppola, catches the flavor, the music, the amorality of the 1920s well enough, but it mistakes F. Scott Fitzgerald's satire of American optimism and materialism for a romance and misfires accordingly. It is partially salvaged, perhaps, by the casting of Mia Farrow as Daisy Buchanan (whose voice cannot sound "like money") and Robert Redford as Jay Gatsby. Redford may get away with wearing a ridiculous pink suit, but he is never convincing as a bootlegger who has "business connections" with the gambler who fixed the World Series of 1919. By his very presence, Redford sanitizes a role, whether it be Jay Gatsby or Roy Hobbes in Barry Levinson's crowd-pleasing adaptation of Bernard Malamud's *The Natural* (1984). And that scrubbed image consequently changes the nature of the character (in both instances) and the meaning of the story itself. Whereas Clayton's *Gatsby* merely fizzled away every so gradually and boringly, Levinson's *The Natural* completely reversed the corrupt and failed conclusion of Malamud's novel in its desperate attempt to demonstrate the possibility of second chances. "Repeat the past?" as Gatsby asserted to Nick Carraway. "Of course you can!" Of course Gatsby couldn't repeat the past in his own lifetime, but ten years later Redford could, as Roy Hobbes in the *The Natural.*

These flawed movie adaptations — or "translations," to use the language Linda Cahir employs in this text — at least played for high stakes. In the first instance, *Gatsby* was crippled by its misplaced fidelity to the original; in the second, *The Natural* was a popular success, but only because it threw any notion of fidelity to the winds. "More important than such faithfulness," however, as André Bazin wrote, "is knowing whether the cinema can integrate the powers of the novel (let's be cautious: at least a novel of the classical kind), and whether it can, beyond the spectacle, interest us less through the representation of events than through our comprehension of them" (7).

For those of us who have thought long and hard about the problems and the process of cinematic translation, the question of fidelity still lingers, since for those attuned to literature and drama, the adaptation will demonstrate what the medium of film can or cannot do, depending upon the imagination of the director and screenwriter. How was the story told? How is it re-told? Is point of view a particular problem because of a first-person narrator (however limited by relationship or circumstance) or a third-person omniscient narrator? Is the story completely told? If not, has it been intelligently abridged, but, if so, what was lost? Do the characters appear much as most readers might expect? Has the thesis or meaning been changed, and, if so, to what degree? Has fidelity to tone and nuance been scrupulously observed? (Consider, for example, Francis Ford Coppola's so-called *Bram Stoker's Dracula* [1992], which turns Lucy Westenra into a slovenly and randy aristocratic tart whose language and behavior is simply over the top by polite Victorian drawing-room standards.) Finally, has the film translation been true to the "spirit" of the original (subjective and problematic though such an assessment may be)?

Consider, as a final example, the case of John Lee Hancock's *The Alamo* (2004). Adapted from history, colored by myth and legend, this film faces not a "literary" challenge, but an historic one, since youngsters raised on this adaptation will no doubt "Remember the Alamo!" accordingly. Did screenwriters Leslie Bohem and Stephen Gaghan and director John Lee Hancock get the story right? Were the characters dressed as they might have been in 1836? Was the casting "right"? Was Santa Anna, who called himself the "Napoleon of the West," as vain and as cowardly, for example, as the actor Emilio Echevarria makes him seem? Did "Jim" Bowie and "Davy" Crockett die as heroically as Jason Patric and Billy Bob Thornton represented them in the film? Does it matter? Isn't it "only a movie," as Alfred Hitchcock once advised a disturbed actress?

Well, yes, not to put too fine a point on it. Historical accuracy (which is to say, historical truth) *does* matter, or it should, if students are to have any real appreciation of Texican history, just as their understanding of *The Great Gatsby* or *The Natural* or Edith Wharton's *The Age of Innocence* or *The House of Mirth* or even *Gone with the Wind* will be influenced by the Hollywood treatment. A good film translation doesn't necessarily have to be exactly "by the book," but many will expect it to be close to the book, rather than an utter betrayal. Celluloid is a notoriously unstable medium in terms of film preservation, but it is a powerful one that makes an impact. All the reading one does of Texan and Mexican history could well be obliterated by the icon of Fess Parker as "The King of the Wild Frontier" for an earlier generation of students raised on television images, or of Billy Bob Thornton as "David" Crockett in John Lee Hancock's *The Alamo*, who might rather fiddle than fight. Likewise, students who have seen *Bram Stoker's Dracula* will have an oddly skewed impression of the relationship between Mina Murray and "Vlad" because Coppola's odd screenplay goes beyond the novel to suggest that Mina is somehow the reincarnation of the Count's wife Elizabeta, who, the newly invented prologue suggests, died a suicide in the Middle Ages while Vlad was out impaling Turks. Cinema is wonderful, and film can be entertaining, but pedagogically it needs to be approached carefully. Fidelity, accuracy, and truth are all important measuring devices that should not be neglected in evaluating a film translated from a literary or dramatic source.

— James M. Welsh
Editor, *Literature/Film Quarterly*

Works Cited

Bazin, André, "*M. Ripois*, with or without nemesis," trans. Bert Cardullo. *Literature/Film Quarterly* 30:1 (2002): 7.

Eberwein, Robert T., "Christian Metz," in *Defining Cinema*. Peter Lehman, ed. New Brunswick, NJ: Rutgers University Press, 1997: 189–206.

Leitch, Thomas M. *The Encyclopedia of Alfred Hitchcock*. New York: Facts on File, 2002.

Thompson, Frank. *The Alamo: The Illustrated Story of the Epic Film*. New York: Newmarket Press, 2004.

Preface

"Content grows from language," film critic Pauline Kael reminds us (*For Keeps* xxii). In other words, we often do not know exactly what we think about a matter until we sit down and write about it. Kael saw this as particularly applicable to the process of writing about movies, since we experience a film as it unrolls, viewing it at the filmmakers' pace, with little time to process what we are seeing. Afterwards, we reflect on the experience, and reflection through writing helps to clarify our position on the film.

Writing about film is similar to writing about astrophysics or plumbing in that all writers need to know something about the subject matter they are discussing. In order to write meaningfully about films, we need sufficient knowledge to structure an informed response. While everyone is entitled to an opinion, skill and art are required to write — or even to speak — that opinion in such a way that it merits another person's time to consider it. *Literature into Film: Theory and Practical Approaches* attempts to increase the skill with which its readers apprehend, appreciate, and express themselves about film, specifically films that are based on literary sources.

Knowledge of film adds to — expands — our experience of a movie. This book is devised to deepen film and literary knowledge in order to deepen one's experience of literature-based films.

Interspersed within each chapter are activities that film students or enthusiasts can use to reinforce and expand upon their understanding of the material being presented. As film is a collaborative art, several of the activities are interactive and collaborative, and accommodate different learning styles. These activities are printed in *italics* and identified with a pointing hand (☞).

Literature into Film establishes contextual and theoretical bases to help the reader understand the complex relationships that exist among various genres of literature and the films that have been made from them. It specifically examines novels, short stories, plays, and poems that have been translated into film. Each of these individual genres raises specific issues that filmmakers must consider when translating the literary work to the screen. This book provides a general overview of these considerations; then it moves to case studies, examining specific film translations of different literary genres.

Literature into Film's overall goal is to teach its readers to recognize the specific attributes of effective literature-based films. In the process of learning concrete methods of critical analysis, readers will also examine the more theoretical aspects of this analysis, i.e., the medium-specificity of both literature and film (their ontology), the nature of film translations of literature, and the consideration of the rights and responsibilities — if, indeed, there are any — that literature-based films have to their parent texts. *Literature into Film* guides the reader through all nature of literature-based films and offers a broad study of both literature and film through detailed, specific examinations of some of the greatest literature-based movies. It provides a comprehensive guide to a variety of literature-based films and a mechanism for formulating aesthetic determinations.

Each chapter of this book is self standing. Each may be read in conjunction with or independently of the others.

Chapter I establishes one of the book's basic premises: All literature-based films are invariably interpretations of their source material. The first chapter creates a simple matrix which explains that film translations of literature exist in three distinct modes: literal translations, traditional translations, and radical translations. The distinctions among the three variant translation modes asserted by *Literature into Film* are explained and illustrated with examples.

While films based on literary works are generally referred to as "adaptations," Chapter I of this text suggests that this complex process can perhaps be better understood if the film is seen as a "translation" of the literature. As readers progress in assessing the merits of what filmmakers are attempting to do in bringing literature to the screen, the distinction between a translation and an adaptation will become a helpful one.

Chapter II explains the language of film, i.e., the fundamental structure and components of a movie that cause it to communicate with an audience in those ways that are unique to the medium. The chapter defines the basic formal properties of movies and establishes parallels between film devices and literary devices, knowledge that is essential to the reader's grasp of what filmmakers are doing when they translate a work from the language of literature into the language of film.

Chapter III examines the film industry and the collaborative work of filmmakers. It discusses the studio system, independent filmmaking, the specific contributions of the members of a filmmaking team, and the various steps involved in bringing a literary work from the page to the screen. In considering the role of the director, the chapter also discusses *auteur* theory and the subsequent response of post-structuralists to auteurism.

Rather than taking an historical approach, *Literature into Film* is formalistic, in the sense that it focuses on the specific forms and permutations of various literary and film genres. Chapter IV sets forth, in the form of a rubric, a theoretical framework for understanding and evaluating any literature-based film. The rubric, introduced in that chapter, readily available in Appendix A, and implemented throughout the remainder of the book, provides a concrete way of exploring the aesthetic merits of all literature-based films and raises important questions in the process. (Examples: Why might it be necessary to create such a rubric? Is the creation of an aesthetic rubric naive? Can the merit of a work of art be measured against such a stable, defined calibrator?) The text includes clearly-phrased theoretical issues and provides specific techniques and systems for analyzing film treatments of literary works. It does so in a way that allows instructors to make their own choices regarding the particular literary/film works they want to use in their courses. To help with this selection, recommended films for students, teachers, and film enthusiasts to pursue are interspersed throughout the book. These lists include literature and films by women and by filmmakers from a diversity of nations. Appendix C specifically identifies Shakespeare plays that have been made into films.

The text also briefly discusses two topics which, though important, are seldom considered in literature to film studies: (1) the role that economic considerations and pressures play in affecting production choices and film outcomes (initially discussed in Chapter II and additionally considered throughout the book's other chapters); and (2) the concept of the unfilmable novel (discussed in Chapter IV).

Intertextuality is an element common to both literature and film, and Chapter V, "Plays into Film," discusses this concept. The chapter also explores the structural parallels of a play and a film and proposes that filmmakers follow in the tradition of either David Belasco or Hugo Musterberg when they are translating a play to the screen. The chapter pays particular attention to Shakespeare plays made into films, and contends that there are three definable and different approaches to filming Shakespeare. These approaches are best represented by the work of Laurence Olivier, Akira Kurosawa, and Franco Zeffirelli, each of whom adheres to significantly different concepts in rendering Shakespeare's plays into film and can stand as representative of a foundational mode of translating Shakespeare to cinema. The chapter also discusses musical theater, the effects of the Motion Picture Production Code on plays translated to the screen, and the inception of theater of the absurd.

Particular challenges arise in translating a short story into a feature-length film, as Chapter VI, "Short Stories into Film," discusses. Rather than requiring the text to be shortened to fit into the movie's playing time, as novels and plays often do, the short story's inherent brevity usually requires that the filmmakers expand upon the material that the literature provides. Chapter VI considers the unique characteristics of this literary genre by discussing Edgar Allan Poe's "Philosophy of Composition" and explores the methods and means by which short stories are translated to the screen. The chapter analyzes film translations of Poe short stories and the parallels between the work of Poe and of Alfred Hitchcock, who, while never having actually made a film of a Poe work, nonetheless claims that Poe's writing exerted a persistent influence on him. The literal film translation of James Joyce's "The Dead" is set beside the radical translation of Ryunosuke Akutagawa's "In a Grove" and "Rashōmon" in this chapter, which also considers classical Hollywood cinema, science fiction, and *film noir*.

Chapter VII, in conjunction with the information in the preceding chapters, prepares the readers of *Literature into Film* to be effective writers. It offers practical suggestions and explanations for different approaches to "Writing about Film." Writers addressing the complexities of literature-based movies need an understanding of the common, constituent codes of cinematic structure (discussed in Chapter II), as well as a strong, well-trained eye that discerns the distinctive elements of a given film's method of literary translation, the subject of Chapter I ("The Nature of Film Translation: Literal, Traditional, and Radical"), Chapter IV ("Novels and Novellas into Film"), Chapter V ("Plays into Film"), and Chapter VI ("Short Stories into Film").

The Foreword to this book is written by James M. Welsh, a pioneering scholar in the area of film adaptation, the editor for thirty-two years of *Literature/Film Quarterly*, and the author of a multitude of excellent books on film adaptations of literature. His insights provide a valuable introduction to the ideas in my text. I have known Dr. Welsh, professionally and personally, for many years. The stamp of his excellence is well known, and I stand indebted for the power, scope, insight, and wit that continually characterize his work and that his Foreword has brought to this book.

CHAPTER I

The Nature of Film Translation: Literal, Traditional, and Radical

"The book is *always* better than the movie."

This presumption is widespread, but it is less a critical determination than a personal bias. A movie based on a literary source is often seen as a secondary work and, consequently, of secondary value. Literature, generally, still occupies a more privileged position in the cultural hierarchy than movies do; and readers often have a proprietary attitude toward the book, an attitude that influences their reception of a film based upon it. They often are disappointed when the movie does not match their concept of what they have read, not realizing that reading, itself, is an act of translation. Readers translate words into images and form strong, private, often vivid impressions of what the book's fictional world looks like and what it all means; words become translated into emotional experiences. When a film does not square with the reader's ideas, images, interpretations — even simple recall — of the book, the movie is deemed de facto deficient and disappointing, spawning the general impression that *the movie just never is as good.*

Sometimes the film is a flawed translation of the literature (*The Scarlet Letter*, 1995; *The Bonfire of the Vanities*, 1987); but often the movie is arguably as good as the book (*Heart of Darkness/Apocalypse Now*, 1979; *McTeague/Greed*, 1924), and on occasion even arguably better (*The Godfather*, 1972; *The Garden of Finzi-Continis*, 1970). Are such qualitative determinations merely arbitrary, the consequence of personal taste, or is it possible to establish a less subjective, more impartial apparatus to help determine the merits of literature-based films? Actually, there are rudimentary and objective bases by which an educated and discriminating viewer can evaluate a film's quality, while simultaneously understanding that art can eclipse all known standards.

The first step in exploring the merits of literature-based films is to see them as *translations* of the source material and to understand the difference between "adaptation" and "translation." While literature-based films are often, customarily and understandably, referred to as adaptations, the term "to adapt" means to alter the structure or function of an entity so that it is better fitted to survive and to multiply in its new environment. To adapt is to move *that same entity* into a new environment. In the process of adaptation, the same substantive entity which entered the process exits, even as it undergoes modification — sometimes radical mutation — in its efforts to *accommodate* itself to its new environment

"To translate," in contrast to "to adapt," is to move a text from one language to another. It is a *process of language*, not a process of survival and generation. Through the process of translation a fully new text — *a materially different entity* — is made, one that simultaneously has a strong relationship with its original source, yet is fully independent from it. Simply put: we are able to read and to appreciate the translation without reading the original source. If we think of a literature-based film as a translation we will come to see that the filmmakers are moving the language of literature — made up of words — into the language of film (the details of which are explained in Chapter II). In doing so, they make choices from within film's syntax and vocabulary.

To think of a literature-based film as a *translation* of the original text is to understand that:

1. *Every* act of translation is simultaneously an act of interpretation.

2. Through the process of translating, a new text emerges — *a unique entity* — not a mutation of the original matter, but a fully new work, which, in form and in function, is independent from its literary source.

3. Film translators of literature face the same challenges, dilemmas, interpretative choices, latitudes and responsibilities that any translator must face.

We have strong presumptions and predilections regarding the proper activities of translators — what they should and should not do when moving the source text from one language into another. We bring these same general presumptions and predilections about the act of translating to our critical reception of a film we watch that is based on a literary work we have read. If we think of these films, however, as translations, perhaps we can stay more mindful of our inherent predispositions and more aware of how our overall translation expectations influence our reception of literature-based movies.

In assessing the merits of any translation, faithfulness to the source text is the virtue most frequently requested, the quality generally most valued. However, the issue of *faithfulness* in translating is a complex one. A translation cannot simultaneously replicate the resonating beauty of the language and its word-for-word meaning. It simply cannot recreate, in a different language, every aspect of the parent text. To what, then, should the translator be *most* faithful? The question is not that of the translation's faithfulness, but of its *faithfulness to what?*

The matter is further complicated by filmmaker and theorist Jean-Luc Godard's position that originality is inevitable in all cinematic translations of literature. For Godard, an insistence on a filmmaker's fidelity to the literary source is based on a false assumption, i.e., that there is a core, stable text which the film can steadfastly translate, instead of, as he believes, an infinite number ways of readings of any one work. For Godard, originality invariably enters the moment someone begins reading the literature; and the unavoidably original way in which one reads a text affects how one translates the work into film.

There is a hierarchy of purpose and intent within the dynamics of translating. In the large and small decisions that attend the work of translating, each individual translator must determine what is most crucial, what is of secondary importance, and what is of least importance: The literal letter of the parent text? Its structure? Its unique music — its rhythms and sounds? Its meaning? Its accessibility to a popular audience? Its *beauty?* While a translator may want to be faithful to all these features of the source text, translation, at its finest, is an art, with the translator's values determining the subtleties of decisions that attend the complex process of translating.

☞ *In translating a literary text into another language, faithfulness of translation is generally the overall goal. However, the matter of "faithfulness" is a complex one, as there are multiple features of the parent text which a translator needs to consider. With the assistance of the explanation above, make a list of the general features, the issues and concerns, that translators must confront in translating a literary text.*

Determine your own translation values by placing those features in order of their importance.

☞ *In a small group, choose any one literary text that has been made into a film. Read the text and watch the film. Select one very short passage (examples: a scene, an exchange of dialogue) from the literature and locate that passage in the film. Compare this single, isolated moment in the literature and in the movie, making any observations about how the film managed its translation of the literature to the screen. What was lost, if anything? What was gained? What unique slant, if any, did the film assume?*

Much like linguistic translations of literature (French into English, for example), film translations are predicated on a hierarchy of purpose. Translators of literature into film confront the same hierarchy of purpose that all translators come up against. However, film more overtly — more boldly, perhaps — announces its translator's agenda.

Many film theorists have classified film translations of literature into any number of modes and practices. The antecedents of such attempts are in literary theory, the most pronounced of which is John Dryden's categorizing translations into three types: line-by-line, paraphrasing, and imitation.* Film theorists and writers as diverse as André Bazin, Geoffrey Wagner, Dudley Andrew, and Louis Gianetti have written on the means and categorical modes by which literature is "adapted" to the screen.

Thus, while the first step in exploring the merits of literature-based films is to see them as translations of the source text, the second step is to understand that there are different, basic translation modes adopted by filmmakers whose source material is a literary text.

Similar to Dryden's categories, this text asserts that film fundamentally translates literature in three distinctive ways. Each of these three different methods bears distinct translation values, aims, and ambitions, and each regards different features of the source text as most vital to preserve when translating the literature into film. These three translation modes are:

1. **literal translation:** which reproduces the plot and all its attending details as closely as possible to the letter of the book
2. **traditional translation:** which maintains the overall traits of the book (its plot, settings, and stylistic conventions) but revamps particular

---

*John Dryden, *Of Dramatic Poesy and Other Critical Essays, vol. 1,* ed. *George Watson* (London: J. M. Dent and Sons, 1962).

details in those particular ways that the filmmakers see as necessary and fitting

3. **radical translation:** which reshapes the book in extreme and revolutionary ways both as a means of interpreting the literature and of making the film a more fully independent work.

In assessing the merits of a literature-based film, an understanding of the three different translation modes is crucial because any evaluation must take into account the mode used in making the film. It is inappropriate, for example, for a radical or traditional translation of a literary work to be held to a literal standard (*Hey.... That's wrong! In the book she had blonde hair!*). A working knowledge of these three types of film translations is significant also because each of us needs to be aware of the biases — the intolerances and preferences — that we may have for one translation mode over another, as these biases could affect our appraisal of a film's merits and deficiencies. Each of us needs to realize that no translation can transcribe every feature of the source text and that a hierarchy of values operates within any translation, including film translations of literature.

☞ *Read any one literary work that was made into a film. Afterwards, watch the film. Analyze the type of translation (literal, traditional, or radical) that the filmmakers are predominantly attempting. Judged in accord with its mode of translation, was the film successful?*

☞ *Compare two or more film translations of the same literary work. What translation mode were the filmmakers predominantly attempting? Do you find that you have a preference for one mode of film translation over another?*

While the three translation modes occupy distinct categories, it is not unusual for a film to incorporate a combination of these approaches, for a traditional translation, for example, to include a radical sequence. However, the overall manner of any film translation of literature is predominantly accomplished in one of these three distinctive ways.

Case Study: Moby-Dick

What makes Herman Melville's *Moby-Dick* especially interesting in terms of film translations of literature is that, curiously, Melville's masterwork has been made in each of the three distinctly different translation modes. People's favorite film version of *Moby-Dick* may tell them as much about the film, itself, as it does about their own translation preferences.

Herman Melville's Book, *Moby-Dick* (1851)

At the beginning of *Moby-Dick*, the narrator, who asks to be called Ishmael (this may or may not be his given name), describes his remedy for despondency. Having experienced the metaphoric "damp, drizzly November of [his] soul," he decided "to get to sea" by shipping aboard a whaling vessel, the *Pequod*. Narrating the story in retrospect, Ishmael recounts the events that occurred aboard his ship, where he experienced wondrous fellowship, extreme peril, and ponderous mysteries.

Of particular interest to Ishmael are the contrasts of human conduct exemplified by the noble savage Queequeg and the enigmatic Captain Ahab. The pith of the story lies in Ishmael's construing of Ahab's supreme obsession with, and implacable pursuit of, Moby Dick, the great white whale that, in the world before the novel, had amputated Ahab's leg, as well as, arguably, Ahab's sexual potency. Ahab believes that Moby Dick is a force of active and willful malevolence and that in annihilating the white whale, he will be striking a significant blow for humankind against a potent manifestation of evil.

Ishmael repeatedly interrupts his story of Ahab's obsessive pursuit of Moby Dick with digressions which, for a short time, interest him more than his principal story. The digressions include matters as diverse as an empirical disquisition on facts about whales to a poetic meditation on the metaphysical significance of whiteness. Each digression interrupts, without apology, the story proper and creates a rupture in the traditional narrative design. Through these digressive intrusions, Melville demonstrates that the human mind does not inherently think in the efficient, linear, uninterrupted, and orderly manner that novelists and filmmakers often impose upon their fictions. In life, we interrupt our own stories, our narrations stray from the story's orderly path, Melville contends, because associations of ideas carry us, momentarily, to tangents that compel our attention.

Thus, the narrative construction of *Moby-Dick*, with its curious and vital digressions, helps shape and inform Melville's complex of ideas, including his considerations of epistemology, cognition, and human psychology, and, more simply, of how the human mind most naturally engages in thought. Yet, not one of the film translations of *Moby-Dick*, from the most literal through the most radical, considers faithfulness to the book's form as a value vital to its rendering of the text. None of the films includes Melville's digressions.

The decision not to replicate *the form* of the source text is a translator's decision. A literary analogy to this decision occurs in translations of Shakespearean plays into another word-based language (Renaissance English into modern Chinese, for example). For a variety of reasons, the translator may not replicate Shakespeare's poetic form, the instances of iambic pentameter present in his work, even though that metrical form helps to shape and illuminate Shakespeare's complexities of aesthetics and character.

The Literal Film Translation of *Moby-Dick*

One manner by which a film renders a literary work is through a literal translation, which reconstitutes the plot and all its attendant details as closely as possible to the letter of the literature. The film stays as near to the written text as is possible, with little or no addition of scenes that were not in the original literary work. In a literal film translation, the filmmakers are duty-bound to follow the original story. Details of character, locale, and custom are recreated, sometimes painstakingly so, and brought to visual life. The movie stands as a facsimile, the best examples of which are memorable in their visual faithfulness to the letter of the text, at the expense, though, of the creative freedom and boldness of interpretation that the two other translation forms display. While the visual details have the extraordinary force of making us feel like we are experiencing the very world that the writer recorded for us, literal translations tend to fail at plumbing the depths of the book's ideas. The 1956 *Moby Dick* is an example of the extreme strengths and weaknesses of a literal film translation.

Produced and directed by John Huston, the movie succeeds, to a degree, in two specific ways: on the story level, because it does a solid job of conveying the novel's drama; and in art direction, because certain scenes get the dense and salty *taste* of Melville just right. The latter is apparent in the film's recreation of The Spouter Inn, of the pious Bildad assigning Ishmael an inhumane portion of the voyage's profits, of the *Pequod* meeting the *Rachel*, and of Queequeg's death reverie. The film's images carry an evocative worth that helps to convey to an audience just why Melville's work is so highly regarded for its amalgam of detail in depicting the nineteenth-century whaling industry.

John Huston's passion for authenticating Melville's literal details is evident throughout the movie in such things as his world-wide search for a real ship that most clearly conformed to the book's specifications of the *Pequod*, in his painstaking recreation of Queequeg's tattoos in accord with Melville's descriptions, and in his insistence that sequences be shot on a turbulent St. George's Channel rather than a set. Warner Bros. was generous in financing this film, funding Huston's taste for nineteenth-century authenticity with the then considerable budget of five million dollars. In processing the film footage for *Moby Dick*, Huston used a photographic technique called "desaturation," a process by which the film's color is muted (chemically desaturated rather than enriched) in an attempt to replicate, in this case, the visual attributes of old whaling prints. When Huston's *Moby Dick* is projected properly on a large screen, the effect of this technique is quite transfixing; however, this quality is all but lost today on the prints now shown on television and in the video and DVD versions currently in circulation. The effects may be recovered if and when the original print is remastered in a way that restores the desaturation of color.

The movie is faithful to the letter of Melville's work, with the two most pronounced exceptions being (1) the initial sighting of Ahab: In the book, Ahab's entrance is delayed for almost 200 pages, while in this film, Ahab is first seen within five minutes of the film's opening, and (2) Ahab's death: In this film, Ahab vaingloriously shouts invectives from atop Moby Dick, where he is pinned by a web formed of his own crew's harpoons and ropes. Huston's movie was made for a popular audience; and, in accord with popular tastes, he chose to heighten the vividness and dramatic intensity of Ahab's demise.

However, the ending was changed for yet another reason. In his translation into film of Melville's *Moby-Dick*, Huston is a literal filmmaker, who, faithful to that sensibility, makes Ahab's final confrontation with the white whale a literal confrontation. In Melville's book, Ahab does not make direct contact with Moby Dick. Instead, Ahab's death comes about when he is caught in the "igniting velocity" of his own *misguided* harpoon rope which catches him around the neck and drags him instantaneously down into the sea "ere the crew knew he was gone." The way in which Ahab dies in Melville's book resonates with meaning, but those Melvillian subtleties of significance just do not translate well within the mode of literal filmmaking that Huston favors in this version of *Moby-Dick*. Thus, Ahab's ferocious battle with the white whale is, ultimately, literalized in this movie, with Ahab, literally, combating the whale in a bravura of direct combat.

The literalness of Huston's film is proclaimed in the opening scene: screenwriter Ray Bradbury, in collaboration with Huston, rewrote *Moby-Dick's* opening paragraph, which is delivered in a voice-over that translates Melville's dense prose into lighter, popular prose, accurate in a literal, if superficial, way. A less literal film approach would not have needed the opening voice-over at all, but would have found ways to have the camera show us what Melville's first paragraph does: the complexities of Ishmael: the damp, drizzly November of his soul; his capacity to apprehend beauty; to comprehend the relational agencies of history; to speak in poetry; and to suffer deeply while playfully self-mocking his own deep suffering.

A strength of Huston's film is that it demonstrates a certain respect — perhaps even a reverence — for Melville's work through its commitment to recording precisely what Melville had dramatized. However, in doing so, the movie stays on the surface of Melville's ideas, never attempting the boldness of interpretation and the creative delineation that are the hallmarks of great literature to film translations. For reasons about which we can only speculate, it was never the intention or design of the 1956 *Moby Dick* to explore Melville's meaning or to find filmic ways of creating the profound beauty and the destabilizing ambiguity of Melville's writing. As literal films characteristically are, the 1956 *Moby Dick* is a synopsis-film. It is *Masterplots* in celluloid, accurate, succinct, but nugatory, void of any ambition to translate into the language of film the equivalents of the stylistic miracles of Melville's writing.

Literal translations do not lend themselves to exploration of the integral meaning of the parent text; in contrast, radical and traditional translations do.

The Traditional Film Translation of *Moby-Dick*

The majority of literature-based films are traditional translations. In a traditional translation, the filmmakers stay as close as possible to the original literary text, while making those alterations that are deemed necessary and/or appropriate. These changes may be made in service of the filmmakers' interpretive insight or stylistic interests, but just as often they are driven by a need to keep the film's length and its budget manageable, and to maintain the interests and tastes of a popular audience. In a traditional film translation of a literary text, scenes are added or deleted as needed; characters are often composites; and the settings are frequently modified in ways that make them more visually interesting or more cost effective. While the film's alterations may rankle those readers of the literature who prefer a literal translation and who find such tamperings to be either *de facto* objectionable or beyond the license and scope of the work and obligations of the film translator, the alterations allow for greater freedom in rendering meaning.

The USA Network version of *Moby-Dick* that aired in 1998 is an example of a traditional film translation of a literary work, in that it maintained the overall traits of the book (its plot, settings, and certain stylistic conventions), but revamped particular details as the filmmakers saw fit. The movie does a commendable job in several ways: integrating Melville's digressions about whales into the sailors' dialogues; representing the hardships of everyday life aboard a nineteenth-century whaling vessel; showing the multinational composition of the crew of the *Pequod*; depicting the cutting-in and processing of a huge whale aboard ship; and having a helicopter-mounted camera register the glories of standing tall in the ship's foretop on a clear, mild day.

However, in spite of its 18 million dollar budget, the film also includes whaling and historical inaccuracies. In this movie, the harpooners sleep in the forecastle with the common mates. Historically, harpooners bunked separately from the rest of the crew. Since their skills were vital to the success of a whaling voyage, the harpooners were treated as a privileged group aboard the whaling ships. Not the equals of the officers, but certainly superior to the common mates, they were normally given bunks in the steerage section of the ship, between the forecastle where the crew lived and the cabins where the officers lived.

A second error, or a product of creative license, in this case, occurs in the film when Ahab pursues Moby Dick into iceberg-filled waters, a handsomely filmed scene, visually interesting and dramatically bold, but an act contrary to the actual practices of American sperm whaling. While the sperm whale's range would include the polar regions, most whalers, certainly those in *Moby-Dick*, hunted whales in more tropical or temperate climates and would never approach the polar caps. The screenwriter, Anton Diether, did research "about Greenland whaling which detailed how those whalers actually trapped their prey under ice floes."* Traditional translations are free to break away from the parent text, and, in this instance, Diether's change created, arguably, a more dramatic sequence in the film by incorporating this whaling practice in scene.

As traditional translations will, this *Moby Dick* alters details of plot and character in furtherance of the filmmakers' interpretations. Whether

*Anton Diether, personal interview, 10 December 2002.

one agrees with the interpretations or not, this film's changes emerge as annotations — commentaries and interpretations — of Melville's work. They make us think about *Moby-Dick* in unexpected ways. This is most apparent in the manner in which this film construes Melville's characters, three instances of which provide pronounced and interesting examples of the film's interpretive constructions, permitted within the agency of a traditional translation.

One of these interesting alterations occurs in the conduct of Starbuck, the first mate and second in command of the ship. In Melville's *Moby-Dick*, Starbuck realizes that Ahab's conduct has transcended all rational and acceptable modes of behavior and that he is clearly placing the *Pequod*'s entire crew in peril of their lives. In response, the "honest, upright" Starbuck debates the moral necessity of assassinating Ahab. In "The Musket" (Chapter CXXIII), Starbuck anguishes over the "unsounded depths" to which he might, perforce, "sink" in killing the captain of his ship. As he struggles with his choice, a violent typhoon, a literal storm, is occurring in simultaneity with the inner storm of his indecision. In a misery of irresolution, Starbuck seeks guidance from God for what he should do, petitioning: "Great God, where art thou? Shall I? shall I —" At the height of his turmoil and at the exact moment that he voices his heavenward petition, the storm curiously subsides. Starbuck receives the report that the ship's topsails are set and that the *Pequod* now "heads her course." As if yielding to the mystical kismet of existence, Starbuck, in Melville's book, quietly sets his assassin's musket (the "death tube") back in its rack and surrenders to the inevitable course that the *Pequod* and all her sailors must follow.

This 1998 film version of *Moby-Dick* includes a sequence in which Starbuck debates assassinating Ahab. While Huston's film also includes Starbuck's consideration, that sequence, as literal translations will, stays on the surface of the dilemma, with Starbuck's cowardice being the deciding factor. ("I do not have the bowels to slaughter thee," he actually explains to Ahab in un–Melvillian language.) In keeping with a traditional translation, the 1998 version alters the parent text, in this case, as a interpretive act that adds more complexity to Starbuck's character. In contrast to the book, Starbuck's deliberation in the film is interrupted by Ahab's delivery of the moving monologue that, in Melville's work, actually appears nine chapters later in "The Symphony" (Chapter CXXXII).

In "The Symphony," Ahab gives Starbuck hope that he will cease in his maniacal pursuit of the great white whale. Ahab articulates a lamentation over "this life I have led; this desolation of solitude" and sees that

sight which is "better than ... sea or sky": the reflection of his wife and
child in the "magic glass" of Starbuck's eye. In the film, Starbuck decides
against the assassination because of Ahab's unexpected enunciation of his
own humanity, his capacity to love deeply, his suffering passion before a
larger moral cause, and his longing for release from his pursuit. Influenced
by the depth of Ahab and by what he, Starbuck, most wants to believe
(i.e., that Ahab will come to his senses and abandon his pursuit of the
white whale), the staid and level, pragmatic and sensible Starbuck makes
the ship's most crucial decision based on his emotional response to Ahab.
In the film's alteration of Melville's book, an interesting complexity is
added to Starbuck's character, generating a weighty example of the inconsistencies and mysteries of human nature that so fascinated Melville.

When asked about this interpretive alteration of Melville's work, the
screenwriter, Anton Diether, explained:

> As to Starbuck's dialogue and his actions, I was trying to complete the arc of
> a character whom I truly wanted to make more assertive and stronger than
> Melville's passive Starbuck. You describe him as "staid" and "pragmatic," but
> I always saw him as deeply emotional and constantly torn over his duty to
> Ahab and his duty to God, as when he produces the knife and cries out to
> God, "Show Yourself to this man ... or give me the strength to do Your bid-
> ding!" But then he's still swayed from murder by Ahab's self-revelation of his
> own folly and ends with: "Is Ahab ... no longer Ahab?" In retrospect, I think
> I was trying to deal not only with Starbuck's inner crisis with obeying a
> madman, but also with his moral conflict between his faith in God and his
> duty as a whaler [Diether, interview].

A second example of the film enlarging on character occurs in its
rendition of "The Candles" (Chapter CXIX). In Melville's book, Ahab
convinces the sailors that he can master the very fires of heaven. Using the
natural phenomenon of the corposants (St. Elmo's fire), Ahab's performance transfixes the crew of *Pequod*, who become an "enchanted crew,"
believing in Ahab's preternatural powers. In the book, Queequeg's particular response to the situation is never made known; yet in the film,
Queequeg, transfixed along with the other sailors, murmurs, as if in devo-
tional prayer, "Me Captain, me Captain, me God" as he falls on his knees
in sacred awe at the feet of Ahab, the masterfully inspiring *performer* of
this theatrical moment.

Throughout Melville's book, Queequeg stands apart, ever-dignified
within his "savage" aspect. He is the crown prince of his island kingdom,
and throughout Melville's text, Queequeg acts in noble, wise, strong, and
kind bearing. For him to become so fully engaged and so hoodwinked by

Ahab's theatrics is an interesting interpretive reading, one which says more about Ahab's character than about Queequeg's. The film's reading of Queequeg's susceptibility to Ahab's theatrics may run contrary to readers' impressions of Queequeg, though Melville never shows us Queequeg's response in this scene; and it is intriguing to suggest the possibility that even Queequeg could fall sway to Ahab in this particular moment. Such a reading asserts that Ahab is *so* dynamic, charismatic, and commanding that even one such as Queequeg could be momentarily susceptible. In the film's alteration of this scene, Ahab's potency — his greatness — is demonstrated and, in doing so, the tragedy of Ahab increases, heightening the awareness of and the sorrow over what he could have been.

When asked about this interpretive alteration to Melville's work, Diether explained:

> My intention was, as you say, to show the extreme of Ahab's power over the men — exaggerate it — even over an island prince whose cultural values were so far removed from white culture. Note that after Queequeg rejects Ahab and resigns himself to death [pages 133–134 of the unpublished screenplay], Queequeg burns his pagan god figure ... "no more god on dis ship." He's forsaken his own god. So it's even more ironic when, under the spell of Ahab's magic, he embraces the Captain as his new god. Simplistic, yes. But I had to show how Ahab prevails over ALL the men, even defiant Queequeg and, even in the end, the doubtful, mutinous Starbuck [Diether, interview].

The film's third interpretive alteration of Melville's work occurs at the end of the film: the ambiguity of the film's final shots of Ahab; dead on the back of Moby Dick, where his body hangs crucified, swaddled in white gauze, his head listing left, in the traditional iconography of the crucified Christ. This image of Ahab resonates, very curiously, even more so in a post–11 September 2001 world which has witnessed the veritable toppling and sinking of the World Trade Center and the resultant, untold sacrifice of innocent lives for a fanatic's cause. Captain Ahab, the fanatical destroyer of lives, is the agent who pulled down the entire *Pequod* in service to his fanatical vision of righteousness. Yet, in this movie, he is ultimately encoded by a supreme visual trope of benevolent conduct, Jesus Christ. If taken literally, the film's interpretive image is inconsistent with the complexities of Ahab created by both the film and the book. The image, instead, may be a darkly ironic comment on Ahab, whose character belies such a single-sided benevolent interpretation as the Christ imagery connotes.

When asked about the imagery, Diether explained:

As for your third point, now that I've looked at the script, it seems that your interpretation of Ahab's final image as a crucified Christ was unintentional. In the screenplay, I describe dead Ahab underwater as just "a pale corpse ... coiled in ropes" as he descends to his watery grave [Diether, screenplay, 175]. That's all. If the filmmakers intended any iconography, I have no idea. I wasn't there, and the director [Franc Roddam] never mentioned it. I can only guess that that particular image may have been an accident. My visual emphasis in the script was actually on the white whale streaking by, the image of a victorious Moby Dick [Diether, interview].

In keeping with the characteristics of a traditional film translation of a literary work, the 1998 *Moby Dick* stays respectfully close to Melville's original text, while making those alterations that are deemed necessary and/or appropriate to the filmmakers' concepts of what they want their translation to achieve. As the 1998 film version of *Moby-Dick* demonstrates, traditional film translations of literature lend themselves to exploration of the integral meanings of the parent literary text, as do radical translations.

The Radical Film Translation of *Moby-Dick*

To many filmgoers who have read the literature that is the source for a film, the least appealing film translation is the radical translation. A radical translation reshapes the literary work in extreme and revolutionary ways as a means of rendering what the translator sees as most integral to the source text; as a way of construing or interpreting the literature; or as a mode of making the translation, itself, a more fully independent work. Radical translations are not unique to film. They occur in word-based translations, also. In translating Ovid's Latin poetry into modern English poetry, Ezra Pound, for example, employed this radical translation method.

Radical translations allow for multicultural explorations of literary texts, as literature generated by one culture can be explored and reconstituted in other cultures. *Bride and Prejudice* (2005), Gurinder Chadha's radical reworking of Jane Austen's *Pride and Prejudice,* transposes Austen's 1813 British novel to contemporary Amritsar, India. Austen's Mr. and Mrs. Bennet become Mr. Bakshi (Anupam Kher) and his ambitious wife (Nadira Babbar), who is anxious to find eligible husbands for their four daughters. Austen's Elizabeth Bennet becomes the smart, headstrong, and beautiful Lalita (India's cinema superstar, Aishwarya Rai), who emphatically announces, counter to her culture, that she will only marry for love. Lalita meets the wealthy, arrogant American Will Darcy (Martin Henderson), Chadha's version of Austen's Fitzwilliam Darcy; and both fall prey to the same false assumptions, prejudices, and lapses in judgment caused by pride that we see in Austen's work. Most notable, however, is how *Bride and Prejudice* incorporates in its radical translation the values of popular Indian cinema: elaborate dance sequences and music are integral; the plot is melodramatic, often romantically so; the story depicts a moralistic universe where good triumphs and true love is rewarded; slapstick humor abides; costumes are elaborate and beautiful, as are the actors who wear them; and the sanctity of family forms a recurring theme. *Bride and Prejudice* is a strong example of how radical translations can harbor multiculturalism.

While taken to various degrees, a radical translation allows for total artistic liberties. The literature's integral meaning, rather than its literal details, is of paramount importance to the radical film translator; consequently, the filmic rephrasing of the parent text, under the codes of a radical translation, permits — even celebrates — the alteration of any or all details that promote the filmmakers' personal vision of the literary work.

While the radical film translation allows for exciting, unlimited possibilities of expression and interpretation, and while it may discover new ways of appreciating old works, it runs the risk of becoming so fully self-expressive and self-involved that we may wonder about — at times even suspect — the motives for its proclaimed kinship with the parent literature. This is especially true of the two radical translations of *Moby-Dick* produced by Warner Bros.: the silent 1926 version, *The Sea Beast*, and its 1930 version, *Moby Dick*.

The Sea Beast uses the conventions of radical film translation in order to capitalize on three things: (1) literature's ability to confer instant status and marketability upon a movie; (2) the slowly emerging popularity of Melville's book at the time; and (3) the 1920s' popular taste for swashbucklers and sea epics in combination with the ever-abiding popularity of the love story. *The Sea Beast* attempts to be all three.

This radical version of *Moby-Dick* principally tells the story of Ahab Ceeley's love for the sweet, pretty, and very young "Faith," a parson's daughter. The movie takes audacious liberties with the novel, adding layers of story and character that simply *never* occurred in Melville's work. When asked to justify the vast liberties that the film took with the novel, a spokesperson from Warner Bros. responded by saying, "The construction of this early history ... is not presumptuous meddling. It is, on the contrary, a laudable act of critical explanation."

While our temptation is to snicker, knowingly, at the spokesperson's

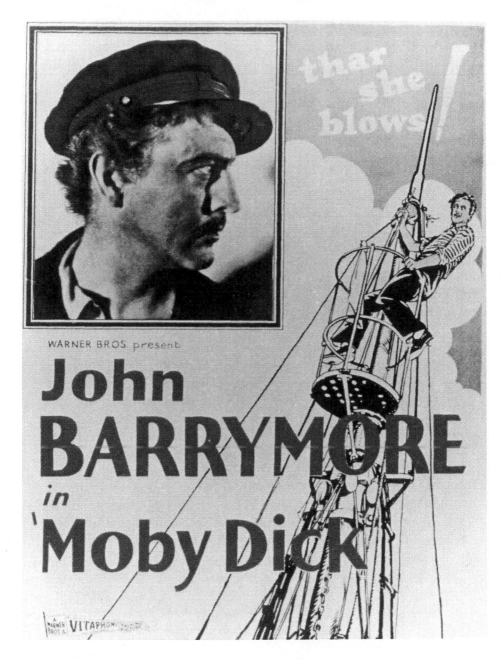

Moby Dick (1930): The original movie card depicting John Barrymore's Ahab as robust, intense, agile, and athletic. The Warner Bros. film is a radical translation of Herman Melville's *Moby-Dick*.

attempt to take the high road in justification of Warner Bros.' commercially motivated alterations of Melville's text, the beginning of this film does construct an early history of Ahab that functions as a prequel of sorts to Melville's text.

In its radical translation of *Moby-Dick*, *The Sea Beast* shows us a young Ahab and, in doing so, makes us think about what Ahab was like prior to his life-altering encounter with the white whale. The film's young Ahab is robust, magnificently festive with masculine agility, and joyously in love. The film's early images of Ahab make its later images, those of Ahab's ruination by the whale, more poignant. In the contrast, we experience the underlying, human reasons for Ahab's rage, and later in the film, when John Barrymore's "Ahab Ceeley" battles the white whale, we have a vested interest in his success.* However, fully antithetical to Melville's vision, *The Sea Beast* ends happily: Barrymore's Ahab kills Moby Dick and returns to New Bedford, where his great love, Faith, waits faithfully for him. The ending raises an issue crucial to the scope and responsibilities of any translation, even a radical one. To what extent, if at all, may the translator recast the integral meaning of the parent text?

Despite mediocre reviews, *The Sea Beast* was popular, largely due to Barrymore's vaunting and flamboyant performance; however, the popularity of Barrymore's Ahab is not an isolated case. All four versions of *Moby-Dick* discussed above make Ahab into a populist hero, a hero complete with the requisite grand scene of grand battle. In each of these films and, oddly, under each of these three different translation modes, Melville's Ahab is reduced to visual cliches. Ahab's charismatic potency and his arrogant suggestion that he is doing battle with nothing less than God are reduced to the non-threatening, rather appealing — arguably, even charming — popular incarnations provided by John Barrymore, Gregory Peck, and Patrick Stewart. Melville's *Moby-Dick* is a perplexing, unsettling work of incidents and ideas, but it is translated, each time, into competent, but pedestrian, film language.

☞ *Read the first chapter ("Loomings") of* Moby-Dick. *Watch the opening of three film versions of the book. Scrutinize the specific sight and sound choices that the filmmakers have made. What was each film translation*

In an attempt to capitalize on the success of The Sea Beast, *Warner Bros. remade it in a sound version titled* Moby Dick *(1930), also starring Barrymore. The plot is essentially the same as* The Sea Beast; *however, Barrymore's Ahab in* Moby Dick *is even more theatrical than his Ahab of* The Sea Beast, *as he uses his voice — which resonates like thunder in a small cove — to simulate Ahab's physical suffering, insanity, and death throes. About his work in this film, Barrymore commented, "Give them torture.... The public loves torture."*

most faithful to? Whenever possible, discuss these issues in terms of the language of film (i.e., the formalistic properties discussed in Chapter II).

Each film version of *Moby-Dick*, to varying degrees, has its strengths, but strengths with pronounced shortcomings, which leads to another question: Do the film versions of *Moby-Dick* disappoint us because the book's rushing complexity of ideas, its iconoclasm of form, its metaphysical intimations, and its daunting length render Melville's masterwork an inherently unfilmable novel?

No. No literary work, not even Melville's *Moby-Dick*, is unfilmable. However, these literary works that are complex texts of form and meaning need to be taken up by filmmakers who have four distinctive attributes:

1. the wisdom and intelligence to understand the most integral elements of the literary work they are translating

2. the technical skill to translate that understanding into the language of film

3. the conceptual creativity and mastery needed to translate an extensive text into a film of palatable length

4. that extraordinary white-heat that fuels *that nature* of creative expression which erupts somewhere beyond the realms of safety and reason.

Case Study: *The Gangs of New York*

Arguably, Herbert Asbury's 1927 book, *The Gangs of New York*, is an unfilmable work, since it is largely a sketch book containing hundreds of characters and scores of quickly reported tales about the emerging underworld in 1840–1863 New York City. Arguably, Martin Scorsese succeeds in translating this "unfilmable work" into film because his work has the above-stated four characteristics. When Scorsese made Asbury's compendium into the film *Gangs of New York* (2002), he did so by conceptualizing the pith of Asbury's work; by getting at the heart of Asbury's subject; by doing so with evident technical skill; by audaciously omitting the largest portion of Asbury's writing, while preserving its integral elements; and by including characters and incidents that were never in Asbury's book. In short, Scorsese succeeded in translating Asbury's potentially unfilmable work by creating a radical translation of Asbury's book.

The film fully changes the form of Asbury's work, turning the book's aggregation of quick facts into a well developed, traditional narrative; it transforms Asbury's non-fiction into fiction; and it unabashedly creates an arresting style apart from Asbury's flatly reportive book. In turn, the film remains faithful to the book's fascination with the times, to its regard for history and historical minutiae, to the book's understanding of human nature, to its unflinching rendering of situational violence, and to its commitment to expose the political and ethical corruption engendered by the unremitting poverty of New York City's Five Points area. As radical translations can, the film may be disappointing to people who, having read Asbury's book, expect to see the literal people and incidents that Arbury describes (i.e., expect a literal or traditional film translation of Asbury's book). Martin Scorsese's *Gangs of New York* is a radical construction, which creates a coherent, fictional story from the fragments of information found in Asbury's historical, violently descriptive, non-narrative pastiche, which was culled from dubious nineteenth-century police records, legends, and solid research. Jay Cocks, who developed the story, concentrates on only two of the many gangs depicted in the book and, in creating the plot, claims to have been "inspired" by a line from Bruce Springsteen's song "Thunder Road," which contains the image of waiting "for a savior to rise from the streets." From that notion of a popular hero, Cocks created the fictional Amsterdam Vallon. Steven Zaillian (*Schindler's List*) and Kenneth Lonergan (*You Can Count on Me*) joined Cocks in writing the screenplay.

Set largely in the Five Points district of old New York (bounded by Broadway, Canal Street, the Bowery, and Park Row), much of the film's action occurs on or near the wharves of lower Manhattan, where Irish immigrants to the United States would first land. The world of Five Points is one of abject poverty, remorseless violence, vice, and political corruption. The immigrants who alight from their ships become environmentally-altered humans, whose only behavioral codes are subservience to the immediate dominant power and survival at any cost. The unremitting tragedy of life in the turbulent and treacherous slums of Five Points is heightened by Scorsese's sparing use of close-ups throughout the film, where we see beautiful faces, human, yet not quite.

As a very young boy, Amsterdam Vallon (Leonardo DiCaprio) witnesses the brutal murder of his father, "Priest" Vallon (Liam Neeson), leader of the Irish gang, the "Dead Rabbits" (from the Gaelic phrase, "dod ráibéid," meaning a violent, angry hulk). In the presence of his son, Priest is beaten and bludgeoned by William "Bill the Butcher" Cutting (Daniel Day-Lewis), the leader of the rival gang, the "Nativists," an anti-immigrant group made up of those born in America, who declare a belief in

Gangs of New York (2002): Directed by Martin Scorsese, with Leonardo DiCaprio (as Amsterdam Vallon) and Cameron Diaz (as Jenny Everdeane), the film fully reconstructs the form of Herbert Asbury's 1927 book by turning the book's historical aggregation of quick facts into a well developed, traditional narrative.

their racial superiority to the Irish. Simply because he is an orphan, Amsterdam is placed in a House of Reform. He returns to Five Points after sixteen harsh years to avenge his father's murder.

The fictional meets the historical as the film recreates the rise of the Anglo-Irish underworld and its relationship to Tammany Hall; the influx of Irish immigrants (at the height, more than 15,000 a week arrived in the New York harbor, many of whom spoke only Gaelic, had no jobs and no money); and the 1863 Civil War draft riots.

Gangs of New York is set in a New York in the midst of the Civil War, where poverty, racial tensions, and lawlessness create an ever-present volatility. The spark that ignites this volatile situation is the institution of a military draft, politically designed to conscript the poor.

In keeping with Asbury's book, Scorsese's film explains that in an effort to recruit more Union soldiers, President Abraham Lincoln issued the Enrollment Act of Conscription (1863). The Act, as written, contained several exemptions, including one for any man who could pay a three hundred dollar "commutation fee." With this clause that favored the rich, and fueled by political adversaries of Lincoln, vehement protests against the draft arose throughout several Northern cities, the most feral and violent of which were the New York City demonstrations. In New York, the newly immigrated, impoverished Irish were competing with free blacks in the North for the same unskilled-labor jobs. They resented being drafted into the Union Army to fight for the emancipation of the very workers who represented the greatest threat to their ever-tenuous financial solvency. The riots, bloody and harsh, lasted for four days. Horrifying acts of racism were committed against free black men and women: beatings, lynchings, and degrading displays of murdered bodies. In response to the upheaval in the streets, the Union Army was called in to quell the protesters.

Gangs of New York recreates the city's draft riots. The film shows the Union soldiers firing directly into the ranks of citizens in a way that calls to mind Sergi Eisenstein's "Odessa Steps" sequence within *Battleship Potemkin*. Scorsese's sequence masters the same sort of potency as Eisenstein's does (see Chapter II). A similar slaughter, a marching militia firing into its own citizenry, occurs in *Gangs of New York*; however, unlike Eisenstein's film, in Scorsese's, no one is innocent — not even the children. Slaughter or be slaughtered is the abiding code of conduct in *this* old New York. The Irish rioters engage in race-based killings, treating the blacks with the same murderous, debasing racism that the Irish, themselves, suffer at the hands of the Nativists. In their rage, they sack and burn sections of the city. (Martin Scorsese makes a cameo appearance at the dinner table in a wealthy home that is looted.) They inhumanely massacre and hang from lampposts innocent black men, while the Union Army responds to the mob's hideous conduct by shooting, at close range, into the unruly band, who are armed largely with only crude clubs and knives. The Irish are clearly out-muscled by the powerful militia in a world where, from the opening to the closing sequence, muscle is the single reigning law. The film cross-cuts between the Union Army's confrontation with the rioters and the confrontation of the two street gangs, the Dead Rabbits and the Nativists. Through this parallel structuring, the film points up the fact that the Union Army's conduct is in keeping with the conduct of the other bands of thugs inhabiting the city; the army is merely another of the many *gangs of New York* who respond in kind to the dehumanizing environment and who rule through might. No one is innocent in Scorsese's film. Not Lincoln's emancipating Union army. No one.

☞ *Read Chapter VII ("The Draft Riots") and Chapter VIII ("The Draft Riots: Continued") in Herbert Asbury's* The Gangs of New York. *Watch the New York draft riots sequence in Scorsese's film. While the overall translation style of the movie is radical, what translation style does the film employ in this particular sequence: literal, traditional, or radical? Support your determination with specific details.*

Throughout the movie, innocence is ripped, often brutally, from every one of the film's inhabitants. Cherubic-faced children witness, up close, the wholesale butchery of their parents; young girls are made prostitutes by their mothers; and pregnancies are ripped from youthful bodies, whose scars are made ever-graphic. Habituation in violence and abysmal poverty decays all notions of human decency, as the film graphically demonstrates. As violent as *Gangs of New York* is, with its moments so difficult to watch without turning away, the beauty of the film, the odd, disturbing beauty of it all, relates in some complex manner to how we, in the audience, do *not* connect in any intimate manner with any of the characters.

We watch example after example of the death of basic, essential humanity in an environment where people are conditioned to behave without the slightest concept of right and wrong. While Amsterdam Vallon and Jenny Everdeane (Cameron Diaz) represent the emerging aspiration to integrity and higher values, they, too, have been conditioned by the violence, corruption, poverty, brutality, and literal and moral disease intrinsic to Five Points. Five Points is a vacuum of values that accustoms its inhabitants to behave in a Darwinian coldness of behavior where brutality is the presumed code of conduct. While we feel a universal sorrow for the conditions depicted, the sorrow is never sentimentalized or even particularized in any one character. This is the boldest move in this bold film.

Gangs of New York is an important film for the question that it asks and for the cinematic ways in which it asks that question: *What makes something human?* The film implies that to be human necessitates a rudimentary understanding of right and wrong. Throughout its two hours and forty-five minutes, *Gangs of New York* graphically depicts how people can adapt so fully to a hostile, diseased, and degenerative environment that they come to resemble rats more than they do humans, not only in their behavior, but, more significantly, in their complete inability to apprehend simple moral notions. The film has a tone sadly accepting of the power of environments and events, largely outside of a people's control, to effect transformations of humans into rats of the wharves.

Asbury's book describes Five Points as once boasting tenements where families lived alongside of the brothels housed on every floor. The thoroughfares of Five Points abounded with thugs and pickpockets, prostitutes and drunkards. It was considered "one of the wickedest sections of the city" as the environment transformed people's nature, destroying innocence and engendering horrors of self-preservation. Scorsese, in his radical translation, is faithful to this integral notion of Asbury's book

Throughout the movie, Scorsese takes on the politics of immigration, of racism in the North during the Civil War, and of New York's Tammany Hall. Depicting the emerging Irish gangs in mid-nineteenth-century New York City, the movie, as described by Scorsese, functions as a "prequel" of sorts to films that portray the subsequent rise of Italian gangs in New York, including his own *Goodfellas*. In keeping with Martin Scorsese's commitment to authentic period detail, *Gangs of New York* incorporates many of the 850,000 authentic artifacts (examples: dishes, combs, children's toys) recovered by archeologists recently excavating in lower Manhattan. The recreation of the Old Brewery (which Asbury describes as the most squalid tenement in New York), the streets of Five Points, and the brothels and saloons is extraordinary. Martin Scorsese reminds us that radical film translations of literature can be expressed through a realistic visual style.

Additional examples of radical film translations of literature that employ a realistic style are Francis Ford Coppola's *Apocalypse Now* (1979), a radical translation of Joseph Conrad's *Heart of Darkness*; Gus Van Sant's

My Own Private Idaho (1991), a radical translation of Shakespeare's *1 Henry IV* and *2 Henry IV* (discussed in Chapter V); and *Clueless* (1995), a radical translation of Jane Austen's *Emma*.

Quite frequently, radical translations of literature reject the conventions of visual realism, preferring to exploit those formal qualities that are unique to film. The filmmaker Ken Jacobs creates an avant-garde film analogy to Hart Crane's poem "The Bridge" (1930) in his mythopoeic film *The Sky Socialist* (1965–1967, revised 1986). Like Crane's poem, which Jacobs had read, *The Sky Socialist* is a meditation on the Brooklyn Bridge as the great mechanical feat of modern times, the display of the majesty of the human spirit, and the manifestation of mystical intimations of the capacity to soar above, while simultaneously spanning and connecting, two separate worlds (the shores). The utter beauty of the bridge is captured, poetically, by both Crane, in his poem, and Jacobs, in his film. Both works show the bridge as holy, uplifting, and awe-inspiring. In both the poem and the poetic film, the bridge represents a hint of the divine in a world apparently divested of all divinity. Both works use the bridge as a means for meditating upon the metaphysical values inherent in matter, and both see the bridge as a symbolic link between the past and the present (Jacobs includes the historical Anne Frank and Isadore Lhevinne in his film). There is a directness of expression in both works, combined with an eloquence, an emotional power, a leisureliness, and, contrastingly, a vigor, created by Jacobs through his dynamic zooming, sweeping, and panning camera. While critics dispute the extent to which Jacobs's film is a direct, yet radical, visual translation of Crane's poem, *The Sky Socialist* arguably functions as much as a meditation on Crane's masterfully beautiful poem as it does as a meditation on the beautifully masterful Brooklyn Bridge.

Other non-realistic, radical film translations of literary works include *Abismos de Pasion* (1953), Luis Buñuel's surreal, radical translation of Emily Brontë's *Wuthering Heights; Andy Warhol's Frankenstein* (1974), a gory, overtly sexual, avant-garde, radical translation of Mary Shelley's romantic novel, *Frankenstein; Naked Lunch* (1991), David Cronenberg's radical translation of William S. Burroughs's book in which the film mixes details from the novel with those of Burroughs's own life and with a fictionalized account of Burroughs's writing process; and *Shrek* (2001), an animated, radical translation that enlarges upon William Steig's short story "Shrek."

☞ *Choose any one literary work that you have read. Think of what aspects of the work your film based on this work would include. Write a two-page story treatment for a radical film translation of that literature. ("Story*

Abismos de Pasión (1953), Luis Buñuel's surreal, radical translation of Emily Brontë's *Wuthering Heights*, with Jorge Mistral as Alexander (Heathcliff) and Irasema Dilián as Catalina (Catherine).

Treatments" are defined in the Glossary and in Chapter III.) Write a meta-text— a reflection on and analysis of— your own story treatment in which you explain what your interpretive ideas and your translations ambitions are.

While radical translations of literature frequently employ a non-realistic style, traditional film translations of literature are, most often, realistic in style. However, when the literature, itself, is not realistic, the traditional film translation will, understandably, depart from realism in an attempt to replicate the style of the literary text. Because these films look radical in their integration of surreal, dream-like, or hallucinatory effects, there might be the temptation to see them as radical film translations of the literature. However, rather than reshaping the literature in extreme or revolutionary ways, as radical film translations do, these non-realistic, but traditional, film translations adhere to the overall narrative characteristics of the literature, which may use, for example, the stylistic conventions of surrealism, impressionism, or modernism. Examples of traditional translations of literature which, in part or in whole, are non-realistic in style because the literature they are translating is non-realistic, include *Steppenwolf* (1974), Fred Haines's traditional translation of Herman Hesse's book which explores the complexities of human personality through the character Harry Haller's dreams, fears, hallucinations, and pleasures; *Slaughterhouse-Five* (1972), George Roy Hill's traditional film translation of Kurt Vonnegut's impressionistic novel, narrated in fragments which incorporate everything from science fiction through French existentialism; and *Fear and Loathing in Las Vegas* (1998), Terry Gilliam's traditional translation of Hunter S. Thompson's savage, hallucinogenic, postmodern satire of the American dream.

More often than not, traditional film translations of literature are realistic in style, a prime example of which is *The Black Stallion* (1979).

A young boy's attaining of his dream is at the heart of *The Black Stallion*, Walter Farley's simple, yet sublime, novel translated in traditional mode into the beautifully simple and sublime 1979 film of the same title. "Did other fellows dream of horses the way he did?" the main character, Alec, wonders early in the book (5). The story is simple: After several weeks' vacation in Bombay, India, a young boy, Alexander Ramsay, attempts to return, via ship, to his home in America. In a terrible storm, everyone aboard perishes, except for Alec and a magnificent, wild, black Arabian stallion, whom he saves from being trapped in the sinking ship. The two are stranded on a deserted island; and, as Alec saved "the Black," the horse saves Alec by towing him through the tumultuous ocean to land, by leading him to fresh water, and by killing a poisonous snake about to attack the boy, who, in turn, saves the horse by finding ways of keeping the Black sufficiently fed. Relying on one another, slowly trusting, and ultimately rejoicing in one another's society, a wondrous fellowship, a kindredness of joy, intuition, and understanding, develops between the two, the boy and the horse.

When they are rescued from their island idyll, their soulful federation continues, despite the new pressures of a civilized environment. With the help of horse trainer Henry Dailey, an aged, but once-successful jockey (as a young man, he rode his horse, "Chang," to victory in the Kentucky Derby), Alec trains the Black to race. The boy's commitment is as strong and true as the training sessions are rigorous. Alec's motivation is love of the horse, which impels him to show the world what he knows to be true: that the Black is not a pugnacious, dangerous, crude brute, but "a stallion with a wonderful physical perfection that matched his ... spirit" (6). Alec is proved correct when the Black wins against the two top ranking racehorses, Cyclone and Sun Raider.

The movie *The Black Stallion* (1979) was directed by the cinematographer Carroll Ballard, who created a cinematic equivalent of the visual and emotional beauty of Farley's novel. Just as the best translators in word-based languages look for *just the right word* and the exactly right sequence of language that gets at the meaning, texture, music, and style of the literature they are translating, Ballard shares the great translators' aspirations; and he succeeds. This film shows us translation as an art.

The Black Stallion abides in pure cinema, i.e., the aesthetic standard that asserts that a film is most successful when it uses, manipulates, and exploits the *image*, alone, unaided (untainted) by extraneous devices of sound. Sympathetic to the values and theoretical position maintained by pure cinema, *The Black Stallion* has a sparse soundtrack, with long stretches of complete silence. Music, sounds effects, and spoken words, when incorporated, are kept minimal. The story is told, almost fully, through images. Camera movement and placement, lighting, shot sequencing and duration, and composition all are combined to translate Walter Farley's magical tale to a magical tale told by a camera. It is not just that Ballard allows the image to tell the story of the boy and the black stallion. He does much more. Ballard maneuvers the language of cinema in order to translate the book's truths of the heart, its mythic powers, its rendering of the inspiring forces of nature, and its profoundly simple understanding of bliss.

The film, *The Black Stallion*, retains the novel's essential plot details: the overall story, the names of the characters, and the locales. Rather than a literal translation, however, it is a traditional translation, since it makes a significant departure from the narrative design of Farley's literary work. Where the book only devotes four of its eighteen chapters to the storm at sea and Alec's and the Black's time on the island, the movie commits nearly half of its running time to those experiences, creating an equal divide between dichotomies: the island and the town, nature and civilization, natural law and human-made law, and solitude and society. In doing so, the film is making interpretive comments on Farley's book. The film is stating that if the bond between Alec and the Black is genuine, as Farley's book asserts, that relationship will survive the pressures and demands of society, as it survived the trials and hardships of nature, free of basic societal resources. Spending equal time in each of the two worlds, the movie *The Black Stallion* visualizes the miracle of the relationship: that it is equally successful when put to the test in antipathetic worlds.

The film also alters one significant detail of story. In the movie, Alec's father dies in the storm at sea. In the book, he is safe in Flushing, New

The Black Stallion (1979): Alec Ramsey (Kelly Reno, left) with his horse trainer and surrogate father, Henry Dailey (Mickey Rooney). Carroll Ballard, the film's director and cinematographer, succeeds in creating a cinematic equivalent of the visual and emotional beauty of Walter Farley's novel.

York, waiting for his son's return from a visit to India with his uncle. This alteration adds the complexity of Alec's loss of and subsequent search for a father, a role subsumed by the horse trainer, Henry Daily (Mickey Rooney). The alteration adds complexity to both Alec's and Daily's characters.

The film also incorporates issues of intertextuality, not only between the texts of the movie and the book, but also between two parallel films: *National Velvet* (1944) and *The Black Stallion*. In *National Velvet*, Mickey Rooney plays Mi Taylor, the horse trainer, who takes the unruly, wild stallion "Pi" and transforms him into a champion race horse (Pi wins the Grand National). Ridden to success against all odds by Velvet Brown (Elizabeth Taylor), the child-jockey who loves the horse, Pi is transformed through Mi Taylor's (Rooney) training and Velvet's dedication much as in *The Black Stallion* the Black is transformed through Henry Daily's (also Rooney) training and Alec's (Kelly Reno) commitment.

Made in 1944, but set twenty years earlier, *National Velvet* functions as a prequel of sorts to *The Black Stallion*, which is set in 1946, approximately twenty years after *National Velvet*. In *The Black Stallion*, Henry Daily makes reference to his riding and training success of twenty years ago. It is as if Mi Taylor from *National Velvet* grows up in *The Black Stallion* and we are able to see what nature of man he ultimately becomes.

Additional examples of realistic, traditional film translations of literature are *The Graduate* (1963), director Mike Nichols's traditional translation of Charles Webb's novel, a film which largely conforms to Webb's construction of events, but transforms the protagonist, Benjamin Braddock, from Webb's object of satire into a somewhat sympathetic anti-hero; *Empire of the Sun* (1984), a traditional translation of J. G. Ballard's novel, in which the film, directed by Steven Spielberg from a screenplay by playwright Tom Stoppard, adheres to the basic elements of plot, but adds darker tones and philosophical considerations to Ballard's book; and *Babette's Feast* (1987), Gabriel Axel's traditional translation of Isak Dinesen's short story, a film which translates not only the events of Dinesen's story, but also the intricacies of her narrative structure and voice, while frequently being brave enough to be silent, to have the images render the complexities of meaning and emotion in Dinesen's text.

Traditional film translations share with radical translations the value of creating an independent work, one that asserts its right to interpret the literary text and to make those alterations judged as financially or artistically warranted. Traditional translations share with literal translations the respect for adhering to the basic narrative values of the parent text. The literal translation values, above all, replication of the literary text.

Examples of literal film translations of literary works are director Chris Columbus's *Harry Potter and the Sorcerer's Stone* (2001) and *Harry Potter and the Chamber of Secrets* (2002) and Alfonso Cuarón's *Harry Potter and the Prisoner of Azkaban* (2004), all literal translations of J. K. Rowling's novels; *Ethan Frome* (1993), director John Madden's literal translation of Edith Wharton's novel (discussed in Chapter IV); *A Room with a View* (1986), James Ivory and Ishmail Merchant's literal translation of E. M. Forster's novel; *Daisy Miller* (1974), director Peter Bogdanovich's literal translation of Henry James's novella; and *The Great Gatsby* (1974), director Jack Clayton's literal translation of F. Scott Fitzgerald's novel.

Consistent with the values of a literal translation, the 1974 *The Great Gatsby* faithfully replicates the details of Fitzgerald's story.* Particulars of character and setting are as Fitzgerald describes them and are depicted with strict fidelity to historical accuracy, down to the crates of oranges and

---

*There are two prior film versions of Fitzgerald's book: 1926 and 1949. All three films of The Great Gatsby were made by Paramount.

lemons that arrive, every Monday, from a greengrocer in New York City to Gatsby's back door.

Set in 1922, Fitzgerald's story centers on Jay Gatsby, born James Gatz, the self-made millionaire, who buys a mansion in (fictional) West Egg, Long Island, to be near the woman he loves: his Platonic ideal, Daisy Fay Buchanan, the wife of wealthy Tom Buchanan. Far from the ideal that Gatsby envisions, Daisy is the embodiment of spiritual desolation, waste, and vacuity. The narrator Nick Carraway describes Tom and Daisy as "the care-less people," the vastly wealthy who "smashed up things and creatures and then retreated back into their money or their vast carelessness, or whatever it was that kept them together, and let other people clean up the mess they had made" (180–81). By the end of the book, Nick Carraway's opinion of Gatsby has shifted. Despite his disapproval of Gatsby's shady associations and dubious means of acquiring wealth, Nick realizes that only Gatsby has retained a genuine innocence and a persistent faith that wonderment and imagination can be actualized. "They're a rotten crowd," Nick announces to Gatsby. "You're worth the whole bunch put together" (154).

Faithful to the letter of Fitzgerald's text, the film shows Nick saying these words, yet they sound ludicrous within the context of a movie in which Robert Redford's Jay Gatsby never assumes the mythic dimension that the character must in order for us to see what Nick ultimately sees in him. Fitzgerald's exploration of impossible idealism and profane materi-alism becomes Paramount's star vehicle for Redford and Mia Farrow; and, in consequence, it becomes consumed by its stars, consumed by the van-ity shots of them and by their sheer unwillingness to enter the depths of and expose the cavernous faults of their characters. The film is all visual literalness and surface, and in an odd sort of way, it conveys the very steril-ity of the characters' lives, their superficial, vain, and self-consumed monied world, by being, itself, the very world it attempts to satirize.

Literal film translations of literature can excite us through their extraordinary capacity to transport us to the very world that the literature describes — to show us, for example, what life looked like amid the luxu-ries of exclusive areas like New York's Long Island in the early 1920s. Lit-eral translations can also frustrate us in their failure to plumb the depths of the literature they are rendering. While traditional and radical film translations are more likely to explore the regions of meaning in the lit-erary text than literal translations do, these two translation modes may frustrate us for their failure to render the literal world that the writer has had us so strongly envision.

☞ *In this chapter, two starting points are suggested for assessing the merits of literature-based films. First, that literature-based films need to be understood as translations of the source material; and, second, that film translations of literature exist in three distinct translation modes: literal, traditional, and radical translations. What are the strengths and weaknesses of each of these translation modes? Which mode do you most prefer? Least prefer? Why should you remain mindful of your translation presumptions and preferences when you assess the merits and flaws of a literature-based film?*

CHAPTER II

The Language of Film and Its Relation to the Language of Literature

What you look hard at has a way of looking back hard at you.
— Ezra Pound

To like what one likes is a valid way of assessing a movie's worth, however, often this judgment is made uncritically, passively, and without solid reasons. In contrast, to know *why* one finds a film to be flawed or fantastic and to be able to see and communicate how it is skillfully or poorly constructed is to experience a broader and deeper sense of appreciation. This deepening of discriminating perception and expansion of critical evaluation begins with a basic knowledge of the fundamental elements of a film and the techniques that are specific to this medium.

Writing in *The New York Times*, Elizabeth Van Ness questions, "Is a Cinema Studies Degree the New M.B.A.?" Film and media images dominate international modes of communication (a heightened example of which, Van Ness explains, is the means by which terrorists and their opponents communicate in intricately "staged" videos). Van Ness asserts that "cinema isn't so much a profession as the professional language of the future" (sec. 2:1). The ability to use, appreciate, and manipulate the language of film, like any language, is enhanced through expanded understanding.

All films share a fundamental anatomy created largely by the specific and defining ways in which the camera is employed. While sound may also be incorporated in a movie and while the various sound tracks (spoken words, music, and effects) may significantly enhance the film, sound is not an essential property of a movie. In fact, for many years (1895–1929), films were silent with, at most, a piano in the movie theater providing the only source of sound.

Movies are fundamentally visual, with the images recorded by a camera or created through computer imaging being their single, essential feature. Images are used in various ways that all amalgamate to produce the particular form and function of a given film; and while each movie is unique in the ways that it utilizes cinematic devices — including sound devices — each film does so by implementing basic properties common to all movie-making. Students of film, like students of any specific discourse, need to know the fundamentals of their subject — its language — in order to move forward in their understanding. Fundamental knowledge for a film student includes an understanding of cinematic structure, its anatomy or form. This knowledge of form is particularly important when given the added complexity encountered in analyzing (or anatomizing as it were) films that are based on literary works.

Knowing the formal properties employed by movies assists us in determining the quality and appropriateness of filmmakers' choices as they translate from the language of literature into the language of film. A knowledge of film trains us to be more alert to the concepts, techniques, and decisions that attend literature-to-film conversions.

Film and literature have aesthetic equivalents in methods and styles. Affinities exist between literary form and cinematic form. Much like literature, a film achieves its distinct style through its organizing and editing methods; its particular rhythms, tones and syntax; and its genre and subject matter.

Viewers consume a film much as readers do a literary work, over time. They turn pages or sit through sequences of shots, with the writer and filmmaker, arguably, more in control of the minimum amount of time that the reader and viewer must initially invest in experiencing the work than, for example, the painter is.

Like a work of literature, a film is the result of the process of composition, the meaning of which is "to make by putting together." Literature and film composition, unlike a painting, for example, both comprise a series of constantly changing images. The compositional structure of both is created from the splicing together of a sequence of smaller units: a paragraph (or stanza) in literature and a shot in film.* Paragraphs, stan-

---

There are exceptions to this general composition principle, i.e., a film including only one shot, a single-paragraph literary work, and, in the other direction, a painting sequence.

zas, and shots simultaneously function as both singular, separate units and as integrated, inseparable parts of the entire work. The splicing together of the smaller units creates the design-whole of the film or the book.

Our understanding of the meaning and significance of the literary or film text can be enhanced through a close reading of the smaller units that form the work. In analyzing a literary work, we look at a paragraph, a sentence, or a single word. Much in that same way, in analyzing a film, we scrutinize a shot, a sequence of frames that make up the shot, or a single frame.

Film is composed of a sequence of still images (frames) that pass through a projector at the rate of twenty-four frames per second. We are able to pause at a single frame (freeze it) and study it, much as we can pause at a single word in a literary work and scrutinize its importance. The frame, like the word, is important both as an isolated, self-reliant entity that yields meaning and as an interdependent element in the entire work.

Like words in a sentence, film frames are placed in a specific sequence. They have a definite syntactical structure; and, as in writing, the sequencing of the frames (which creates the film's particular syntax) helps to create the work's clarity of meaning and definition of style. Like words in a sentence that combine to make a paragraph or like lines of poetry that together form a stanza, frame sequences compose a shot; and shots combine to make the entire film much as paragraphs combine to make a book.

A shot is the amount of film footage exposed in a camera from the time that the camera is turned on until it is turned off. The running time of a shot is called its duration. Before a shot is incorporated into a film, its duration, as originally recorded by the camera, may be shortened, the film material literally cut in the process of truncating the shot. Thus the term "cuts a film" is synonymous with editing a film. Individual shots are selectively edited and then each of the individual, edited shots is spliced (edited) together to compose the whole film. A variety of editing practices are traditionally used which include hard and soft cuts, fades, or dissolves. Shots are visible on the screen as the intervals between these cuts, fades, or dissolves.

A 35 millimeter film camera, the commercial standard for theatrical releases, is able to hold in its canister one thousand feet or approximately eleven minutes of film. (The film feeds through the camera at ninety feet per minute.) A shot in film (in contrast to a shot made by a digital moving camera, for example), therefore, has a maximum playing length of eleven minutes. Once it is edited into a film, a single shot, thus, can be no longer than eleven minutes. Theoretically, a shot can be as short as one frame, which runs one twenty-fourth of a second. The splicing-in of one frame is an editing possibility, but it would be impossible to be seen by a spectator watching it on a screen. Film mythology is replete with stories of short frame sequences (twenty frames or fewer) depicting propaganda or selling products, being spliced into feature films in such a way that the images are not consciously visible to the audience, yet are said to work quite effectively on the subconscious. Theodore Rosak's book, *Flicker*, is a fictional study of this very phenomenon and has at its core the sinister, yet risible and ironic, theme that *there is more to film than meets the eye*.

Film shots, like literary paragraphs, interact with those that precede and follow them. The smaller units (the shots, the paragraphs) are connected in a series (of shots/paragraphs) to form a single, coherent unit of dramatic action, a shot sequence in film or a chapter in a book. The shot sequence, like the book chapter, is a self-contained group of related scenes. It presents a small portion of the overall events that occur within the entire dramatic structure. In film jargon, a shot sequence is frequently referred to as a "chapter" since both have the same structuring principles. They are separate parts into which the film or book is divided, numbered, and often given a title; and they are unified according to a specific set of dramatic, aesthetic, or ideological values.

The final cut of a movie (the conclusive editing) assembles the various shot sequences into their appropriate succession. However, most films are not shot in the sequence in which they appear in the final cut of the film. Instead of being shot in sequence, a movie is filmed according to its shooting schedule which is structured around such practical concerns as the availability of the actors; the need to complete at the same time all shots set in the same location, no matter where they chronologically appear in the completed film; the terms of permission for use of exterior and interior locations; and the availability of an unoccupied sound stage.

Director Bill Paxton explains that in establishing the shooting schedule for *Frailty*, he only had the principal actors, Matthew McConaughey and Powers Boothe, for a few weeks, so he had to shoot all the scenes involving those two actors according to their very limited availability. The two actors, McConaughey and Boothe, play pivotal characters who appear throughout *Frailty* (2001). *Frailty* tells a dark and twisting story of Fenton Meiks (McConaughey) who confesses to FBI agent Wesley Doyle (Boothe) that Meiks's younger brother, Adam, was the "God's Hand" serial killer that the FBI has been searching for. Filmed fully out of sequence, *Frailty* delivers a logical and coherent narrative, created, in part, through the work of very worthy editing.

In making *The Age of Innocence*, director Martin Scorsese had to schedule his filming, in part, according to the availability of real buildings that he wanted to use. Based on Edith Wharton's Pulitzer Prize–winning novel set in Old New York's grand society of the 1870s, *The Age of Innocence* (1993) is a period piece, which adds the complexity of maintaining historical accuracy to the filming process. Known for his scrupulous attention to authenticity in details, Scorsese and his pre-production team rigorously researched locations. Their work was rewarded. The Pi Kappa Phi fraternity house in Troy, New York, was used as wealthy Mrs. Mingott's 1870s New York City home and the current Philadelphia Academy of Music served as the old New York Academy of Music. Both locations are remarkably similar to Wharton's descriptions of these places, as are the redressed interiors of the Tilden House on Gramercy Park (now the National Arts Club), which became the Beauforts' house and ballroom in the film. Filming at those locations was scheduled around the availability of the sites and, later, those shots were appropriately edited into the film.

Traditionally, it is the job of the film editor to determine the sequence and duration of a movie's shots; and a film is successfully edited in proportion to the art and precision with which the shots are integrated. The film editor often works in close alliance with the director to determine the form that the final cut takes.

The director Alfred Hitchcock notoriously played a large part in the editing of his films, and he is highly regarded for the exactness with which his movies are edited. Hitchcock is credited for never holding a shot for a single frame longer or shorter than was needed to create the desired effect. This is praise that, while exaggerated in its literal specificity, is not exaggerated in its critical intent. Contemporary film editors study Hitchcock's cutting strategies, as do students of film. They repeatedly watch shot sequences to deepen their appreciation of the editing choices: the manner by which shots are sequenced and integrated, the methods of transitions used between them, and the precision of each shot's duration. Hitchcock's editing is amazingly refined and passes unnoticed by an audience swept up in the suspense created, in part, through his highly skilled editing sensibilities.

The length of time that a shot runs in a film varies much in the same way and for the same substantial reasons that paragraph length varies in a book. A writer creates variations in paragraph length in order to communicate information suitable to that paragraph and to modulate the work's stylistic textures, its music, tones, and rhythms. Filmmakers vary the duration of shots for the same reasons: to create modulations of rhythms (visual and auditory) and to convey appropriate and sufficient information. Shots longer in duration, composed, literally, of longer strips of film, produce slower rhythms, as would long, complex sentences in lengthy paragraphs. Shorter shots, like simple sentences in short paragraphs, produce a more rapid rhythm.

☞   *Select any film by Alfred Hitchcock and then a short sequence of shots within it. Count and number each shot, then clock the duration of each within the given sequence. Study the effect that duration has on the rhythms created and the dramatic information communicated by each shot within the sequence.*

It is vital for film students to be able to see where a shot begins and ends and to see how it functions within the shot sequence and the film, overall. The capacity to see individual shots is a foundational step in understanding the structure of a particular film. It develops an awareness of and appreciation for shot duration and editing strategies; and it fosters the ability to engage in "close readings" of film. Film, like literature, lends itself to close readings, i.e., the scrutiny of the various details and elements of the work, the practice of which sharpens and clarifies our capacity to see the film or literary text more fully.

To this end, director Martin Scorsese, who regards himself as a perpetual student of film, will study shot sequences of other directors to analyze how the mechanics available to filmmakers can be employed to create the miracles of film beauty visible on the screen. In interviews with him, many of which are available on the Internet through simple searches, Scorsese speaks openly of what his analysis yields and how he incorporates into his own work what he has learned from close scrutiny of other directors' strong films.

Good films, like good literature, are enhanced through effective editing. The editing in both literature and film may, but does not have to be, the result of a collaborative effort. Professional editors may be brought in or writers may edit their own work much as producers or directors may cut their own films. In literature and in film, the final editing occurs once the preliminary work is completed, that is, when the entire draft is written or the full filming is finished.

However, in both literature and film, editing also occurs as an integral part of the entire process of composition. From the first word or from the first shot, writers and filmmakers are employing structuring devices, ever-deciding how to organize — edit together — the small and large units that make up their completed work. Both writers and filmmakers frequently employ an initial structuring device: an outline for the writer and a storyboard for the filmmaker. (Many DVD versions of movies contain storyboards among their extra features.) A storyboard is series of sketches placed in sequence, much like a comic strip, that provides a visual outline for the entire film. An example of a storyboard can be found in Appendix B. In literature and in film, the structuring methods — the design — by which thoughts, images, and ideas come to follow one another are the result of a complex process, only some of which occurs consciously.

The various revisions, minor and major, that a paragraph may go through in the process of composition are analogous in film to the multiple takes. A take is the single, uninterrupted filming of a specific shot. In the course of filming, several takes are normally recorded and numbered separately, and the best one (or a portion of it) is edited into the movie. A director may decide on multiple takes for any number of reasons: a desire to film the shot from different angles, an actor's mistake, a shift or flaw in lighting or sound, an interest in having the actors perform the same shot in various ways, the intrusion of visible crew or equipment into the frame, a change in the script, or a continuity mistake.*

A significant structuring method common to both literature and film is the manufacturing of transitions between one paragraph or one shot and another. Transitions are created through edits that join shots together in a film or paragraphs together in literature. There are two methods by which the writer or the filmmaker edits together, or arranges, as it were, the smaller units that form the complete work. In film these editing practices are called continuity editing and montage editing, but the same, basic essential editing principles operate in literature, also.

The first of these methods, continuity editing, connects each paragraph or shot in a sequence to the subsequent shot or paragraph by creating a logical continuation of the action and/or themes or ideas. In writing, this continuity occurs when the transitions between paragraphs develop in a logical, clear, and smooth manner. A writer will use transi-

---

*A simple Internet search for "continuity mistakes" will yield several sites that list these errors. Examples of continuity mistakes include: Spider-Man (2002): Peter Parker first learns he can climb walls after running out of his school. In that shot sequence, Peter is wearing different shoes on the wall and on the roof. The Lord of The Rings: The Return of the King (2003): Midway through the movie Frodo is hurt and has a scar on his lower right cheek, close to his chin. Several times throughout the film the scar changes position and size.

tional devices between paragraphs to link a new phase of the idea or the action with the phase discussed in the preceding paragraph. The transitional devices used in writing include repetition and expansion of key words, ideas, or actions or the incorporation of mechanical connectives such as: thus, however, accordingly, nevertheless, and as a result. Effective continuity transitions are, ironically, most successful when they call least attention to themselves, when they occur naturally and unobtrusively within the cadences and tones of the writer's style. A writer who composes according to continuity values certain compositional qualities: the consistent sustaining of a smooth, clean progression from paragraph to paragraph and the avoidance of jolting leaps that appear illogical, unclear, discordant, or messy.

Continuity editing in film has the same goal: to have the movie progress (transition) from shot to shot in a smooth, clean progression that is most successfully accomplished when most unnoticed. In film the objective of continuity editing is to create the illusion that the movie is not made up of a series of short, separate shots, but that it is, instead, one ongoing, unspliced (seamless) whole. Continuity editing is accomplished by deploying those specific editing procedures which conceal or minimize the transpositions from one cut to the next, in effect making the edit as unnoticeable as possible. In continuity editing, shots are spliced together to follow the story's movement, to direct the audience's attention to specific objects and actions, and to present and enlarge upon repeating visual motifs. Much as writing incorporates certain mechanical devices to sustain the continuity of the work, film employs specific structuring devices to sustain its continuity. The fundamental editing devices used to structure and maintain visual or dramatic continuity are shown in Table 1.

☞ *The ability to see these principal editing devices at work is a developmental skill that occurs by training the eye to see them. This training, like any training, is strengthened through repetition. Train the eye to see the nature of editing devices by selecting any film and then a sequence of shots within the film. Scrutinize and write down the particular methods by which the individual shots are edited together. The more this exercise is done, the more you will understand editing methods and the more your appreciation will deepen for the skill and/or deficiencies in a given film's editing practices.*

Not all literature and not all films are organized in accord with the methods and the values of continuity editing. Some instead employ (in part or in whole) a very different approach, montage editing. Montage edit-

Table 1.
Principal Continuity Editing Strategies

Editing Device	Description
match on action or match on movement	the editing together of shots to create a continuation of a dramatic action or a particular physical movement across a cut to the subsequent shot
match on a line	the editing together of shots which cut from a line that is spoken to what is referred to by the speaker or shots which cut back and forth between speakers in accord with the rhythms of their lines
eye-line match	the editing together of shots which cut from a character to what that character is seeing
match on an object	the editing together of shots which carry an image of a person, place, or thing across a cut to the subsequent shot
cross cuts	the editing together of shots that jump back and forth between two or more locations, causing the audience to see a relationship between events, which often happen concurrently
fade	the transition between shots created by the gradual disappearance of an image (a fade-out) or the gradual visual strengthening of an image (a fade-in)
dissolve	the transition between shots created by a fade-out to a fade-in

ing is the rhythmic cutting of sentences or shots based on images and emotional responses in relationship to one another. Rather than arranging the paragraphs or shots in accord with narrative progression, as continuity editing does, montage creates its stream of shots or paragraphs based on the associational relationship of one image to another. In literature this montage effect is created through writing techniques employed by literary impressionism and its close associate, stream of consciousness.

Stream of consciousness is a style employed in prose fiction in which the inner thoughts and feelings of a character are presented as they occur. It attempts to create a record of the conscious experiences of a character as a continuous, flowing series of images and ideas running through the character's mind. Literary impressionism is a highly personal mode of artistic expression in which the subject is presented as it appears to the artist's individual temperament rather than as it appears in actuality.

Kate Chopin employs the techniques of literary impressionism in her book *The Awakening*. Bold for its day (the book was published in 1899), *The Awakening* tells the story of a married woman, Edna Pontellier, who finds, outside of her marriage, a sexual fulfillment she has never known. Chopin implies the sexual act rather than openly depicting it. It occurs, discreetly, in the white space between the ending of one chapter (Chapter XXII) and the opening of the next one. The physical details of the adulterous assignation happen "off camera," as it were, in a literary equivalent of film's fade to black.

In the subsequent chapter of the book (Chapter XXIII), Chopin breaks with the stylistic convention of continuity narration that she has employed throughout the novel. She writes a brief, single-paragraph chapter that describes the *impression* that the experience has had upon Edna, her confusion of conflict in the aftermath of her prodigious first fulfillment, her first infidelity. Chopin creates a stream of impressions by linking images and emotional responses, by creating a montage of impressions, where each leads into the next, not by continuation of the story, but by an association of images and feelings edited into the literary text much as film footage is assembled in montage.

Stream of consciousness composition, which often, but does not always, employ impressionistic descriptions, also assembles words much as montage editing assembles film, through an association of images, ideas, and emotions rather than a continuity of story. The term "stream of consciousness" was first coined by William James in *The Principles of Psychology* (I, 239) and refers to writing that focuses on inner awareness rather than on outward exposition. Stream of consciousness assembles free associations, psychological conjunctions of words, and psychic impressions. The writing is often delivered in waves upon waves of words (Virginia Woolf titles one of her stream of consciousness novels *The Waves*) which often include characters' interior monologues. The story does not move forward by means of novelistic incident, but, instead, through slow and meditative introspection. Often there is a use of verbal repetition that may become incantatory. (*Yes I said yes I will Yes*, Molly Bloom affirms in James Joyce's stream of consciousness novel, *Ulysses*.) Stream of consciousness collides concepts, symbols, and images which are so personal to the character (or writer) as to be indecipherable with concepts, symbols, and images so universal as to be personally felt by the reader. The chaos of undifferentiated minutiae and the clarity of the vast importance of minutiae simultaneously spill forth in the character's stream of thoughts, constructed of a literary syntax that, at its most radical, rejects the very organizing principles traditional to continuity narration. James Joyce composed *Ulysses* in accord with the techniques and values of stream of consciousness.

Set in a single day, *Ulysses* is the story of Leopold Bloom's wanderings through the streets of Dublin on June 16, 1904. (Bloom's travels parallel Odysseus's journey home in Homer's *The Odyssey*.) While a large portion of the book is told as a straightforward narrative — Bloom going about his daily activities — the work shifts throughout between external narration and characters' inner responses and meditations. The methods by which this inner discourse (this stream of consciousness) is rendered varies, growing more complex as *Ulysses* progresses.

Feeling increasingly alienated from his modern world, Bloom returns home that night, where he falls asleep beside his wife Molly. The last forty-five pages of *Ulysses* are Molly Bloom's interior monologue, a punctuation-free and powerfully sensual, nocturnal outpouring of her carnal meditations. Molly's monologue, with its musical affirmation of life (*his heart was going like mad and Yes I said yes I will Yes*), underscores Joyce's own affirmation of the redemptive powers of sexuality, kindredness, art, and love. Molly's great monologue is not the work of a logical, orderly progression of thoughts stitched together by an invisible order. Her monologue is not a seamless continuity of story and ideas. Instead, it is a speech that calls attention to its own methods: a rapid-fire succession of images, feelings, and impressions, a montage of words.

☞   *Read a passage from Molly Bloom's soliloquy from* Ulysses. *Scrutinize the specific ways in which Molly's free associations are the masterful work of James Joyce's organizing principles which create associational relationships that move from one image, memory, or emotional response to the next. Read the passage several times; look at it. Hear it. Try to see how Molly's soliloquy is a methodical construction created from the rhythmic and visual values of montage editing.*

☞   *Watch any one of the following:* Grand Isle *(1991) a traditional translation of Kate Chopin's* The Awakening; Ulysses *(1967) or* Bloom *(2003, video-shot), traditional translations of James Joyce's* Ulysses. *In what ways, if at all, do the filmmakers approximate the impressionistic technique of Chopin or the stream of consciousness technique of Joyce?*

Much like stream of consciousness and literary impressionism, montage editing in film often creates a rapid-fire, wave-upon-wave succession of images, rhythms, and impressions. The rhythms can also be slowed or can be repeated. The patterned repetition of images, words, rhythms, or music in a film can create a meditative, sedating, or incantatory effect, much like effect of the repetition of a mantra. The meditative, incantatory power that montage editing can have on the viewer is evident in the film *Koyaanisqatsi* (1983), where the simple repeating tones of minimalist music punctuate the montage of contradictory images showing the "life out of balance" state of the modern world.

In montage editing in film, transitions between shots are not meant to be smooth. They jolt and jar, colliding noticeably, sometimes violently, instead of blending, elegantly and unobtrusively. Links between the shots are not created by using editing strategies that preserve the dramatic continuity, but, instead, are created from the ways in which the images, themselves, relate, or have a relational value, to one another. (See Table 2.)

Table 2.
Fundamental Montage Editing Strategies

Montage Editing Principle	*Example*
formal	a low angle shot followed by a high angle shot or a close-up followed by a long shot
ideological	a shot of a crowd of workers on a Chinese communal farm followed by a shot of a crowd of shoppers at an upscale American mall
emotional	a shot of the American World Trade Center's towers standing tall followed by a shot of the towers crumbling
political	a shot of a dove of peace followed by a shot of a hawk attacking or a shot of American military tanks in Iraq followed by a shot of a peace protest
abstract or impressionistic	a shot of billowing white clouds against a blue sky followed by a shot of an erupting volcano against a dark and fiery sky

Montage creates an association of images in an effort to create a unity of effect. Refusing to construct fabrications of linear, dramatic, pseudorealistic time desired by continuity editing, montage, instead, aspires to create emotional time. To this end, time may be mechanically altered —

slowed down or sped up — to underscore the emotional value of any given experience. The toppling of a building may happen in slow motion to accentuate the long-lasting effects of the devastation; a winning touchdown may be sped up to point up how elusive and fleeting the moment is.

The theoretical basis for montage editing was first articulated by the Soviet filmmakers of the 1920s, who were inspired by the principles and energy generated by the Russian Revolution of 1917. To these early film theorists, Lev Kuleshov, Alexander Dovshenko, Vsevolod I. Pudovkin, Dziga Vertov, and Sergei Eisenstein, the very stuff of film should be charged with revolutionary vigor. Sequentially, as well as ideologically, the revolution in film theory followed the Russian political revolution, and like the Soviet Marxist revolutionists shortly before them, the film theorists were influenced by the writings of Georg Wilhelm Friedrich Hegel, especially his teleological account of history with its dialectical explanation of historical development.

History is dynamic to Hegel. It is ever-moving, ever in flux. Historical progression is a responsive energy to what immediately came before. It is a dialogue between two contradictory states or two opposing concepts. In Hegel's dialectic, one concept (the thesis) invariably collides with its opposite (the antithesis) and the two interact to form a new concept (the synthesis). The synthesis of opposites gives rise to a new thesis which, in turn, collides with a new antithesis and sets in motion the ongoing dynamic of thesis, antithesis, and synthesis. Hegel's understanding of dialectics gained prominence in creative discourse, most notably among the Soviet film theorists, whose ideology and aesthetics insisted that, if the function of art is to depict truth, Hegelian dialectics can and should infuse art.

To the Soviet film theorists, thesis and antithesis — contrast, conflict, and dissonance — led to meaningful reconciliation (synthesis). Their position was in stark contrast to what they saw as the false reconciliations, the pat endings, and tidy narrative progressions with their illusion of linear time that the movies of the day, edited according to the polite rules of continuity, were delivering. Following and expanding upon the earlier work of V. I. Pudovkin, Sergei Eisenstein proposed that editing was the singular most significant feature in elevating a movie from banal entertainment to art, from facile escapism to truth. Whereas the shot is the basic unit in continuity editing, the collision of two shots — the thesis and the antithesis — became the essential unit for Eisenstein. Shots were to be cut according to dynamic juxtapositions, to couplings based on visual

Battleship Potemkin (1925): The tremendous wrong done by the Czarist militia firing on its own citizens becomes enlarged into the very conflict of history itself in Sergei Eisenstein's powerful images and rhythmic montage editing in the "Odessa Steps" sequence.

conflict. This montage editing strategy, with its attending aesthetic and ideological values, infuses the greatness of the "Odessa Steps" sequence in Eisenstein's *Battleship Potemkin* (1925).

 Battleship Potemkin tells the story of the justifiable mutiny of the crew aboard the Czarist naval ship, *Potemkin*, and the subsequent support of their mutiny by the citizens of Odessa, Russia. The "Odessa Steps" sequence within *Battleship Potemkin* recreates that historical moment when the citizens, rallying in joyous support of the mutiny, are confronted by the Czarist militia, which responds to their celebratory conduct by marching in and firing shots at their own citizens gathered on the grand Odessa steps. A slaughter of innocent citizens follows. Shots collide: peace and violence, light and dark, laughter and hostility. Visual patterns are constructed in accord with the dialectic of thesis, antithesis, synthesis. A static mid-shot of a soldier, with the dominant visual interest located in the left of the frame, is followed by a static mid-shot of his adversary, a mother, with the dominant visual interest on the right of the frame. The synthesis of the two shots is the third: a long shot showing the soldier in the center of the frame, gun raised, moving aggressively toward the mother. That synthesis shot becomes the new visual thesis, which is followed by its antithesis: a close-up of the mother, moving in frightened reaction to the militant movements of the soldiers.

Throughout the "Odessa Steps," any sequence of shots can be bracketed-off and studied, with the same results: the editing occurs in strict adherence to the values of Soviet montage. Shots are cut to a definite rhythm. There is the linking — the clashing collision — of visual opposites: long shots are followed by close-ups; high angle shots by low angles; vertical lines by horizontal; left side dominated images by right side dominated images; gentleness with violence; and, always, the allegorical and literal use of light with dark. To heighten the emotional effect of the rampage, Eisenstein mechanically alters time, slowing down and stretching out the time that it takes a carriage holding a baby to roll down the long steps of Odessa. The enormous wrong enacted by the Czarist militia against its own citizen becomes enlarged into the very conflict of history, itself, communicated through the powerfully rhythmic montage editing of the "Odessa Steps" sequence.

☞ *Watch and count off the first twenty shots of the "Odessa Steps" sequence in* Battleship Potemkin. *Scrutinize them. Write out the specific ways in which the shots are edited together according to their oppositional visual and emotional qualities.*

The "Odessa Steps" sequence from Eisenstein's *Battleship Potemkin* is a virtuosity of Soviet montage. However, the political ideology and practices promoted by Soviet montage were challenged by subsequent filmmakers. In a sense, montage theory underwent its own Hegelian dialects as the "thesis" of Soviet montage was challenged by its own "antithesis," American montage.

Rather than adhering to the ideological and aesthetic value of montage as the visual collision of opposites, American montage, developed in the 1930s and 1940s, sees montage editing in terms of pragmatism. American filmmakers of this period realized that montage has the great practical, *functional* value of being capable of collapsing time and space, using devices like fades, dissolves, wipes, jump cuts, and superimposition to telescope events. In American montage, incidents that occurred over a span of years and over several locales can be collapsed into a matter of minutes — even seconds — of movie running time without the importance of the events and the intervening passage of time being lost. In some cases, the significance is even intensified through the compression of time created through the editing. A masterful example of American montage is the "breakfast table" sequence in Orson Welles's *Citizen Kane* (1941).

Citizen Kane tells the story of newspaper mogul Charles Foster Kane's rise and fall from power. (On one level the film is a biting satire of William Randolph Hearst.) Kane is fully incapable of sustaining a close relationship with another person, due, in part, to the early betrayal of his mother, who signed over the custody of her fortune and her young son to a bank trustee. In the course of his life, all of Kane's friendships and marriages (there are two) invariably disintegrate.

The disintegration of his first marriage is conveyed in the film's most famous montage sequence: the breakfast table exchange. Constructed of a series of five quick vignettes, all of which occur at the couple's breakfast table, the 135 second sequence spans the sixteen years of Kane and Emily Monroe Norton's marriage and chronicles its regrettable deterioration. The first vignette shows the couple early on in their marriage. All is well and married life is pleasant. The affectionate prattle of the couple's dialogue, their physicality, and the camera's movement animate the first sequence, as do their youth and promise. The warmth of the early marriage is captured by a two-shot, which holds both Kane and Emily in the same frame together, close and affectionate.

In each subsequent vignette, the warmth diminishes. The composition of the vignettes grows more static; the animated vitality of early marriage disintegrates. The couple's conversation grows more clipped as their intimacy and trust lessen. By the second vignette, the two-shot which held the couple affectionately in the same frame is replaced by each character alone in the frame: a series of one-shots, largely cut on the line, pointing up the growing alienation of the husband and wife. By the final vignette, the two-shot recurs, but to a very different effect. The couple has grown cold and estranged, and the frame that they share, ironically, registers the death of their union.

The disintegration of Kane's first marriage is delivered through this series of five vignettes that are edited according to continuity within the vignettes, but according to American montage between the vignettes. The transitions between the sequences are made by a flash pan, where the camera pans so rapidly that the images are blurred as they "flash" by. The sixteen years of Kane's marriage and the complex reasons for its demise are compressed into a little more than two minutes, with the flash pans going by at the speed by which life, itself, sometimes seems to pass.

Unlike continuity editing, which seeks to splice the shots in such a way that the editing is unobtrusive and creates the illusion that the film

Citizen Kane (1941): The composition of this two-shot shows that Charles Foster Kane (Orson Welles) and his wife, Emily Norton Kane (Ruth Warrick), have grown cold and estranged, and the frame they share, ironically, registers the death of their union. It contrasts an earlier scene, where the couple, at the beginning of their marriage, share a tighter two-shot, depicting their then closeness and affection.

is all of a piece, montage editing, in all its permutations, with its flash pans, jump cuts, and superimpositions, calls attention to the fact that film is composed of a series of separate shots, usually cut to a distinct design and/or rhythm.

    ☞   *Watch a television commercial that has been edited according to the principles of montage. Is the editing Soviet or American or a synthesis of the two? If it is Soviet montage, inspired by the values of a Marxist communist system, what ironic historical progression (what dialectic) has occurred?*

    Most current films employ a combination of continuity and montage by selecting the editing practice that is most appropriate to the particular sequence in the film. An early example of the integration of continuity and montage editing is the classic, silent, surrealist film, *Un chien andalou* (1928), which uses continuity editing, ironically, to debunk the notion that life proceeds in any contiguous, logical manner.

Directed and written by Luis Buñuel in conjunction with Salvador Dali, *Un chien andalou* respects the customs of traditional narrative film, while simultaneously communicating a surrealist vision. In the opening of the movie, Buñuel uses just enough continuity to make us assume that we are watching a popular thriller, then, in most unpredictable ways, he divests the narrative of all expected progression. The shots are cut on the image in an altered montage practice that arranges the sequences in an apparently illogical, random manner. Buñuel's editing shows that he is interested in a different mode of a logic, "dream logic," or the "logic" that is readily acceptable to us when we dream. He understood that dreams conform to meaningful patterns of association. They have a design and a meaning which might be understood, in part or in full, through close analysis, even psychoanalysis. Human psychology interested Buñuel much more than the dialectics of history. *Un chien andalou* is a study in the capacity of film to recreate and to explore dreams, with their own lexicon of images and their own structure of time and space that defies all conscious temporal notions.

Un chien andalou reinforces the surrealist doctrines of the illusion of rationality and of the strange, perhaps even malignant, animus that can lurk beneath an ordinary surface (themes that David Lynch would later take up in *Blue Velvet*). The very normality of the opening continuity sequence (the normal-appearing man, the balcony, the moon) makes the man's violent, unprovoked, and senseless act even more shocking. *Un chien andalou* also demonstrates the power of film to induce automatic and strong physical reactions to illusions projected on a screen, an effect that would be replicated in everything from the French New Wave (1959–1966) to *The Blair Witch Project* (1999).

The technology available to a filmmaker affects the result of what we see on the screen. The invention and development of a lightweight camera that could be hand-held freed filmmakers to shoot almost anywhere with a minimum of setup. Especially useful for shooting documentaries, the hand-held camera became appropriated by the French New Wave, whose filmmakers saw in its technology the capacity to create the verisimilitude, the rawness and realism of life, the *cinéma vérité*, that they sought. The hand-held camera could record the spontaneity, the "reality," of what was occurring.

Rather than carefully composing the elements of the shot prior to filming it, the hand-held camera was used to record whatever passed in front of the lens. Under such conditions, things go in and out of the frame, naturally, haphazardly, sometimes even blocking the dominant view. The footage that is shot is invariably shaky, as it is impossible to keep the lightweight, hand-held camera fully steady. Recording every shimmy and shake of even the most stable human hand that is holding it, the hand-held camera can intensify the illusion that what is on the screen occurred, just as it was recorded by the cameraman who really was there, filming it. Whether in the French New Wave or a film like *The Blair Witch Project*, the rawness, the lack of visual refinement, of the hand-held camera technique — sometimes, its very bogusness, its highly constructed and *directed* reality — paradoxically can heighten the sense of realism the viewer experiences. Viewing extended footage, dominated by a pronounced shaking of the camera, often provokes a visceral response, causing the viewer to feel dizzy or nauseous.

The invention of the Steadicam combined the mobility of the lightweight, hand-held camera with the visual steadiness of a mechanical mount, producing footage that allows the hand-held freedom of movement for the camera operator without the jostled, shaky outcome that was earlier inevitable.

In the early stages of movie-making, the camera did not move at all. It was fixed on a stationary mount. As the technology developed, the camera's capacity to move became more sophisticated, but the camera's movement can still be defined in seven basic ways, as shown in Table 3.

Whether the camera moves or is stationary, it records images on film frames, each of which has its own distinct composition. When referring to a film's composition, the term mise-en-scène is used to describe the arrangement of all the elements within the frame, a term that originated in theater to describe all the stage components. Much as it does in theater, the *mise-en-scène* is composed according to particular styles. For example, classical composition stands in contrast to the compositional style of *cinéma vérité*, where realism is most highly sought and framing allows for inclusion of all the visual messiness of real life. In classical film composition, however, the *mise-en-scène* will appear balanced, elegant, and centered. The human body normally will occupy the middle of the frame; and even while the figure moves, he or she will be kept centered by a camera that pans or tilts in accord with the character's movement. Vacancy in the frame will often be reserved for characters who will enter momentarily. In film, the visual components that form any *mise-en-scène*

Table 3.
Basic Camera Movements

Camera Movement	*Description*
pan or panorama	the camera remains fixed on a stationary mount, but moves on a horizontal axis, side to side
tracking or dolly	the camera is attached to a mount that moves on a horizontal axis, along tracks, attached to a motorized cart, or on the back of a moving vehicle
oblique or tilt	a fixed camera is tilted so that the images recorded appear to lean diagonally
zoom	the camera's lens moves, pulling in toward or back from its subject
crane	the camera is attached to a bucket affixed to the arm of a crane
aerial or bird's-eye	the camera is placed at a great height, as attached to a helicopter or a plane
hand-held	the camera is held by the camera operator, who can take it anywhere that he or she can go

include standard theatrical elements: lighting, set design, make-up, costumes, actors, and arrangement of the objects on the stage or within the frame. *Mise-en-scène* is also comprised of purely cinematic components: the nature of the film stock (its grain, its absence or presence of color), the angles at which the subjects are being shot, and the distance the subjects are from the camera.

The distance that the subjects are from the camera results in the quantity of frame-space occupied by the subjects. If a camera is extremely close, the space within the frame will be dominated by a single subject. The closer the camera is to the subject, the more intimate and subjective the image appears, while the farther the camera is, the more remote and objective the effect. The distance of the camera from its subjects is defined in six basic ways, which use as a reference point the amount of the human body contained within the frame. (See Table 4.)

No matter the distance from the camera, each shot is accomplished in one of basic five angles. (See Table 5.) Camera angle refers to the position of the subject matter in relation to the camera lens, and it is created by the specific manner (the angle) by which the camera is pointed at its subject. Each camera angle produces a particular psychological effect upon the spectator.

Table 4.
Basic Camera Shots

Camera Shot	Description
extreme close-up	a portion of the human face; a small portion of an entirety or the entirety of a small object
close-up	the full human face, an entire small object, or part of an object
medium (mid) shot	the human body from the waist up, the full figure of a seated character, or the visual equivalent of another object
full shot	the human body, head to toe, or the visual equivalent of another object
long shot	the camera placed approximately twenty-five feet from the body or the dominant object
extreme long shot	the camera placed a long distance away from the body or the dominant object, even a quarter mile or farther

---

☞   *Choose a movie that you are familiar with. Select a sequence of ten to twenty shots from it. Analyze the passage you selected in terms of the angles at which the subjects are being filmed and the distance the subjects are from the camera. What psychological effects, if any, are created through the various uses of distance and angles? Watch the sequence several times. Try to see other compositional elements: set design, actors, camera movement, and arrangement of images within the frame. Based on all the choices made regarding these elements, determine the extent to which you find the sequence to be successfully filmed and edited.*

None of the compositional elements that the director arranges will be recorded by the camera if the set or locale is not sufficiently lighted. Lighting is crucial to both the quality of the image that the camera captures and the atmosphere that is created in the shot. Film is a technology-based medium and like most of the elements of film, lighting grows ever-more complex and sophisticated with technological changes that allow for greater versatility. However, whether in the technological sophistication of the twenty-first century or in the beginnings of film, the major source of lighting in the frame is referred to as the key-light.

Table 5.
Basic Camera Angles

Camera Angle	Description	Effect
high angle	the camera is placed above the subject and angled down	makes characters appear diminished, threatened, or vulnerable, as the camera presses down upon the subjects
low angle	the camera is placed below the subject and angled up	empowers characters, heightening their dominance or importance
eye-level or straight-on	the camera is positioned five or six feet from the ground and directed straight at the subject	is the most neutral of the angles
oblique angle	the camera is tilted or skewed	creates the affect of psychological imbalance, inebriation, or pending horror
aerial or bird's-eye	the camera is positioned above the subject and at a great height	communicates a lot of visual information regarding location, but has a diminishing effect on characters, rendering them negligible, unimportant

While early movies were filmed outdoors in natural light, when filming moved indoors, to closed studios, the use of key-light became vital. Even in early films, key-light is seldom, if ever, created from just one isolated literal light, but, instead, from a composite of lights, designed to blend into one lighting effect. Key-light is augmented by fill-light, which is employed "to fill" any unlit or unevenly lit areas of the frame insufficiently illuminated by the dominant ("key") light source.

Key-light can be defined in two extremes: high-key and low-key, each of which has a different look and creates a different effect. High-key lighting refers to a bright, even light, with very few shadows or pools of light. Low-key lighting uses subdued lighting that is less bright. With literally less light illuminating the subject, the scenes look darker. Shadows are prevalent, and areas of deep and dark textures and pools of light emerge. The visual relationship of light and dark within the same frame is referred to as contrast. In high-contrast, the disparity of dark and light is pronounced, the dark is deeper and the light is brighter, sometimes piercingly so. The combination of low-key and high-contrast lighting is popular in suspense films, a genre in which danger lurks in shadows and the world seems inhabited by extremes of good and bad, signified in the visual shadows and the extreme contrasts of light and dark.

Film, like literature, is classified according to **genre**, and no matter whether the work is fiction, non-fiction, docu-drama, or verbal or visual poetry (film examples: *Koyaanisqatsi*, *Meshes of the Afternoon*), the work invariably carries, even if only sometimes tangentially, a theme, or integral meaning. The discussion of integral meaning will inform subsequent chapters in this work.

Most films based on literature, both fiction and non-fiction, are narratives; they relate (narrate) a story, an event or series of events. (A non-fictional example of this would be the film *A Beautiful Mind*, based on the book biography of the same title written by Silvia Nasar.) A narrator is always present in the narration, and, although we may not be aware of the narrative voice, it is ever at work. The perspective through which the action is viewed is referred to as the point of view. Most narrations are told from either the first person or third person point of view, with second person narration being very rare.*

A first person narration is a story told by a major or minor character in the story who experienced the events. "If you really want to hear about it, the first thing you'll probably want to know is where I was born, and what my childhood was like, and how my parents were occupied and all before they had me," the character Holden Caulfield states at the opening of J. D. Salinger's novel *The Catcher in the Rye*, a work which uses Holden's impressions of life to question whether he is crazy in a world that is sane or if he is sane in a world painfully crazy in its lopsided values (the same theme Emily Dickinson considers in her poem, "Much Madness Is Divinest Sense"). Words in the novel (such as "I," "my") and the various points of reference confirm that *The Catcher in the Rye* is being narrated by a character within the story.

First person narration is also used in film where words, most often via voice-over narration, establish that the story is being told from the point of view of a character who experienced the events about to unfold. Stanley Kubrick's film *A Clockwork Orange* (1971), based on Anthony

---

Second person point of view is a story told from the perspective of "you," an example of which is Lorrie Moore's "How to Become a Writer." The use of the second person is much more widespread in electronic fictional forms (i.e., interactive fiction, literary hypertext narrative, or hyperfiction) than it is in conventional paper-based fiction.

A Clockwork Orange (1971): Alex de Large (Malcolm McDowell, center) and two of his London "droogs" at the Korova Milkbar. Director Stanley Kubrick used low angles in filming Alex to confirm his sense of sovereignty in his world of ultra-violence.

Burgess's book of the same title, is centered on the Beethoven-aficionado leader of a London gang that steals, rapes, and murders to assert their freedom against the conformity of a "clockwork" society. (Burgess wrote the novel, which incorporates graphic gang brutality, after an assault on his wife resulted in the loss of their expected child.)

The film begins with a voice-over narration that clearly situates it in a first person narration, consistent with the book's narrative voice. However, the film uses cinematic devices in addition to verbal ones to show that the events are refracted through the experiences and sensibilities of the main character, Alex de Large (Malcolm McDowell). The recurrent use of low angles that confirm Alex's sense of sovereignty, of long shots that frame his brutal acts of physical aggression depicted as if balletic movements seen on a stage, of editing in which the basest acts of violence are cut to the rhythms of Rossini music, and of lenses that distort what is actually occurring, all help render the film's point of view: the inner life and values of Alex, his distorted, lordly, nihilistic perspective.

The film is focalized through Alex, showing matters as he sees and responds to them. His narration is a futuristic nightmare in which survival of the fittest becomes the mode of entertainment, with brutality and devastation the fashion. Alex is iniquitous and sees iniquity all about him. The horror of it all is exacerbated by the first person narrative perspective that reveals how indifferent Alex de Large is about the atrocities he commissions. It is likewise, paradoxically, exacerbated by our experiencing, through Alex's own eyes, society's equally horrifying means of "rehabilitating" him. Both the film and the book, *A Clockwork Orange*, exemplify the writer Henry James's critical conviction that point of view is the single most significant compositional element for establishing the meanings of the text.

Kubrick's bleak social commentary is made more forceful by the events being filtered through Alex's values and responses; but, while *A Clockwork Orange* is told from Alex's point of view, the camera does not always position itself to record matters as Alex literally sees them. Instead, the camera exposes the psychological result of how Alex sees rather than the literalness of what he is actually viewing. When Alex refers to himself and his "droogs," for example, the camera focuses on them, showing us the imperious Alex as he sees himself.

This is not the case in *The Lady in the Lake* (1946), a traditional translation of Raymond Chandler's novel. In keeping with the novel, the film is constructed around a first person narrative in which all the events are shot just as the main character and narrator, detective Philip Marlowe, sees them. The movie is composed of all subjective shots, where the camera is placed in such a way that it replicates what the character (Marlowe) would be viewing. The only time that the viewer sees Marlowe is when he looks at himself in a mirror. *The Lady in the Lake* was an experiment in having the camera sustain first person point of view narration.

Literature and film are also narrated from the third person point of view. Third person narration is frequently told from an "omniscient" perspective, that is, from a vantage that is all-knowing about the events and the characters' inner responses to them. E. M. Forster's novel *Maurice* is a sensitive study of a young man's coming to terms with his homosexuality, a bold topic for its day. (The novel was completed in 1914, but its publication was suppressed until a year after the author's death in 1970.) Narrated in third person by an omniscient narrator, the novel takes us to private moments of incident and emotions. Poised to see and understand all facets of Maurice's story and its underlying importance, the omniscient narrator leads the reader to see the integrity of the characters and their alliances and creates a plea for universal compassion, understanding, and tolerance of differences.

In 1987 the production team of James Ivory and Ishmail Merchant

The Lady in the Lake (1946). The original movie card advertising "the most amazing screen development since the Talkies" refers to the film's sustained use of the subjective shot, where the camera is placed so that all events are seen from the point of view of only one character, Philip Marlowe (Robert Montgomery).

made a film of *Maurice* in which the camera, in conjunction with the screenplay, functions omnisciently, conveying events and their import with the knowledge, awareness, and understanding that is crucial to an omniscient perspective. The film also maintains the wit and clarity that define Forster's writing.

Not all third person narrations are omniscient. Third person point of view can also be "limited" or restricted to the understanding of one circumscribed perspective. Jane Austen's *Emma* is narrated in third person, but done so through the limited perspective of incidents and responses being filtered through the eyes of the central character, Emma Woodhouse, a feature maintained in the film *Emma* (1996).* We are led to understand Emma fully because we are led to apprehend those qualities that do not appear through her surface conduct. We come to sympathize with Emma rather than criticize her. Viewed from a different perspective, Emma would be unlikable, as her avocation is manipulating the romantic lives of others, done less from warmth of feeling than from superiority, self-centeredness, and boredom. The same story would be very different had it been focalized through the sensibilities of a different character in the novel, such as Mr. Knightly, Frank Churchill, or Jane Fairfax. As Henry James understood, the meaning of the text would be radically altered by the alteration in narrative perspective.

The point of view in literature and in film does not necessarily remain stable, consistent, throughout a work. It can shift throughout the text, as it does in William Faulkner's novel *The Sound and the Fury*. The first three sections of *The Sound and the Fury* are narrated by each one of three different characters (the Compson brothers), with the fourth section narrated from a third person omniscient point of view. In a sense, the novel tells the same story four times, as each of the four narrations recounts the same essential family history. However, the shifting points of view demonstrate that to tell a story differently is to tell a different story.

This same concept structures the film *Memento* (2000). The plot is fairly standard as *Memento*, ostensibly, is the story of a man who is searching for his wife's killer. In the course of the film, however, the telling of the story is not standard at all. The same basic story is told twice. The black and white segments are focalized through the husband's point of view in traditional chronology and the color sequences are narrated in reverse chronology from a third person omniscient perspective, with the editing integrating, inter-splicing, the two different modes of narration.

In film, the camera becomes the pen that creates the narrative perspective. Point of view is created largely through camera placement. When the camera is placed to show us what and how a character sees, the camera is filming from a first person point of view. Alfred Hitchcock understood, intricately, the camera's capabilities to narrate from a first person point of view, a perspective that he utilizes throughout *Rear Window*. In contrast, the camera can function omnisciently, also, taking us to privileged

For an extended discussion of point of view in Emma, *see Wayne C. Booth's* The Rhetoric of Fiction, *Chapter Nine: "Control of Distance in Jane Austen's 'Emma.'"*

incidents, revealing characters' inner responses, and prevailing over traditional notions of time and space.

A camera can work in ways that are similar to a writer's pen, an observation resulting in the concept of *caméra-stylo*, a term coined by the film theorist, Alexandre Astruc, in 1948. Much as a camera can function as a pen, a pen can function as a camera. The term *caméra-stylo* applies to those literary compositions in which the writer's pen (*le stylo*) works uncannily like a camera. A most classic example of this is Gustav Flaubert's *Madame Bovary*, in which the book's point of view is ever-modulated. The narrator of *Madame Bovary* is, intermittently, very intimate with Emma and then very distant, remote, creating effects that are much like a lens of a camera that records events in intimate close-ups and also in more objective long-shots. Flaubert's pen provides highly visual representations of locations and of the people who inhabit them. Like images recorded by a camera, his work is kinetic and imagistic, with transitions between sentences, paragraphs, or episodes combining the techniques of both continuity and montage editing.

When we watch a movie, the work of the camera carries us forward, as if the sequences of frames were one sentence after another after another. As in reading literature, the experience of watching a movie may involve us fully in the reality being depicted. We occupy the time and the space of the film, as if transported. If someone near us in a theater so much as rustles a candy wrapper, we may grow annoyed, as the noise ruptures our relationship to the screen, pulling us back to the disappointing reality that we are, after all, just sitting in a movie theater, watching a film.

CHAPTER III

The Film Industry and the Collaborative Work of Filmmakers

In the stillest moment of your night, you must ask yourself a question:
If it were denied to you to create, would you truly die?
— Rainer Marie Rilke, *Letter to a Young Poet*

Movie-making is big business. It is expensive, arguably the most expensive art form. In contrast, literature is, arguably, the least expensive art form. All that is needed to create a literary work is a pen and paper. Literature can be, and normally is, produced by a single writer, who needs to secure no approval outside of his or her own. Film is produced in a very different way. The collaborative nature of movie-making requires a certain amount of agreement among the entities involved. More crucially, since production costs are so high, even in the most modest of budgets, if a film is to be made, its worth must be sold to the financiers, that is, the studio or private funding source that believes enough in the merits of the project to bankroll it, hoping, of course, for a monetary return on its faith.

The film industry in America is a huge financial enterprise, a multi-billion dollar industry, with film outstripping aircraft parts, agricultural products, and computer components as our largest national export, accounting for the largest single factor in reducing America's national trade deficit. In film, art and commerce meet, sometimes symbiotically, as one enriches the other, and sometimes hostilely, as the contrary values of art and of commerce conflict and collide. With such large financial concerns at stake, filmmaking is certainly a commercial enterprise in which the means of production is accomplished under one of two systems: the studio system and the independent system.

The studio system emerged in Hollywood in the mid– to late 1910s. Prior to its inception, the division of labor on a film was not clearly established. It was not unusual for one person to do most of the principal jobs: write the script, raise the money, direct the film, act in it, and even operate the camera, whether he or she was good at each of these areas or not. With one person doing all the jobs, the system was inefficient, area expertise was unknown, and overall quality was sporadic. The rise of the studio system simultaneously gave rise to film specialists, people hired to do one thing, to learn it well, and to expand upon that knowledge over time and through repeated practice. Under the studio system, a specialized labor force was developed. Scriptwriters, producers, directors, editors, cameramen, and actors were cultivated as experts in their trade. Since they worked only on that portion of the film claimed by their specific job, the studio system increased productivity, creativity, and consistency of quality while diminishing production costs.

The Hollywood studio system and Henry Ford's assembly line emerged almost simultaneously. Both the auto and film industry had the same essential goal: mass production; and both industries were fueled by a vast love of the product that was being produced and by the zeal for the newness of it all. They also were fueled by vast financial ambitions. Six principal film studios emerged: Famous-Lasky Corporation (which became Paramount), Metro Pictures Corporation (which became Metro-Goldwyn-Mayer or MGM), 20th Century Productions (which became 20th Century–Fox), United Artists, Warner Bros., and Columbia Pictures Corporation.

Each studio had its own principal actors and utilized the "star system," in which a movie was structured, promoted, and marketed around the star who appeared in it. The star system was *quid pro quo* capitalism, in which actors, desiring the career-enhancing security and the backing of a major studio, signed contracts in which they were guaranteed work, a negotiated salary, and suitable publicity in return for agreeing to work exclusively for that one studio on those projects that the studio selected and deemed most appropriate. Each studio cultivated its own stable of stars. The studio system made and shaped the stars by changing their names and recasting their images, creating scripts exclusively for them, manufacturing publicity, and keeping their indiscretions far from the public's knowledge. Under the star system, publicity could make or ruin a star. Gossip was a marketplace commodity, with Louella Parsons and

Hedda Hopper, the two leading newspaper gossip columnists, wielding incredible power over the professional lives of actors in Hollywood. Times change. Today, the very stories that could previously hurt actors under the star system can help them, as the ethos of the contemporary film industry asserts that there is no such thing as bad publicity.

Under the early studio system, the producer was the most influential force in shaping the artistic values and moral precepts of a given film. He made every crucial decision regarding a movie. The system was hierarchical, with the producer fully in charge of the project. The means of production was the producer's exclusive domain, and, as such, he wielded control over the scriptwriters, directors, actors, and cinematographers, who functioned in accord with the producer's, not the director's, cinematic conceptions.

Each studio had its own mogul, the *über*-producer, who had to calculate and recalculate, create and recreate an industry that was growing and shifting with each day. While there was a fundamental similarity among the studios and even among the pictures that they produced, each studio also developed its own special niche.

Paramount Pictures was headed by Adolph Zukor, who felt that motion pictures fell into three categories: Class A movies, sophisticated, costly, and artistic; Class B movies, solid stories with recognizable actors; and Class C movies, cheap and tatty. Zukor discovered that Class B movies were the most successful (profitable and suitably entertaining), and, consequently, Paramount Pictures began specializing in the production of so-called "B movies." Warner Bros. and Fox exhibited the first talking-pictures. Metro-Goldwyn-Mayer built opulent movie theaters, "movie palaces," and began to produce the types of suave, engaging, and charming films, often musicals, that would be appropriate to those surroundings.

Each of the leading studios understood the power and the value in studio ownership and control of the movie theaters that exhibited the films. Studio ownership of the theater meant that the studio had a distribution system in place, a ready market in which to exhibit all the movies — good or bad — produced by that studio, to prolong the duration of a picture's run, and to insist that no film be exhibited at the theaters except those produced by the parent studio. Thus, the studios not only competed by attempting to produce more successful movies than their rivals, but they also competed, sometimes ruthlessly, to acquire and develop theater chains, since in doing so they gained control over the three fundamental divisions of the industry: film production, distribution, and exhibition.

Louis B. Mayer was the MGM executive in charge of production, and it was Mayer who hired Irving Thalberg as vice president in charge of production. Thalberg managed the actual activities of MGM's moviemaking. He chose the projects, assigned the specific producers who oversaw the daily details of production, selected the cast, the script, and the director, whose role, under the early studio structure, was incidental to that of the producer in the overall design and outcome of the movie. Thalberg helped create the standard and the style for MGM. The roster of films produced under his authority demonstrates the uncanny instincts, savvy, and love he had for cinema. (These films include *Gone with the Wind, The Wizard of Oz, The Philadelphia Story, Duck Soup*, and *Grand Hotel*.) The stars he cultivated include Greta Garbo, John Barrymore, Cary Grant, Elizabeth Taylor, Clark Gable, Judy Garland, Joan Crawford, the Marx Brothers, Jimmy Stewart, and Mickey Rooney. While the team of Mayer and Thalberg surely was driven, sometimes unscrupulously so, by the ambition to make the kind of money that kept MGM a super-studio, they also were filmmakers at heart, who knew the industry from the ground up, who were creative with film, whose professional roots stretched deeply into all aspects of the industry, and who believed, to some vital extent, in their MGM motto: *Ars Gratia Artis*, or art for the sake of art.

MGM today has become part of a conglomerate, largely run by business people with business values. The conglomerates are multinational constructions built for business and profit. Their holdings at any given time are the result of the constant flux of mergers and acquisitions, of small fish being eaten by larger fish, who, in turn, are devoured by even larger ones. The distinct standards, styles, and artistic bearing that once distinguished one film studio from another are lost in a milieu of an ever-shifting corporate ownership that has little knowledge of and appreciation for filmmaking. The conglomerate simply acquires a film studio among its varied other holdings and looks to the film studio as a tool to drive corporate profits. Production decisions within this corporate culture are bottom line, held to the crucial standard of the proposed film project's potential to generate strong revenue. By this benchmark, a good picture is one that makes money and yields power and glamour for its executives, and a bad picture is one that loses money and its attending perks, power and glamour. Operating within these narrow standards, the money-making motive can overwhelm all other concerns, rendering bitterly ironic the image of Louis B. Mayer and Irving Thalberg's MGM lion, roaring with the motto *Ars Gratia Artis* encircling his head like a halo.

Films that are not made by a studio are made independently. Independent films ("indies") are made with financing that is raised privately, outside of studio backing. While they do not have the security of large studio funding, they also are not subject to studio control. At least in theory, a greater amount of artistic freedom and experimentation is possible in independent productions. The budget for an independent film is normally much lower than that of a studio financed commercial release, so there is not the same pressure to secure large box office returns. The filmmakers can take more risks, addressing topics of more narrow interest, experimenting with film forms that go beyond the orthodox, and breaking away from formulaic plot. New and emerging technologies, including the affordability of digital moving cameras and computer programs for editing moving images, are expanding possibilities for independent "filmmakers" who are willing to work outside of the medium of film.

Producers of independent films have two large problems to conquer that producers of studio-sponsored films do not. First, the producers must secure the money necessary to complete the projects; and, second, they must find a distributor, that entity who will sell their film to theaters, making it known and making its exhibition desired. It is possible to make a movie that will never get distributed and, thus, never be seen, just as it is possible to write a book that will never be published and never be read. As writers, perhaps, may need to make compromises that make their writing more marketable, more publishable, filmmakers must also compromise. In both cases, the market place — the concessions that will attract a distributor or a publisher to invest money in the work — influences composition.

The distributor is responsible for the cost of making all the film prints and of circulating the prints among the theaters, both of which are very high-priced enterprises. Distribution also entails the expense of advertising, which includes market research and publicity campaigns. In return for its investment, the distribution company secures a percentage of both the theatrical and rental profits. Once production of an independent film is completed, there is the great risk that it will never be seen by the public, that it will never find a distributor. For the independent producer, film festivals (Cannes, New York, Telluride, Sundance, etc.) have become vital because that is where many distribution deals are made.*

It can happen that an independently made film becomes distributed

---

*Each of these film festivals has a Web site, which can be located through an Internet search by simply keying into a search engine the festival name.

Sideways **(2004): Paul Giamatti (second from left, as Miles) and Thomas Hayden Church (as Jack) with director Alexander Payne (standing).**

by a large studio. *The Piano* (1993), *Pulp Fiction* (1994), and *The Blair Witch Project* (1999) were produced independently, but studio-distributed or distributed by a satellite company of a studio-anchored corporation. These satellite companies (examples: Sony Pictures and Fox Searchlight) do not produce movies; instead, they market and distribute films that were produced independently. *Sideways* (2004) was produced independently, but distributed by Fox Searchlight.

Directed by Alexander Payne as a strong, traditional translation of Rex Pickett's *Sideways: A Novel* (it is Pickett's first novel), the movie stands as a strong example of the ever-blurring lines between studio films and indies. *Sideways* was nominated in the Best Picture category of both the Academy Awards and the Independent Spirit Awards, a much-regarded awards ceremony that honors independent films.*

While studios and their satellite companies can and do distribute films that they did not produce, the opposite is also true. It is also not

*The Independent Spirit Awards were founded in 1984 by the non-profit Independent Film Project. Originally called the FINDE ("Friends of Independents"), the name was changed in 1986 and is often simply referred to as "the Spirits."

unusual for a studio to decide against distributing a film that it has made, determining that the distribution costs cannot be justified by the film's bleak box office prognosis. In such a case, the film is shelved, never to be seen, or it is salvaged by direct sale to cable television or straight to video. With the distribution stakes so high, the pressure on an independent feature film to conform more to popular tastes becomes exacerbated, and the filmmakers become more cautious, less willing to experiment as radically, and more open to degrees of conformance.

Securing the funding necessary just to make an independent film may also require compromise. It is not unusual, for example, for an independent film to feature a famous name star, who may be all wrong for the role, but whose popularity quotient increases the odds of the movie finding production financing, a distributor, and stronger terms in the distribution deal that is struck. What also may occur is that a successful, popular actor wants to swell his or her image by having a role in an upscale, small independent film. Again, the actor may not be at all suited for the part, but he or she is willing to finance a portion, if not all, of the film's production costs through a corporation owned by the actor. The financing provides the green light for the project that the producer and director want to complete. In exchange for the corporate funding, which is not readily associated with or traced to the actor's name, he or she secures the desired part and requests script adjustments and shooting alterations that accord with how the actor wants his or her character portrayed. In the process, the independence of independent feature films suffers.

We want to believe that independent films, the indies that we feel are artistically superior to studio films, are pure cinema and are free of the compromises, market concerns, deals, and concessions that drive films manufactured by conglomerates. In many cases they are superior, prodigiously so.* But filmmaking is politics and film production often is political, constructed from a series of compromises in a world where we so want to believe that there are no compromises in art.

Small budget, independent films traditionally do not have the same distribution path that blockbuster features have. They usually will not open on three thousand screens in multiplex theaters nationwide. Instead, they will appear in the limited engagements of small art houses where there is often the kindredness of a like-minded audience, but just as often the liabilities of an antiquated projection system and a retrograde screen

*There are many Internet sites that provide lists of the best independent movies ever made, and a simple search for the "greatest independent films" will lead to these sites.

that may not do justice to the color, lighting, sounds, and textures of the print.

On rare occasions, a film that began as a small release in independent art houses will grow popular, via word of mouth, and its run will be expanded to include extended-run screenings in large theatrical chains, as happened to *My Big Fat Greek Wedding* (2002). The film is based on Nia Vardalos's comedic, one-woman stage show about a clamorous Greek family's fusion with a staid WASP family. Made on the very modest budget of five million dollars and released initially in limited run in small theaters, *My Big Fat Greek Wedding* grew so popular that it became a feature in multiplexes and has grossed in excess of two hundred million dollars.

A film produced for five million dollars is made on a different scale than a film that is produced for fifty million dollars. A crucial question that small budget, independent feature films raise is whether their merits should be assessed in *the same aesthetic way* as films with ten times the production budget. A case in point is *The Age of Innocence* (1993) and *The House of Mirth* (2000). Both films are period movies, based on novels by Edith Wharton. *The House of Mirth*, an independent film, was made for a fraction of the production budget of *The Age of Innocence*, made by Columbia Pictures.

Completed for eight million dollars, *The House of Mirth*'s total production cost was approximately what *The Age of Innocence* was allotted simply for its distribution and exhibition expenses alone. Yet, critics often hold the films side by side, discussing the merits of each in the same way, as equals, attempting the same scale, the same opulence of set design, the same access to authentic locales, and the same cinematic effects. While the comparisons of these two contemporary Edith Wharton films may be understandable, such comparisons are also, arguably, unreasonable. The point is not that small-budget, independent films should be held to a lower aesthetic standard than large-budget, studio films; but, instead, belonging to a different mode of filmmaking, small budget films should be held to the aesthetic criteria appropriate to what they are attempting.

The budget constraints under which independent films frequently must operate may, oddly, conspire in their favor, compelling the filmmakers to devise creative, innovative ways of producing desired effects on limited funds. Terence Davies's *The House of Mirth* is a case in point. Filming cost-effectively in only nine weeks and largely in Glasgow, Scotland, which is made to appear as 1905 New York City, the filmmakers made a series of intelligent choices that reduced production cost. For example, a key scene, set on a yacht off the cost of Monte Carlo, is shot with characters lounging in ship chairs in front of a blue screen and a canvas that effects the ship's awnings. A more expensive production may have lingered on the lush details of the yacht and on the spectacular views of the Mediterranean coast. *The House of Mirth*'s less extravagant, more minimalist, approach works well. While maintaining authenticity of locale, it politely insists that the audience focus on what is important: not on the distracting details of wealth, but on the dynamic currents and undercurrents occurring between the two characters, Lily Bart (Gillian Anderson) and Bertha Dorset (Laura Linney).

Independent films frequently will, perforce, maneuver in any way they can to keep production costs to the bare bone. Sound and camera equipment may not be state of the art. Shooting ratios, the average number of takes a director orders for a given shot, will be lower in direct proportion to the limits of the budget. Where a commercial film can afford to have a 30:1 ratio, an independent film may only have a 3:1 shooting ratio. Additionally, large-budget films are able to purchase that particular film stock which yields the visual effects most desired. Independent films may have to purchase whatever film stock is inexpensively available. This can mean that the footage shot comes from different batches or, worse, from different film companies. The variations in film batches and in film companies create variegations, inconsistencies, in the visual *personality* of the film material. While the variations may pass unnoticed to the untrained eye, the amalgamation of technical liabilities that the independent film must assume can have an aggregate effect.

No matter whether a film is studio or independently produced, the filmmaking process is collaborative. Literary composition, in contrast, is largely solitary. Film is such a collaborative art that there is no one way in which a movie is brought to completion. While the synergy is unique to each film, every feature movie seen in release goes through the same five basic steps: development, pre-production, production, post-production, and marketing.

Development is that initial phase in filmmaking where the worth of a proposed film project is determined. In development, an established director may approach financiers with a concept or a property; or an independent director may have written a script that he or she longs to film. Just as often, the proposed film project may begin as a story treatment, a brief explanation of the salient properties of the idea: the basic story, as well as clear descriptions of setting, characters, and, at times, casting requirements. A treatment is often the writer's only chance to pitch his or her idea, and, as such, the treatment will not only explain the story's basic structure, but also provide a hook, a pithy statement or gimmick that sparks interest in and/or points to the uniqueness of the project. Story treatments may be narrated in story form, but normally they are structured dramatically, scene-by-scene. This scene-by-scene structure delineates the basic narrative design and eventual shot sequence of the proposed film project. While a treatment can be over 40 pages long, the average length is well under twenty pages.

☞ *Choose a short literary work that you think has filmmaking potential. Develop the first phase of the project by writing a story treatment that contains a hook . (An internet search for "story treatment" will yield several examples.) Citing the names of real actors, include proposed casting for the principal parts. Cast the parts in each of three ways:*
   A. focusing solely on profit and selling possibilities
   B. focusing solely on the artistic vision and aspirations of the work
   C. creating an alliance between art and business

If the story treatment is of convincing merit, the next step is for it to be turned into a screenplay, which may or may not be written by the person who initially wrote the treatment. A general rule for a screenwriter to follow is that one page in the script is equal to approximately one minute of screen time. With this in mind, few scripts exceed one-hundred and twenty pages.

Not all film projects begin as story treatments. Instead, the project may begin as a script that finds it way to a producer, a story editor, or a development director. The process of having a script get serious attention is circuitous, but it can occur because the script received a positive response from a reader in the production company's story department, that division that reads scripts that are submitted and writes an evaluation and recommendation for each one. No matter the route, the principal way that an idea is sold is in having a treatment or a script that the financiers understand and see as profitable. If they do not understand the script, odds are the financing will not be forthcoming, the film will not get made, and the vision will die a protracted death, as the writer holds out hope against the lack of response, the indecision, the stallings, the unreturned phone calls, and the ambiguous silence that attends having his or her work under consideration.

Once a script secures the much-desired appropriate interest, it may be rewritten several times by several different people. After an acceptable script has finally been completed, the project is further developed in terms of budget projections and market analysis. In the final phase of development, a draft stripboard is created that depicts the shooting schedule by calculating the approximate number of days needed for each shot sequence and the most efficient way to film the required shots.

When the development phase is completed, the film moves into pre-production, which involves all the work that must be done prior to filming. In this phase, the production team is assembled, the cast and crew are hired, locations and usage permits are secured, details of set design are determined, and, if the budget allows, rehearsals commence. A legion of people may be involved in the details of pre-production, all of which occurs before the cameras ever start to roll. Overseeing the selection, recording, and manipulation of sound (sound editing), the sound designer, the principal author of the film's soundtrack, in conjunction with the director, creates a plan for how the film will sound, much as the production designer and cinematographer plan how the film will look. The director, often in conjunction with the art department, will construct a storyboard (see "Suggested Activities" in Chapter I and the storyboard example in Appendix B). A storyboard is the blueprint or visual depiction, frequently via simple cartoons, of how the camera is to render each shot: what the essential framing strategies should be, where the camera is to be placed, and how it is to move. The Internet and movies in DVD format are replete with examples of storyboards. Internet searches will yield everything from studio-created storyboards to those produced by budding young filmmakers, working inexpensively in home video or digital moving cameras.

Once the details of pre-production are wrapped up, the film is ready to move into production. Production includes essentially of all the activities that occur in the filming of the movie. Shooting schedules that detail the times, dates, and locations for filming are finalized. Daily call sheets that tell the cast and crew, each day, where to report and what is to be done are posted. Sets are constructed; lighting is designed and integrated; costumes, make-up, and hair styles and colors are determined and created; locations are analyzed and utilized for optimum effect; and the cinematographer works closely with the director to achieve the desired results. A second unit may be created to film less crucial, but necessary, scenes. For example: the drama proper is happening inside of a car, where the actors are speaking. It is the job of the second unit to shoot the same model car (without the actual actors) riding down the highway at the same time of day. While second units free the directors and their crew from the more pedestrian tasks of production, second units also add significantly to production costs.

During production, the dailies (or rushes) are screened at the end of shooting each day by the producer, director, editor, and the principal actors. The screening of the dailies is necessary to determine the success of the day's work, what errors may have occurred (is a microphone visible?), and what scenes need to be reshot. The unscheduled reshooting of scenes compromises the overall shooting schedule, often causing costly delays, making production over-schedule, and resulting in the principal reason for a movie's expenses exceeding its budget. In the process of screening the dailies during production, the editors begin their work. They determine and tag what exact takes of each shot are most successful and in what sequence they want the shots to occur. One take of a shot will be selected over another because of the quality of its composition, the skill of its performances, and the absence of errors.

Once the filming is complete, post-production commences. Post-production involves all those activities necessary to get the film into its final polished form. During post-production, the film is edited to a final cut and all extraneous sound (music and effects) is added. The sound designer integrates every sound that is heard in the film, as the sound designer's team mixes the effects, music, and dialogue to match appropriately with the images. During post-production, any additional, necessary footage may be shot or reshot, special effects will be integrated, re-recorded dialogue will be dubbed-in, titles and credits will be added, and the answer print will be completed. The answer print is the prototype of the film, the last version that is constructed after the film has been edited and the sound has been added. Prior to making the definitive prints that will be circulated in theatrical release, the producer, director, and cinematographer examine the answer print in post-production to catch any part of the complete film that needs changes.

Once the labor of filmmaking is completed, the movie must be marketed to be seen. Marketing involves all the distribution and exhibition arrangements: advertising, publicity, film prints, contractual arrangements made with movie theaters, and the production and terms of sale and rental of video and DVD versions. Theater chains (e.g., Loews, Sony, Clearview) bid on the exhibition rights of a given film, and in return for the agreed-upon fee, the distribution company licenses the theaters to run the movie for a specified number of screenings over a specified period of time. Independent theaters (those single movie houses privately, not corporately, owned) normally acquire their films through booking agencies, who recommend films appropriate to that theater and negotiate the terms of exhibition on behalf of the movie theater.

Film is collaborative, made of the cooperative efforts of all the people involved in development, pre-production, production, post-production, and marketing. As much as each film has its own distinct collaborative methods, yet conforms to these same basic production and distribution steps, the specific jobs that people do on films are particular to the methods and dynamics of the individual movie while, simultaneously, definable as basic tasks common to all filmmaking.

In filmmaking, job lines invariably blur. Actors may help to write the screenplay; screenwriters may suggest lighting and camera set-ups; and the director or the producer may play a large role in the editing of the film. The cast and crew, perhaps on location and far from home, may eat together and live together, with the common denominator being the film they are all making together. Each evening members of the production team, everyone from the director and the principal actors through the grips, may informally meet and brainstorm about the following day's work, each adding his or her own distinct directorial opinions. Yet, at least hypothetically, film production follows a basic pattern, with the attending jobs having definite, definable, clear-cut, and unique functions that need to be fulfilled.

The producer of a film is responsible for pitching the initial idea to the studio executives or independent financiers. Producers also must target their market (is this film best as a theatrical release, as a made-for-television movie, or as a cable television release?). Under a studio system, the pitch is usually made to a "development executive" (also called a "creative executive"), who, in turn, will assess its worth, possibly suggest changes, and, once convinced of its merits, attempt to sell it to upper management. The process is not so very different in book publishing, where the writer (often operating through an agent) must determine which publisher is most suited to the type of book being written. Once the appropriate publisher has been targeted, the writer will submit ("pitch") a book proposal (similar to a movie treatment) to an acquisitions editor (similar to the creative executive), who will assess its merits, perhaps suggest changes, and, when and if appropriate, recommend its publication to upper management.

Once the initial idea is approved, a screenplay needs to be written, if it has not already been. Screenwriting is a microcosm of filmmaking, in that it is often done collaboratively. One screenplay, credited to one person, could actually be the work of several people, as area experts are brought in to work on different aspects of the same script. One person may be good at writing dialogue, another at humor, another at dramatic development, and still another at simply polishing the proceeding drafts.

It is not unusual for a director to write the entire script. Preston Sturges is an early example of the creative dynamism possible in the writer as the director of his or her own work. Certain writer/directors (Kevin Smith, for example) will generously post their screenplays on an Internet site. Shooting scripts, the version of the screenplay written for filming, will, to varying degrees, include shot setups: actor's instructions, lighting, camera placement (angles and movement), sound effects, and sound sources (example: off screen or "OS").

Screenplays have their origin in either original material or source material (examples include news events, biographies, or literature). A screenplay based on a literary source, invariably, cannot include all the details of the literature or the film would be prohibitively long. The screenwriter must make decisions regarding what should be included and omitted from the source literature. Each inclusion and each deletion is an act of interpretation, as the writer, in small and large ways, is determining what he or she sees as the essential worth intrinsic to the literary text. The movie viewer may not agree with all of the screenwriter's decisions. However, the decision to include or omit certain scenes is generally made because of two factors: (1) The material selected efficiently and intelligently advances the necessary details of story and character, while omitting extraneous details; and (2) The material selected helps shape the screenwriter's ideas of the integral meaning of the literary text. A first step in screenwriting is organizing the original story into brief, sequential scenes, to which dialogue and visual descriptions will subsequently be added.

☞ *Choose a short story or a novel with limited action. After reading the literary work, make a list of what scenes from the literature you would include in a film. Look at the list and organize the scenes according to the chronology with which you would have them appear in the film. Not everything from the literature can be included in the film. Each decision you make to include a scene or delete a scene is an act of interpretation. Consider your reasons for including and omitting certain scenes. Based on your reading of the literature, what is the dominant idea, the integral meaning, that you hope your screenplay will communicate?*

Once the film concept is accepted and the script secured, the producer, traditionally, hires the director, whose job is to superintend all aspects of the filmmaking process, from pre-production through post-production. The director, in collaboration with the casting director and the producer, will determine the cast. The director must communicate his or her concepts about the film to the set and costume designers, the location scouts, the scriptwriters, and the actors, who, in a collaboration of ideas, will take the director's conceptions and preferences and render them in their own work. While creativity is key to masterful directing, so are strong communication, organization, and management skills.

In contemporary cinema, the creative function of the director is more pronounced than it was in the early days of movie-making, giving rise to the general perception that the director is the dominant creative force in a film and that the other collaborators on the movie are largely assistants, albeit significant ones, to the director. This presumption is the driving argument of "*auteur* theory," i.e., the idea that within the collective endeavors of filmmaking, there is a creative signature that emerges, which is, most often, that of the director's.

Under *auteur* theory there is a guiding, dominant, creative identity that is responsible for the essence and personality of the work. The *auteur* (French for author) of a film may be the producer or the actor (Charlie Chaplin would be an example); but, most frequently, it is the director. The director, functioning as author, integrates all the elements into one composite design, much as the author of a book may integrate the ideas or actual work of others into his overall composition. The initial *auteur* arguments were put forward in the 1950s in the journal *Cahiers du Cinéma*, first by Eric Rohmer, then in expanded form by François Truffaut, and then in further refinement by André Bazin.

Auteur theory emerged as an outcome of a distinct historical moment. During World War II, with the German occupation, American films were prohibited from being shown in occupied France. With the end of the war, all the American films from the preceding decade became available. In France, a vast interest in American cinema emerged. The number of films suddenly available was sizeable, but the rental cost of each movie was directly proportionate to the popularity of the specific title and the amount of time that the film was held (much like modern day video and DVD rental practices that are based on *per diem* fees). Therefore, it was not uncommon for multiple films to be screened on the same day, at the same theater, but available only for that single day. Compendious screenings, especially popular at the *Cinémathèque Française* in Paris, became *de rigeur* for the enthusiast of American films.

In consequence, film aficionados would watch several films over several hours each day, and since the films were often bundled according to a commonality, it was not unusual for films made by the same director

(John Ford, William Wyler, Howard Hawks, Alfred Hitchcock, or Orson Welles) to be viewed in succession over a very short period of time. These were the circumstances under which François Truffaut, André Bazin, and Jacques Doniol-Valcroze first studied American films and, in part, out of which emerged in 1951 the film journal *Cahiers du Cinéma.*

Watching a sequence of films by the same director in such tremendously concentrated circumstances lent itself to having viewers see and describe distinct recurring patterns of design, theme, cinematic habits, and uniqueness of style in the movies made by certain directors. *Cahiers du Cinéma* established its then-radical position toward film, when, in January 1954 (issue no. 31), François Truffaut wrote his now-famous essay, "*Une certaine tendance du cinéma français.*"

Truffaut's essay criticized the tendency in French film to privilege the writer as the single most influential force in the creation of a film. The abiding trend in France was the "*tradition de la qualité,*" or the adapting into film of high-culture (quality) literary works. The adapter, or screen-writer, was viewed as the dominant creative force, forging his or her vision of the parent literary work, with the other members of the production team, including the director, functioning as technical assistants in service to the writer's concepts. Enlarging significantly upon an argument forwarded two years earlier in *Cahiers* by Eric Rohmer, writing on filmmaker Jean Renoir, Truffaut argued that *the director*, not the writer, is the vital force that shapes a film. The director integrates the various film techniques, creates the film's style, and structures the film's themes, which are often delivered in visual, not verbal, codes.

Truffaut called for a *cinéma d'auteurs*, in the sense that the "author" of a film must, necessarily and logically, be that entity who works most fully in the *medium* of film. The writer, working with the language of words and in the medium of the written word, in not the author of a movie; the director, working in the language and medium of film, is. The authors of cinema, thus, are not the writers, but the directors. In the case of certain great directors, largely American ones (Orson Welles, Howard Hawks, John Ford, Alfred Hitchcock), the director is the artist of great works of film, much as great writers, painters, and composers. Truffaut further held that authorship is vital to cinema. Subsequently, the journal's position became "*la politique des auteurs,*" or the policy of the director as the author.

Cahiers du Cinéma's *auteur* position as "*la politique*" subsequently became very significant beyond the specific *auteur* concept that the journal was embracing. What became validated was film theory, itself, as a body, as a discourse, rigorous, intellectual, and, thus, worthy of academic attention. Movies, previously viewed as the artifacts of low culture, slowly gained entry into the discourse of high culture.

Auteur theory, thus, was important, in part, for introducing and validating the worth of film studies in universities, since it legitimized cinema as discourse in a way the academy could understand. Among the first film courses offered in colleges were *auteur* classes in which the works of great directors were studied much like the academy has always studied the great works of great artists. What was once a radical assertion, *Cahiers du Cinéma*'s endorsement of director-based *auteurism,* is now the discourse of general acceptance as it has become an everyday, popular practice to refer to and to discuss films in terms of their directors.

The concept of *auteurism* was first introduced in America by Andrew Sarris, an American writer and film critic. His initial article, "Notes on the *Auteur* Theory in 1962," appeared in *Film Culture* (winter 1962/63) and established Sarris as an early leading advocate of *auteurism* in American film discourse. In direct response to Sarris's advocacy of *auteur* theory, the American film critic Pauline Kael argued that the *auteur* theory is fundamentally different from the traditional attention critics have always given to an artist's body of work because, simply, the production of a film is not analogous. Film, instead, is a complicated, collective effort. Kael further asserted that this is particularly true in Hollywood. She explained that the *auteur* theorists do not understand "how confused and inextricable are the roles of the front office, the producers, writers, editors, and all the rest of them — even the marketing research consultants who may pretest the drawing power of the story and stars — in Hollywood" ("Circles and Squares," 23).

The famous and very public Andrew Sarris and Pauline Kael debate (1962–1963) over *auteur* theory is only one example of the complexities of this issue, which were enlarged upon by the arguments presented by Ernest Callenbach in *Film Quarterly* and the editorial board of *Movie* magazine. The debate continues today, causing the Directors Guild of America Inc. (DGA), the dominant labor union comprised of directors, assistant directors, production managers and assistants, to contend officially that film is a director's medium.

Notwithstanding the DGA's labor position, what is the critical stature of *auteurism* as discourse?

Arguing against any *auteur* approach to a text, Roland Barthes wrote "The death of the author" (1968). In that work, Barthes asserts that language, composed of linguistic or visual codes, speaks, not the author.

Barthes's approach is rooted in Ferdinand de Saussure's work in semiotics, the study of sign systems — of complexes of codes (which, again, may be linguistic or visual). The act of *reading* (a book, a painting, a movie, even the world — any text) is an activity of decoding the signs that are included in that particular text. Semiotics explains that sign systems consist of the "signified," which is the concept that is represented, and the signifier, which is the mode of representation. The signifier is not, literally, the author, but rather the complex network of codes from which meaning is constructed. Barthes argues that we mistake the person of the author for the text. He further explains that "a text is not a line of words releasing a single 'theological' meaning (the 'message' of the Author-God) but a multi-dimensional space in which a variety of writing, none of them original, blend and clash" (211). To Barthes, no one person is the source of author-ship. A text's unity, he argues, lies not in its origin, but in its destination, i.e., in the reader, who does not *construe*, but rather *constructs* the text.

Barthes's theory adds another dimension to the consideration of the soundness of attributing authorship of a collectively produced work to any one, individual person. Barthes is a post-structuralist. Post-structuralism generally maintains that there is not a self-referential core text, the mean-ing of which is fixed and determinable, i.e., composed of stable *structures* of meaning, the truth of which is apprehensible and determinate. For post-structuralists, no essential core text exists that ensures the correct, definitive reading of a given text.

Other forms of post-structuralism concur. Reader/response theory holds that all readers of a text (any text — literary, cinematic, or other-wise) are writers — *ecritures*-of each of the works approached; and decon-struction theory, under the advocacy of Jacques Derrida, maintains that any given text is open to an infinite number of readings, whose signification is constructed, not by the author, but by the reader. Further, Derrida asserts that translations are fully independent works. In "Letter to a Japa-nese Friend," he maintains: "I do not believe that translation is a second-ary and derived event in relation to an original language or text." Thus, for Derrida, a film translation of a literary source is a fully independent entity.

☞ *Read Derrida's "Letter to a Japanese Friend," full-text copies of which are available on the Internet at several locations. In this work, he argues that a translation is not secondary to the "original" text. Do you agree with his position? What implications does his stance have for film trans-lations of literature? Under Derrida's position, what obligations, if any, does the film have to the parent text? Use "Letter to a Japanese Firend" to help clarify and formulate your opinions on what status a film translation holds in relation to its original text. Present your conclusions and opinions in an oral presentation.*

☞ *The theoretical differences and positions maintained by the various post-structuralist theories are complex and fascinating. These theoretical positions lend themselves to in-depth study. Research any one of the theories. Read actively by formulating critical responses to the ideas. Present your findings and evaluations in an oral presentation.*

Any discussion of *auteurism*, thus, opens a fundamental, theoretical question that extends beyond the specificity of *auteur* theory: Does the person of the author construct a text composed of recurring, common elements whose patterns we can discern and whose substance has stable meaning, independent of our perceptions, as the *auteurists* hold; or is each reader the author of a text whose signification he or she constructs? Are there patterns, structures, and conclusive meaning created by an author and inherent in a text, whether or not the inhered meaning is apprehended by the reader, as the *auteurists* hold; or is a text's meaning actively constructed by the reader-author, as the post-structuralists assert? Are the concepts mutually exclusive? Is the great wonder of art that it contains multitudes and accommodates paradoxes? Perhaps as we watch a movie, the collective "author" is simultaneously present and not present in the film because a film is simultaneously a text with its own, individual personhood and a series of codes whose meaning we readers and viewers invariably and variously construct.

Amid all the debate regarding *auteurism*, one fundamental issue is generally agreed upon. *Auteur* theory has the capacity to distort critical judgment, to tempt the *auteurist* critic into the determination that a bad film made by a great director must, in some measure, be a great film, worthy of close study. Pauline Kael's overall assessment of *auteurism* may simply be the most sensible. Kael writes, "I assume that anyone interested in movies uses that director's name as some sort of guide, both positive and negative, even though we recognize that at times he is little more than a stage manager.... There is no rule or theory involved in any of this, just simple discrimination; we judge the man from his films and learn to predict a little more about his next films, we don't judge the films from the man" ("Circles and Squares," 23).

A director, given *auteur* status or not, seldom works in isolation. A vital collaborator in the filmmaking process is the cinematographer. The cinematographer, or director of photography (DP), oversees all the factors involved in the literal filming of the movie, and, in conjunction with the director, creates the appearance — the mien and style — of the movie. Largely responsible for achieving the look of the film that the director wants, the DP's choice of lighting, lenses, film stock, filters, colors, camera settings, motion, angles, and even processing must all integrate to attain the desired compositional values and visual effects. The DP is responsible for appropriately lighting the shots, and, as such, supervises the work of the "gaffer," who oversees the layout and operation of the electrical schemas required by the lighting designs.

The gaffer must calculate the amperage needed for all the lighting specifications, maintain the appropriate generator at each location, and wire the scenes so that no electrical apparatus is visible in the shots. The best boy (also referred to as the "best person") is the primary assistant to the gaffer. A great amount of time on a movie set is needed to rig and adjust the lighting. Often the best boy, implementing the plans of the gaffer, will work on setting up the lighting for the next scene, while the gaffer attends to all the immediate needs of the scene being shot. The DP, who designs the lighting necessary to achieve the desired photographic effects, works closely with the gaffer, the best boy, and any of the grips, the general handyworkers, who may be rigging the electrical equipment, constructing the lighting scaffolding, or building the sets in accord with where and how the camera will move to film the scenes.

The cinematographer, thus, is the *director* of many of the technical aspects involved in filming, including the intricate subtleties and complexities of lighting (interiors and exteriors). The job involves much, much more than just running the camera, making the title "Director of Photography" more fitting, and more generally used, than "cinematographer." Oddly, the DP (also known as the "first cameraman") often does not even actually operate the movie camera. The "second cameraman" does, while the DP supervises — directs — all the myriad filming details required before, during, and after the cameras are rolling.

☞ *Watch the closing credits of films that you admire. Write down the names of the producers, directors, cinematographers, editors, and screenwriters. Research several of them (past or present). Assemble your ideal team of filmmakers (the producer, director, cinematographer, editor, and screenwriter) who will collaborate in making a film of a literary work of your choice. Most filmmakers prefer and work more effectively in particular genres, such as drama, action-adventure,*

*suspense, romance, comedy, and science fiction. In making your choices,
consider the extent to which your production team will be assembled
in line with the genre that you have chosen.*

The director of photography works closely with the production
designer (a.k.a. the art director), whose integration of sets and costumes
creates the visual environment and the dramatic atmosphere appropriate
to the genre, mood, historical accuracy, and style of the film. Coordinating the efforts of the art department and the construction crews, the production designer oversees the designing, building, and dressing of sets;
the acquisition of necessary props; and the integration of costuming. From
pre-production through post-production, the director, the DP, and the
production designer collaborate to produce and integrate those exact elements that create the film's overall look, that authenticate the setting, that
establish the characters, that clarify the story, and that communicate the
tone, textures, and themes of the film.

☞   *Watch Bram Stoker's* Dracula *(1992) for features of production design.
Study and write out:*

1. *the ways in which colors are encoded. Specific colors are associated with particular characters and communicate character
   traits. Colors also define the boundaries between the two dis-
   parate worlds, Mina's and Dracula's.*
2. *the different effects created through lighting and set design when
   natural (outdoor) settings and when interior settings are used.*
3. *the manner by which costuming and make-up define character
   and advance the story.*
4. *the ways in which the film incorporates the particular features
   of Gothic horror: the intimation of something dark and foreboding, the feeling of impending doom, occurring in a romantic and opulent milieu.*

Once the final cut of the film has been established (once the "cut is
locked"), but prior to its printing in multiple copies, the work of the sound
track is finalized. The sound that has been recorded on the "production
track" is reviewed and, when necessary, portions of the dialogue are
replaced through a process called looping. The segments that need to be
re-recorded will be projected on a screen for the actors to see as they speak
their lines and attempt to synchronize their dialogue with the images. The
newly recorded spoken words will be incorporated into the film by a sound
engineer, who breaks the dialogue down into smaller auditory units. If

the looping is successful, there is a seamless match of the words with the images.

An actor's voice may be replaced, in full or in part, by the voice of another actor. In making *To Have and Have Not* (1944), Lauren Bacall's singing fell short of the necessary quality. A professional singer was brought in, but since Bacall's speaking voice was so low, a male, Andy Williams, was selected to dub her singing and did so convincingly. The film *Singing in the Rain* (1952) has another interesting example of looping. Set during the transition of silent to sound movies, *Singing in the Rain* includes the story of a silent screen star, Lina Lamont (played by Jean Hagen), who has a voice so unpleasant that Kathy Selden (played by Debbie Reynolds) is asked to dub her lines in the new sound film that is being made within *Singing in the Rain*. Ironically, Reynolds's own voice, as she dubs the Lina Lamont passages, was not suitably sophisticated for the role, so, even more ironically, Jean Hagen spoke the passages in the movie that show Kathy Selden (Reynolds) dubbing Lina Lamont (Hagen). Perhaps most illustrative of the magic of looping is *Greystoke: The Legend of Tarzan, Lord of the Apes* (1984), in which Andie MacDowell, playing the leading role of Jane, was found to have such a strong southern accent that Glenn Close was brought in to loop all of MacDowell's spoken words.

In the final phase of film production, sound effects must also be added and synchronized. Sound effects libraries that archive a vast array of recorded sounds are housed within studios or operate independently, charging fees for the use of their collection. However, instead of using pre-recorded effects, a particular film may want to produce sounds specific to that movie, in which case a sound engineer is hired to record the effects that are required.

Brian de Palma's film *Blow Out* (1981) tells the story of a sound-effects man (John Travolta), who, while attempting to record the noises needed for a B horror movie, records proof, in the form of the background sound of a blown-out tire, that the death of a United States senator was not accidental. In the course of solving the murder mystery, the movie provides information about how sound effects work in the film industry. *Blow Out* functions also as a sound-effects metatext, in that it specifically, self-referentially, and self-consciously examines the nature, status, and function of sound effects through the meta-language of using sound, itself, to describe and comment on sound.

While the sound effects in any given movie must be accurate, they must not overwhelm the sequence or function in ways that are inappropriate to the overall style and timbre of the film. The sounds must match the images accurately and credibly (a singing bird should not sound like a frog), and the *effects* of the sounds must be consistent with the intent and mood of the scene. This is the *art* of sound effects. The pitch, the volume, the duration, and the subtlety or aggressiveness of the sound must integrate suitably with the purpose and meaning of the film, with its style, manner, tone, and technique. The decision of what sounds should be omitted becomes as crucial as what sounds should be included, the sound of silence being as vital in the film as the engineering of sound. The judicious, skilled, and creative ways that both sound and silence are used in a film creates, by degrees, the art of sound design.

☞   *Watch David Lynch's film* Blue Velvet *(1986), a movie highly regarded for its use of sound. As you watch it, listen to the sound effects that are incorporated, noting what is included and what is omitted. Listen for the volume, the modulations, the duration, and the subtlety or aggressiveness of the sound effects. Note instances where sound is used in an exaggerated realism. (Why?) Write out how specific sound effects and sound effects in general function in the movie's overall style and tone; and how sound functions within your concept of the integral meaning of the film.*

In addition to sound effects and dialogue, a sound track often includes a third component: music. Music is used to create a mood, to describe a character, to complement a setting, or to heighten the effectiveness of the image. *Apocalypse Now* (1979) contains a strong example of music having an amplifying affect on the drama.

Set during the Vietnam war, *Apocalypse Now* shows us Lieutenant Colonel Kilgore (Robert Duvall), a maniacal air cavalry commander, who orders and leads a napalm attack on a Vietnamese village because it located on the best beach for surfing, a particular interest of his squad. Kilgore's imposing formation of assault helicopters fires into the population of women, children, and small animals, with a heinous exhilaration of annihilation that is amplified by the rousing music of Richard Wagner's "Flight of the Valkyries" blaring from the helicopters' loud-speakers.

Sometimes music can over-amplify or over-inflect the images, as, arguably, Max Steiner's score does in *Dark Victory* (1939). While we think of music as heightening the visual affects, the opposite can also be true. Music, itself, can become inflected by the accompanying images on the screen. This occurs, for example, when the young Judy Garland sings "Somewhere Over the Rainbow" in *The Wizard of Oz* (1939). It occurs also in the movie *The Piano*, where the composer, Michael Nyman, cre-

Apocalypse Now (1979): Guided by a crazed photojournalist (Dennis Hopper, left), Captain Benjamin L. Willard (Martin Sheen, foreground) and Jay "Chef" Hicks (Frederic Forrest, right) cautiously survey a jungle outpost leading to Colonel Walter E. Kurtz's compound.

ates a piano score that is supposed to be written by the film's central character, Ada (Holly Hunter). Nyman, commenting on his composition, explains, "I had to write the music of another composer ... someone who was obviously not a professional composer or pianist, so there had to be a modesty about it. Except that Holly Hunter played Ada playing the piano with enormous dedication and intensity." The intensity of Holly Hunter's performance charges the music, inflecting it, heightening and deepening the emotional power and resonance that issues forth from Ada's piano.

Film can be powerful, amazingly so. Since movies are fundamentally and essentially visual, they have the faculty, the remarkable faculty at times, of showing us surroundings far different from our own. Film helps us *see* foreign worlds, cultures, and values. We witness, in the extraordinary minutiae of detail that is uniquely possible in film, the physical properties of ethnicity: the faces, the clothes, the terrain, the food, the religious practices, the government, and the everyday routines.

Through film, we can hear the different music of other languages, without losing the necessary translation into our own language (via subtitles) that film uniquely allows. Film guides us through an understanding of the sublime diversity of this planet, as well as the fundamental commonality inherent in all apparent human diversity.

The emotional power of a film, the long-term, resonating effects that it can create, its capacity to engender cross-cultural sympathy, its deftness at manipulating — even exploiting — our emotions, its ability to depict and to remind us of the unthinkable horrors committed by human hands, and its power to restore faith — in short, the tremendous capacities of film — are the result of the blending of many, many, many talents, whose distinct contributions are taken for granted once the theater lights go down and the projector rolls and the audience settles in.

It is to the credit of all the collaborators on a film, major and minor, that their individual contributions disappear in the integrated sum we see as *the movie*.

CHAPTER IV

Novels and Novellas into Film and an Aesthetic Rubric for Film Translations of Literature

A vital step in exploring literature-based films is to understand that a film based on a literary work carries its own distinctive ideas about the book, and that filmmakers, creating such a movie, take on the responsibility of attempting to capture and translate those essential qualities which they perceive to be present in the literature, a medium with a separate and independent life. No matter if they are working in a literal, traditional, or radical translation mode (discussed in Chapter I), the filmmakers, we hope, are motivated by something more intrinsic to the specific work than literature's generic ability to supply a convenient fund of stories, characters, and proven successes — or literature's power to confer a certain seal of stature and respectability upon the movie. We hope they see something so worthy, distinctive, and inherent in the source text that it fires a need to reshape that particular work of literature into film.

Thus, the most successful films based on literary works translate the words into images by both *interpreting* and *exploiting* the source text. The literary text is strip-mined for the riches the filmmakers can use to promote their own vision of the work, and, as a result, the film that emerges, like any translation, is a separate entity, with a life of its own, but a life fertilely tethered to its literary parent. Our own reading of the literature might differ radically from the filmmakers', but in the most effective literature to film translations, the filmmakers, equipped with definite ideas about the source text, are true to the literature, faithful in *their fashion*.

In the most notable novel-to-screen transitions, we sense that the source work kindled strong views in the filmmaker. It provoked definite ideas and impressions which resulted in a film that translated the literature in such a way that the movie emerged as a self-reliant text, an accomplished and individualistic offspring of the novel. (For example, the novel should not have to be read for the film to be understood, much as the novel, translated into English from Spanish, should not have to be read in the original language.) The relationship — the lineage — of the two must be evident. If the film becomes so distinctly independent of, or antithetical to, its literary source that no parenthood is noticeable other than, for example, a shared title, then the movie simply ceases to be a literature-to-screen translation, and any claim to that pedigree is made for reasons that, for the literature or film scholar, are purely speculative.

Films exist as independent works of art; however, when film scholars, critics, or students explore the meaning and merit of a novel-based film, they may add the intricacy of seeing the movie in specific relationship to its literary source. In the process of doing so, one text, the novel or the film, is not privileged over the other. One is not, *de facto*, more important, held in higher regard, or inherently better. Instead, the novel and the film are seen as independent entities, to be assessed independently and, simultaneously, to be explored inter-relationally.

Studying the novel and the novel-based film hinged together, one to the other, allows for an illumination the sort of which occurs in a diptych. Normally the province of painting, a diptych is composed of two, separate, independent canvases or panels. These two, similarly shaped panels depict antithetical states of the same basic theme (example: Youth and Old Age). The canvases are placed side by side; and the interplay between the two pictures yields insights about each individual picture that studying the canvases in isolation might not achieve.

In a successful diptych, when the panels are set side by side, motifs in the second evoke and comment on the first, even as the first evokes and comments on the second. Each canvas illuminates the other. Our contemplation of each separate panel becomes enhanced, perhaps deepened, when set beside its contrast; and in the process a third insight is yielded: the real, but previously unconsidered, similarities and sympathies present beneath the particular disparities. The most successful diptychs, much like the best metaphysical conceits, work because, while the boldness of the coupling *might* startle us (much as a radical film translation placed in comparison to the source novel might), the diptych guides us toward discoveries of unities that were previously unconsidered. At heart, a diptych is constructed from the hope that the viewer is willing to consider and explore what happens when thematically allied, but differing, works of art are set side to side.

When we set the allied, but different, novel and novel-based film side to side, each, hopefully, illuminates the other. The hinging together of the two works helps us to see, perhaps in deeper and more critical ways, ideas, motifs, and aesthetic practices within each of the two, separate, individual works. The novel may help us understand the film more thoroughly, much as the film may help us understand the novel more fully and guide us to see the book in new ways. Examining the works together, however, not only aids our appreciation of each separate work (the novel and the film, separately), but also yields a third consideration: the insights and concepts that emerge through consideration of the relationship of the two works.

When we examine the novel and the novel-based film hinged together, we look at them relationally, much as we do when we consider the two separate paintings combined as a diptych. We examine them intertextually, exploring the complex relationship of the book and the film. This intertextual study of the two works may provoke insights that an isolated, separate consideration of each work could not have yielded. In the process of intertextual considerations, we form critical appraisals of the film and of the book.

The critical evaluation of a film translation of a novel should not be purely arbitrary. Instead, it needs to be grounded in an informed aesthetics, a defined standard against which all critical appraisals of literature-based films are gauged. At its most basic and constitutive, four fundamental qualities contribute to the success of a literature-based film. These four characteristics are:

1. The film must communicate definite ideas concerning the *integral* meaning and value of the literary text, as the filmmakers interpret it.

2. The film must exhibit a collaboration of filmmaking skills (the details of which are provided in Chapter II).

3. The film must demonstrate an audacity to create a work that stands as a world apart, that exploits the literature in such a way that a self-reliant, but related, aesthetic offspring is born.

4. The film cannot be so self-governing as to be completely independent of or antithetical to the source material.

This four-point rubric forms the foundation — or, perhaps, the starting point — for an evaluation of the merits of film translations of all literary genres.

The first point of the rubric states: *The film must communicate definite ideas concerning the integral meaning and value of the literary text, as the filmmakers interpret it.* An aesthetically successful, literature-based film will be more than a plot summary of the book. It will do more than visually recap the story told in the words of the literature. Instead, the movie will communicate definite ideas concerning the meaning and value of the literary text, as *the filmmakers* interpret that meaning and value. The success of the film should not be measured against the degree to which the viewer agrees with the filmmakers' interpretive notions about the source literature, but, instead, against the degree to which the filmmakers successfully communicate their ideas.

Exemplary of this point is William Wyler's *The Heiress*, his film version of Henry James's novel *Washington Square*. Wyler cast beautiful Olivia de Havilland as Henry James's plain, rather homely, character, Catherine Sloper; and while de Havilland is the antithesis of how most readers imagine Catherine, she is magical in communicating the meaning that Wyler finds central in James's novel: even great beauty, like de Havilland's, can appear drab when self-esteem is obliterated by the crushing forces evident in the wealthy New York society of late nineteenth-century Washington Square.

When filmmakers' ideas about a novel differ from a viewer's, when filmmakers alter plot details or place stress on themes that a viewer may consider secondary, the viewer may criticize the film as "unfaithful" to the book. Such a judgment presumes that there is a core novel that can be "faithfully" brought to the screen rather than its contrary position: that there is an infinitesimal number of ways that readers and filmmakers construe and visualize the work that they are reading.

☞   *Determine where you stand on this theoretical issue: Is there a stable, core text which, with enough persistence and knowledge, we can apprehend and which filmmakers can be "unfaithful to," or do we readers each construe the text in varying and different legitimate ways? Is there a solid, knowable essence — a true and fixed meaning — to each novel, or is there an infinite number of ways that readers construct a work of fiction? Does the latter construct render absurd any attempts for a filmmaker to be "faithful" to the essence of a work whose meaning can never be constant and universally agreed upon?*

When filmmakers translate a novel to the screen, they cannot include every detail of the book, since that would make the movie prohibitively long. Films traditionally operate within a prescribed duration (a feature film is normally two hours or so in length), and movies are normally viewed, from beginning to end, in one sitting. Novels are not limited by the same durational constraints as films, and, unlike the watching of a movie, the reading of a novel is often completed in a series of sequential sittings. In this regard, reading a novel is similar to watching a serialized movie.

The length of a novel in relationship to the length of a feature film necessitates that the filmmakers make choices regarding what will be included in the movie. In the process, characters and events may be omitted, narrative gaps may be filled by scenes and personae that did not appear, or even exist, in the novel, and dialogue from the book may be mixed, to varying degrees of success, with dialogue constructed by the screenwriter. These alterations could prove disappointing if the filmgoer expects to see on the screen exactly what occurred in the novel. To this end, serialized productions of novels, many hours in length and shown over several consecutive weeks, may prove more satisfying, since these "large canvas" productions can be and, normally, will be more faithful to the literal details of the novel. This may be one reason for the ongoing popularity of the *Exxon-Mobil Masterpiece Theater* productions, broadcast on PBS television stations.

The *Masterpiece Theater* productions, characteristically, depict the novel efficiently and accurately, faithfully adhering to the details of the story as the book describes them. These productions are reverential in their approach, but, in their reverent reluctance to alter the novel in filmic ways or to attempt anything more than a literal, word for word rendition, they hover on the surface of the book's meaning, much as *Masterplots* or *Spark Notes* summaries do. A novel is more than its storyline, but when the film insists upon such obeisant, literal fidelity, it often shrinks the novel into merely a pictorial story.

In rendering the literal details so faithfully, many of the *Masterpiece Theater* productions, ironically, fail to render the novel's complexities of meaning. Examples of *Masterpiece Theater* productions which are weak in this vital way include Leo Tolstoy's *Resurrection* (1971); Daniel Defoe's *Moll Flanders* (1997); Charles Dickens's *David Copperfield* (2000); Gustave Flaubert's *Madame Bovary* (2000); Willa Cather's *The Song of the Lark* (2001); and Esmeralda Santiago's *Almost a Woman* (2003). Each of these *Masterpiece Theater* translations of the novel retells the book's plot in a way that is generally true to the story, but superficial in its treatment.

These productions are weak in *communicating definite ideas concerning the integral meaning and value of the literary text, as the filmmakers interpret it.* However, while each is weak in exploring and rendering the richness of ideas in the novel — the textures of thought and the psychological complexity of character — they are important for their power to keep that very literature alive in popular culture.

The Unbearable Lightness of Being (1988) is another example of a novel-based movie that is weak in communicating anything near the complex of ideas that are present in the novel (*Nesnesitelna lehkost byti*) written by Milan Kundera and published in 1984. The film is adept, however, in its recreation of Prague just prior to and during its invasion by the Soviet Union and in its incorporation of actual documentary footage of that 1968 invasion into the footage shot for the film.

Set in 1968 Czechoslovakia, the novel is a modern narrative, elliptical in structure and intellectual in its themes which are played in counterpoint through both the personal and the historical, i.e., the fictional histories of the characters and the factual historical context within which their stories unfold. Kundera's novel explores the destructive effects of life under a totalitarian regime, the conformity, self-interest, fear-driven failure to question, and survive-at-any-cost behavior that such an intimidating and formidable autocracy breeds. Constructed around a romantic quadrangle, the novel tells the intertwining stories of Tomas, a surgeon who approaches sexuality with light and pleasurable detachment; his lover, Sabina, an artist as dedicated to non-commitment and personal freedom as Tomas seems to be; Tereza, the ever-loyal and rooted young woman whom Tomas marries while continuing his affair with Sabina, and Franz, the earnestly faithful university professor who loves Sabina and with whom she is also having an affair.

Involved in a series of light, sexual relationships, including his long-term one with Sabina, Tomas, who lives and works in Prague, meets Tereza while he is visiting a small Czech town. She follows him back to Prague, where she and her heavy suitcase eventually move in. Tomas loves Tereza, who is the substance and the weight of love, its intimacies and responsibilities, provoking Tomas to ask about life, itself: *Is it better to be with Tereza or remain alone?* Vacillating in his answer to this significant question, Tomas marries her, but he is unable and unwilling to give up his mistresses. Tomas's perpetual womanizing causes Tereza great anguish. The lives of Tomas, Tereza, Sabina, and Franz are further complicated by the arrival of Soviet tanks in Prague on August 21, 1968. With the horror of Soviet occupation, Tereza and Tomas escape to Geneva, Switzerland, where Sabina is already living. Tomas resumes his surgical practice in a Swiss hospital; however, when his continuous philandering becomes

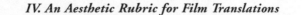

The Unbearable Lightness of Being (1988): Tomas (Daniel Day-Lewis) and Sabina (Lena Olin). Enormous use is made of mirrors and reflecting surfaces which reflect, distort, and fragment reality. But these symbols throughout the film are unbearably heavy in their obvious attempt to be artfully light.

unbearable to Tereza, she returns, alone, to Czechoslovakia. Then, in search of Tereza, Tomas also returns. His growing emotional awareness parallels his growing political awareness, and when Tomas refuses to repudiate an anti–Stalinist paper he wrote earlier, the Soviet-controlled communist Czech government prohibits him from practicing medicine, and Tomas works, instead, as a window washer. Tereza, Tomas, and their beloved dog Karenin (named, ironically, after Tolstoy's Russian autocrat) move to a farm, where they find short-lived satisfaction and peace, which ends when both Tomas and Tereza are killed in an accident.

Often ironic in tone, the novel warns of the dangerous oppression and fearful emptiness of Eastern European life under communist control. (In 1968, when the book is set, the author, Milan Kundera, was a professor of literature in Prague, Czechoslovakia. That August, the Soviet tanks invaded Prague and established complete control, and Kundera lost his teaching post largely because of his writings, which were subsequently banned.) In a world where human choices are nullified by absolute subjugation to external forces and where the political context demands unquestioning conformance and fosters the worst of human conduct (survivalism and self-interest), existence seems to lose its substance — its weight. Life becomes unbearably light, in an existential sense.

In the novel, weight and lightness are represented by a series of opposites: wife and mistress, commitment and independence, home and expatriation, loyalty and betrayal, tenderness and violence, and intimacy and sex. Kundera understands that while weight can crush, it, alone, will give rise to "life's most intense fulfillment." Sabina lives a lightness of being, one of Sabina-centered freedom, self-interest, and non-commitment. She lives unencumbered. Her lightness translates into a certain indifference to fidelity that frees her to leave her family and her lovers, even while her actions do great harm to them. By contrast, Tereza lives the weight of being, but as the loyal and genuinely loving wife of Tomas, she, not Sabina, is the agency of his ruin, as her unwillingness to live in exile in Geneva compels Tomas's return to Czechoslovakia. Thus, Tereza, the mirror-opposite of Sabina in commitment, fidelity, and responsibility, signifies the weight of moral obligation in a Kunderian world of physics in which weight and lightness paradoxically can effect the same result.

Kundera's narrative design is central to one of the book's central themes and presents a crucial matter for any film translation of this novel to consider. Critic Stephen C. Cahir explains:

> In the novel Tomas's story is told by an unidentified narrator who has
> thought about him for many years and admits that only in light of reflection

is he able to see the situation clearly. This narrative method is central to Kundera's theory, borrowed from Nietzsche, of "eternal return," i.e., the ability to return endlessly to an experience, relive and, if desired, change it. In the acts of reflection and story-telling, the narrator has the capacity to revisit events, even change the choices that were made, see what would have happened if different decisions had been made. Kundera argues it is this capacity for "eternal return," a capacity which the narrator (art) has but Tomas (a "real" person) does not, which gives the necessary weight to life. Without eternal return life's experiences are unbearably light. Kundera's narrative device, central not only to the aesthetic but also to the philosophical core of the novel, presents an immense problem for any cinematic translation of the novel. However, the movie handles this problem by simply dropping the device and reconstituting *The Unbearable Lightness of Being* as if it were a novel principally about story [444–45].

However, it is not Kundera's aesthetic, political, or philosophical theories that interest the filmmakers. The story predominantly does. The movie makes some unsubtle attempts to translate some of Kundera's complex of ideas into visual symbols. A bowler hat once owned by Sabina's grandfather represents the personal past, historical tradition, and the stable artistic forms which Sabina's painting seeks to reconstitute. Enormous use is made of mirrors, reflecting surfaces — all manner of things which reflect, distort, and fragment reality. But these symbols throughout the film are unbearably heavy in their obvious attempt to be artful; and Sabina's erotic dance with her hat — as with almost everything in the film, even the symbols — is tuned into sexuality, which is filmed throughout to enhance the beauty of the actors' bodies: Daniel Day-Lewis (Tomas), Lena Olin (Sabina), and Juliette Binoche (Tereza).

The film is more interested in the story of the characters than in the story's larger import. It is visually attractive (the cinematographer is Sven Nykvist, who worked on several films with Ingmar Bergman), but, from beginning to end, the movie concentrates on the sexuality, jealousies, and perturbations of its central characters, with their actions, as with most events in the film, lacking a thematic purpose. In the book, actions are connected to larger themes and questions; and while particular challenges to film are present in the distinct way that Kundera weaves each word of his novel, in the film Kundera's prose, his characters, and situations function to serve the superfluities of a soap opera, albeit a beautifully filmed one.

The film *The Unbearable Lightness of Being* fails in conveying the complex of ideas that are present in the novel, a task essential to the work of a literature-based film. Examples of films that demonstrate the filmmakers' understanding of a given novel's integral themes are listed in Table 6.

Table 6.
Successful Film Translations of
Novel's Integral Meaning

Film's Title	Director	Novel's Title	Author
Greed (1924)	Erich Von Stroheim	*McTeague*	Frank Norris
The Blue Angel (1930 version)	Josef von Sternberg	*Professor Unrat* (*"Professor Trash"*)	Heinrich Mann (older brother of Thomas Mann)
All Quiet on the Western Front (1930)	Lewis Milestone	*Im Westen Nichts Neues*	Erich Maria Remarque
The Informer (1935)	John Ford	same title	Liam O'Flaherty
Dodsworth (1936)	William Wyler	same title	Sinclair Lewis
The Grapes of Wrath (1940)	John Ford	same title	John Steinbeck
Rebecca (1940)	Alfred Hitchcock	same title	Daphne du Maurier
Double Indemnity (1944)	Billy Wilder	same title	James M. Cain
The Best Years of Our Lives (1946)	William Wyler	*Glory for Me*	MacKinlay Toland
The Bicycle Thief (1948)	Vittorio De Sica	same title	Luigi Bartolini
The Third Man (1949)	Carol Reed	same title	Graham Greene
The Idiot (1951)	Akira Kurosawa	same title	Fyodor Dostoyevski
Miracle in Milan (1951)	Vittorio De Sica	*Toto il Buono*	Cesare Zavattini
Strangers on a Train (1951)	Alfred Hitchcock	same	Patricia Highsmith
The African Queen (1951)	John Huston	same title	C. S. Forester

→

Film's Title	Director	Novel's Title	Author
The Apu Trilogy (1956–1959)	Satyajit Ray	*Panther Panchali* and *Aparajito*	Bibhuti Bhusan Banerjee
Jules et Jim (1962)	François Truffaut	same title	Henri-Pierre Roche
To Kill a Mockingbird (1962)	Robert Mulligan	same title	Harper Lee
The Leopard (Il Gattopardo) (1963)	Luchino Visconti	same title	Giuseppe Tomasi di Lampedusa
Tom Jones (1963)	Tony Richardson	same title	Henry Fielding
The Graduate (1967)	Mike Nichols	same title	Charles Webb
M*A*S*H (1970)	Robert Altman	same title	Richard Hooker
Death in Venice (1971)	Luchino Visconti	same title	Thomas Mann
Deliverance (1972)	John Boorman	same title	James Dickey
Carrie (1976)	Brian de Palma	same title	Stephen King
The Man Who Fell to Earth (1976)	Nicholas Roeg	same title	Walter Tevis
Kàos (1984)	Paolo and Vittorio Taviani	*Novelle per un anno*	Luigi Pirandello
Apocalypse Now (1979)	Francis Ford Coppola	*Heart of Darkness*	Joseph Conrad
Being There (1979)	Hal Ashby	same title	Jerzy Kosinski
Tess (1980)	Roman Polanski	*Tess of the d'Urbervilles*	Thomas Hardy
The French Lieutenant's Woman (1981)	Karel Reisz	same title	John Fowles
Blade Runner (1982)	Ridley Scott	*Do Androids Dream of Electric Sheep?*	Philip K. Dick
Fast Times at Ridgemont High (1982)	Amy Heckerling	*Fast Times at Ridgemont High: A True Story*	Cameron Crowe
The Makioka Sisters (1983)	Kon Ichikawa	same title	Junichiro Tanizaki

→

Film's Title	Director	Novel's Title	Author
Carmen (1983)	Carlos Saura	same title	Prosper Mérimée
A Passage to India (1984)	David Lean	same title	E. M. Forster
A Room with a View (1986)	James Ivory	same title	E. M. Forster
Empire of the Sun (1987)	Steven Spielberg	same title	J. G. Ballard
Black Rain (Kuroi Ame) (1989)	Shohei Imamura	same title	Masuji Ibuse
Raise the Red Lantern (1991)	Zhang Yimou	Da hong deng long gao gao gua	Su Tong
Bram Stoker's Dracula (1992)	Francis Ford Coppola	Dracula	Bram Stoker
The Player (1992)	Robert Altman	same title	Michael Tolkin
Schindler's List (1994)	Steven Spielberg	same title	Thomas Keneally
Dead Man Walking (1995)	Tim Robbins	same title	Sister Helen Prejean
Get Shorty (1995)	Barry Sonnenfeld	same title	Elmore Leonard
Il Postino (1995)	Michael Radford	Burning Patience	Antonio Skarmeta
Emma (1996)	Douglas McGrath	same title	Jane Austen
Clueless (1996)	Amy Heckerling	Emma	Jane Austen
The Portrait of a Lady (1996)	Jane Campion	same title	Henry James
L.A. Confidential (1997)	Curtis Hanson	same title	James Ellroy
Beloved (1998)	Jonathan Demme	same title	Toni Morrison
The Virgin Suicides (1999)	Sofia Coppola	same title	Jeffrey Eugenides
Chocolat (2000)	Lasse Hallström	same title	Joanne Harris
Crouching Tiger, Hidden Dragon (Wo hu cang long) (2000)	Ang Lee	same title	Du Lu Wang

→

Film's Title	Director	Novel's Title	Author
Lord of the Rings: The Fellowship of the Ring (2001)	Peter Jackson	same title	J. R. R. Tolkien
Lord of the Rings: The Two Towers (2002)	Peter Jackson	same title	J. R. R. Tolkien
Alias Betty (2002)	Claude Miller	The Tree of Hands	Ruth Rendell
Balzac and the Little Chinese Seamstress (2002)	Dai Sijie	same title	Dai Sijie
Catch Me If You Can (2002)	Steven Spielberg	Catch Me If You Can: The True Story of a Real Fake	Frank Abagnale, Jr., and Stan Redding
Adaptation (2002)	Spike Jonze	The Orchid Thief	Susan Orlean
Lord of the Rings: The Return of the King (2003)	Peter Jackson	same title	J.R.R. Tolkien
Mystic River (2003)	Clint Eastwood	same title	Dennis Lehane
City of God (2003)	Fernando Meirelles and Kátia Lund	same title	Paulo Lins
Whale Rider (2003)	Niki Caro	same title	Witi Ihimaera
The Manchurian Candidate (2004)	Jonathan Demme	same title	Richard Condon
The Motorcycle Diaries (2004)	Walter Salles	(fictionalized biography) The Motorcycles Diaries and "With Che Through Latin America"	Ernesto Che Guevara / Alberto Granado
Enduring Love (2004)	Roger Mitchell	same title	Ian McEwan
Sideways (2004)	Alexander Payne	Sideways: A Novel	Rex Pickett

☞ *Read any one of the novels listed in Table 6. As you read, engage the text in interpretive ways. What are the essential ideas that the novel is conveying to you? Watch the film. What are the essential ideas that the movie is conveying? Does the filmmakers' understanding of a the novel's integral themes correspond to yours? Does the film do an adequate job of translating the novel's fundamental concepts?*

On occasion, a film will transform a novel which is shallow in ideas or facile in form and/or style into a more complex and interesting work. In such cases, the fiction functions much like a sketch that an artist does in preparation for a painting. Like the preparatory sketch, the fiction is the preliminary step in a process of pictorial reproduction that progressively reconfigures and transforms the original material. Studying films which transform two-dimensional literature into more complex works can deepen our awareness of the visual inventiveness possible in film. Examples are listed in Table 7.

For a novel-based film to be successful, the integral meaning of the book needs to be expressed through *a collaboration of filmmaking skills*, the second point of this aesthetic rubric. Since film is largely a collaborative art form, each of the components must work in an aesthetic harmony of vision. The screenwriter, the cinematographer, the director, the art department, and the actors must all bring distinctive skills that mesh with the skills of the others. At its best, filmmaking is the aesthetics of *e pluribus unum*: out of many, one unified work.

This collaboration of skills is evident in *The Manchurian Candidate* (1962), a film which has been honored by the American Film Institute as one of America's 100 Greatest Movies. *The Manchurian Candidate* is a traditional translation of Richard Condon's 1959 novel of the same title.

Condon's novel presents an uncompromisingly cynical opinion of the workings of politics. His brutally critical stance is integral to the novel's meaning, and the film conveys, with force and ferocity, the weight of Condon's dark convictions. The screenplay (by George Axelrod) remains true to the literal details of the story, while integrating much of Condon's prose in with the characters' dialogue. While the 1962 film does soften the novel's references to drugs, sexuality, and the incestuous history of the protagonist, Raymond Shaw, his unconscionably ambitious mother; and her father, the film never backs off from the book's greater significance: showing the vastly iniquitous machinations carried out by politicians who look so respectable in their outward aspect.

The story centers on Raymond Shaw (Laurence Harvey), stepson to Senator John Iselin, who is campaigning for vice president. A recipient of the Medal of Honor for his upstanding and courageous actions during the Korean War, Shaw has been so honored for his heroic conduct as the com-

Table 7.
Movies That Transform Novels
into More Complex Texts

Movie/Year	Director	Genre	Book	Author
The Wind (1927)	Victor Sjostrom	melodrama	same title	Dorothy Scarborough
Tobacco Road (1941)	John Ford	social realism	same title	Erskine Caldwell
Forbidden Games (*Jeux interdits*) (1952)	René Clément	anti-war	*Jeux interdits*	François Boyer
Diabolique (1954 version)	Henri-Georges Clouzot	suspense	*C'elle qui n'etait plus*	Pierre Boileau and Thomas Narcejac
On the Waterfront (1954)	Elia Kazan	drama	same title	Budd Schulberg
Invasion of the Body Snatchers (1956 version)	Don Siegel	science fiction/ McCarthy-ism satire	same title	Jack Finney
The Searchers (1956)	John Ford	western	same title	Alan le May
Touch of Evil	Orson Welles	suspense	*Badge of Evil*	Whit Masterson
Vertigo (1958)	Alfred Hitchcock	psycho-sexual thriller	*D'entre les mort*	Pierre Boileau and Thomas Narcejac
Psycho (1960)	Alfred Hitchcock	psycho-sexual thriller	same title	Robert Bloch
Dr. Strangelove (1963)	Stanley Kubrick	dark comedy	*Red Alert*	Peter George
Walkabout (1971)	Nicholas Roeg	aboriginal adventure	same title	James Vance Marshall
The Godfather (1972)	Francis Ford Coppola	dynasty crime drama	same title	Mario Puzo
Raging Bull (1980)	Martin Scorsese	bio-pic	same title	Jake LaMotta
Ghost World (2001)	Terry Zwigoff	cartoonized novella	same title	Daniel Clowes

mander of a squadron of captured American soldiers. Later, however, we learn that, rather than having saved his platoon, Raymond Shaw is actually a political assassin, guilty of killing two of his own men, an act he has been psychologically programmed to forget. Brainwashed and fully reconditioned by communist leaders attempting to destroy American democracy, Shaw, the highly decorated war hero, is actually a helpless puppet of communist chieftains. He is their perfect killer since he is devoid of all hesitancy, guilt, and memory of his crimes.

Like the novel, the film is less about the literal 1950s cold war politics of communism and democracy and more about the corruption that Condon believes is inherent in all political practices. Like the novel, the film is constructed around mounting suspense, based on intricacies of plot. One of these intricacies involves concurrent action in which two men from Shaw's platoon, Capt./Maj. Bennett "Ben" Marco (Frank Sinatra) and Cpl. Alvin "Al" Melvin (James Edwards), independently of one another, experience the same recurring nightmare. In the film, their dream is conveyed in a memorable sequence which is created, in part, by an uninterrupted pan in which the camera tracks a full 360 degrees.

The director, John Frankenheimer, in collaboration with the cinematographer, Lionel Lindon, works to great effect, using high speed, monochrome film and integrating, with wonderful success, techniques that they learned from watching *Citizen Kane*: deep focus, wide angles, and chiaroscuro lighting. Like *Citizen Kane* (also shot in black and white), *The Manchurian Candidate* incorporates overlapping dialogue, and montage and shock editing, the last of which creates a wonderfully unsettling and unpredictable rhythm to the entire movie.

The Manchurian Candidate, now considered a classic of American film, would not have been made had Frank Sinatra not succeeded in having then-president John F. Kennedy intervene. Kennedy reassured Arthur Krimm (president of United Artists' distribution department and finance chairman for the Democratic Party) that he was a fan of Condon's novel and was untroubled by its subject matter being brought to the screen, as it was. However, from the early 1970s through 1988, the movie was unavailable. Sinatra had bought the rights to the film and forbade its exhibition in any form. While Sinatra has never explained why he prohibited screenings of *The Manchurian Candidate*, most film historians speculate that the presidential assassination that occurs in this 1962 film, which might never have been made had Kennedy not given his imprimatur to the project, is a painful reminder of J.F.K.'s actual assassination which occurred within a year after the film's release.

The Manchurian Candidate demonstrates a successful collaboration of talents — direction, acting, production design, editing, and sound — resulting from the particular chemistry of the particular elements assembled for that particular movie. However, the successful integration of filmmaking skills may also be the result of a team who have worked together frequently in collaboration. Examples of cinematic teams that work together frequently include those assembled by filmmakers as diverse as James Ivory/Ishmail Merchant and Kevin Smith. The Merchant/Ivory and Smith films bear the imprint and values of a repertory system. Different from the Merchant/Ivory productions, which most frequently are based on literary texts, director/producer Kevin Smith's films are based on original screenplays, which he writes himself: *Clerks* (1994); *Mallrats* (1995); *Chasing Amy* (1997); *Dogma* (1999); *Jay and Silent Bob Strike Back* (2001); *Jersey Girl* (2003); and *Fletch Won* (2003).

In contrast to Kevin Smith, producer Ishmail Merchant and director James Ivory often work specifically from novels which they translate into film with the assistance of their screenwriter, Ruth Prawer Jhabvala. Their novel-based collaborative films are listed in Table 8.

Merchant/Ivory/Jhabvala productions are, unfailingly, traditional film translations of novels, with a preference for location, rather than studio, shooting, and a competent manner of depicting layers of character complexity and theme. Demonstrating a consistently adept integration of the collaborative elements of movie-making, their films are ever-pleasant, even if they do hang a bit limp, at times, as in the case of *The Bostonians, Mr. and Mrs. Bridge, Surviving Picasso,* and *The Golden Bowl.*

☞ *Select any one novel-based film by Merchant/Ivory/Jhabvala (see Table 8) or any other production team. Paying particular attention to the collaborative nature of film, watch the movie closely from beginning to end. Choose a sequence of scenes approximately ten minutes in length. Watch that sequence several times. Scrutinize the details of acting, screenwriting, cinematography, make-up, set design, sound, and editing (reread portions of Chapter II for guidance). Are there any notable weaknesses? Does the sequence evidence a sustained mastery of separate skills which synthesize into a composite work in which no one element is dominant?*

Whether the film is the result of a production team who have never worked together before or one that has a sustained history of collaboration, a successful novel-based film will demonstrate a synergy of skills that

Table 8.
Novel-based Collaborative Films
of Ishmail Merchant, James Ivory
and Ruth Prawer Jhabvala

Movie/Year	Book	Author
Heat and Dust (1983)	same title (winner of the Booker Prize)	Ruth Prawer Jhabvala
The Bostonians (1984)	same title	Henry James
A Room with a View (1986)	same title	E. M. Forster
Mr. and Mrs. Bridge (1990)	Two separate novels: *Mr. Bridge* *Mrs. Bridge*	Evan S. Connell
Howard's End (1992)	same title	E. M. Forster
The Remains of the Day (1993)	same title	Kazuo Ishiguro awarded the O.B.E. (Order of the British Empire) for literature in 1995
A Soldier's Daughter Never Cries (1998)	same title	Kaylie Jones
Surviving Picasso (1996)	same title	Arianna Stassinopoulos Huffington
The Golden Bowl (2000)	same title	Henry James
Le Divorce (2003)	same title	Diane Johnson

yields something more than a movie which is a respectful synopsis of the book or a superficial, if even visually lovely, summary of the story.

As the third point of this aesthetic rubric states, a successful novel-based film will establish a certain remove from the novel. The film will demonstrate a certain *audacity to create a work that stands as a world apart, that exploits the literature in such a way that a self-reliant, but related, aesthetic offspring is born.* The successful novel-based film should be able to exist apart from the book, much as a foreign language translation of a novel can. Much as the successful foreign language translation will preserve what is integral from the original novel by utilizing what is appropriate — what is beautiful and effective — from the translation language, a film will do the same. It will utilize what is beautiful and effective from cinematic language, while retaining what is essential from the novel.

The great Japanese director Akira Kurosawa does just this in *Ikiru*

(1952), his radical film translation of Leo Tolstoy's novella *The Death of Iván Ilych* (1886). Tolstoy's nineteenth-century story, set in Russia, is recast by Kurosawa (who directed the film and co-wrote the screenplay) to mid–twentieth-century Japan, with very few of the literal, specific episodes from Tolstoy's novella ever being actually incorporated into the film. Nonetheless, Kurosawa's movie is a miracle of translation for what it does create on the screen that matches what Tolstoy created on the page. Both *The Death of Iván Ilych* and *Ikiru* (the Japanese for "*To Live*") are imbued with what the Japanese call *mono no aware*, the deep beauty apprehensible, paradoxically, in the sadness of life, the delicate sublimity one feels before the fleeting nature of all things. Both works chronicle with remarkable artistry one ordinary man's dark night of the soul and the serene and tender resolution that results.

Like *The Death of Iván Ilych*, *Ikiru* tells the story of a government bureaucrat who, having led a most bourgeois and proper life, learns that he has terminal cancer. His impending death brings about a painful questioning of his life. In both *The Death of Iván Ilych* and *Ikiru*, the protagonist of each work, Tolstoy's Iván Ilych and Kurosawa's Kanji Watanabe (Takashi Shimura), wonders if the life he has led might have been lived in vain, a thought that initially seems implausible since each man assumed that to live so properly and so correctly, as he did, was to live as one should. Ilych, like Watanabe, confronts the additional anxiety from wondering if "his life was not what it should have been"; and, then, was there enough time left to rectify a whole life lived so mistakenly, one filled with such a terrible hollowness and mundanity of values? Finally, both protagonists come up against the ultimate question: What is the point of it all, anyway, if it all, in the end, simply ends in death?

In his stark confrontation with their impending death and the questions that it raises, Ilych and Watanabe each pass through five, distinct emotional phases: shock, depression, isolation, escapism, and acceptance. These phases are similar to the stages of dying that were subsequently described in the pioneering research of Dr. Elisabeth Kubler-Ross, making Tolstoy's and Kurosawa's understanding of the universality of death — of the internal, emotional process that is the dying experience — rather uncanny. During the emotional process that Iván Ilych and Kanji Watanabe undergo, each reflects on the tremendous love he feels for his son and the coinciding grief he suffers over his alienation from his child; and each man suffers the loss of his wife, Watanabe's wife having literally died and Ilych's being so fully alienated from him as to be dead to him. The great physical and moral suffering that Ilych and Watanabe undergo brings about a transformed awareness of the meaning and value of human existence. Each realizes that there is the potential for change and for action as long as one is alive. Each man turns for solace to a young underling whom, neither man, when healthy, would ever have deigned to engage on a personal level: Ilych to his servant Gerasim, and Watanabe to Toyo (Miki Odagiri), the child-like young girl who once worked in his office. The simplicity, faith, and joy with which Gerasim and Toyo live, their happiness in making others happy (the young woman, Toyo, finds great delight in making wind-up toys for children), teach Ilych and Watanabe the master-lesson of humanity, the lesson of Otherness.

Rather than transposing to the screen the literal details of Tolstoy's story, the characters, action, setting, and narrative structure, *Ikiru* functions as a meditation on Tolstoy's text, Kurosawa's reflection on Tolstoy's meaning. In altering the book's literal details, while retaining that which is fundamental and integral to Iván's experience, *Ikiru* heightens the universality of *The Death of Iván Ilych*.

In each work, a man who has attained a certain financial and professional success and who has comported himself in strict adherence to what his society has asked of him, learns that he is to die. The circumstances in each work compel fundamental questions. Thus, foundational to both the book and the film are crucial considerations of how one ought to live, of what gives shape and value to existence. In Tolstoy's work, written shortly after his own Christian conversion, Iván Ilych finds "the light," which is faith, a transcendence in God. Kurosawa has thought long and hard about Tolstoy's answer, and, in his film, he carries on a conversation with Tolstoy, as if to say: *Yes, yes ... but personal salvation can come in another form.* That form is humanism, service to *the Other*.

Kanji Watanabe decides to do one meaningful act before he dies. Maneuvering through layer upon layer of bureaucratic red tape, he brings about the building of a children's playground in a once disease-breeding swamp.

The film is divided in half. The first section is devoted to Watanabe's awareness that he is dying and to his eventual realization of how he ought to have lived his life, and the second section is the wake that follows his death. In that second section, political officials and colleagues who are in attendance attempt to share credit for the creation of the park brought about by Watanabe, alone. The hypocritical, insincere, and self-serving tone of the wake changes decidedly when the group of mothers, who earlier had petitioned ineffectively for the rehabilitation of the contaminated land, arrives and the women express genuine grief over Watanabe's death. Subsequently, Watanabe's colleagues, having consumed a lot of sake, vow, teary-eyed, that they will emulate his example. Yet, when they return to work the very next day, they resume their same deadening patterns of behavior, as Iván Ilych's colleagues do in Tolstoy's tale.

Throughout the movie, close-ups function as depth-psychology. The distinctive work of the camera (Asakazu Nakai is the cinematographer) utilizes black and white photography to create portraiture in which every face seems to hold the complexity of a novel. This is evident even with the most minor characters, who are shot in a variety of low, high, straight-on, and oblique angles, each creating an impression of a distinctive, specific character. The camera is frequently kept static, with straight-on shots of Watanabe, punctuating the static nature of his life. The non-sentimental, direct way in which Watanabe's life and death are portrayed works as a cinematic equivalent of Tolstoy's writing style.

When Nakai's camera is in motion, with the visual vitality and vigor created by its tracking, panning, and elevator shots, the movement heightens the contrast from the death-like stillness and heaviness of the frequently stationary camera. Aided by the film's editing, humor occasionally prevails, as in the sequence involving the group of distressed mothers attempting to have City Hall clean up the disease-ridden drainage area of their neighborhood where their children are getting sick. Incorporating the technique of American montage, with sequences edited together through wipes, the women are shuffled to over a dozen different departments only to be sent back, in the end, to the exact same department where they first began.

Sound and silence are used to great effect throughout the film. Early on, Watanabe, stunned by the news of his terminal cancer, walks home from the clinic in a state of shock. He is so internally focused on what he has just learned that nothing from the external world registers — no sounds, no sights. As he crosses the street, Watanabe almost walks into a moving truck that he does not see. He is jolted to a halt by the sudden, loud blaring of the truck's horn. We are startled, too. The entire sequence is silent, something so subtle that we may not have noticed until the blasting horn jolts Watanabe (and us) back to the external world of sounds and objects.

Sound is frequently used simply, beautifully, and musically, as when Watanabe's memory carries him back to moments shared with his young son, which provokes him to whisper over and over again, as if were a mantra or a prayer, the name of his boy: *Mitsuo ... Mitsuo ... Mitsuo....*

Music in *Ikiru* is incorporated with a profound simplicity, as when the aged, dying Watanabe listens to strains of "Happy Birthday" sung by happy, healthy children; when two prostitutes sing a popular song ("Come On-A My House"), raucously off-key and fully out of sync with what Watanabe is feeling; and when "The March of the Wooden Soldiers" is heard in the background as Watanabe struggles to explain his dire situation to the young girl who has secretly nicknamed him "the Mummy." However, the most memorable music in the movie is that of the simple strain, "Life Is So Short."

The song is first heard as the opening credits roll, and then, again, in the night-town section of the film where Watanabe, seeking pleasures and experiences he had previously always shunned, is escorted to various tawdry and arcane nightspots by a hack writer (Yunosuke Ito) he has met. In one of the nightspots, the piano player asks for requests, prompting Watanabe to ask for a song from his youth. He begins to sing, in a quiet, deeply affecting voice, with each word of "Life Is So Short" registering on his face in a far different, deeper, and disturbing way to him now than the words of the ditty did when he was young. The song is reprised at the end of the film, where a policeman (Ichiro Chiba) at Watanabe's wake describes having seen Watanabe the night that he died. As he speaks, the camera cuts to what he saw: Watanabe in the park he made possible, peacefully — serenely — swinging on a child's swing, quietly singing "Life Is So Short" as snow falls.

Ikiru is simply one of the most beautiful films ever made. Kanji Watanabe dies in a state of wise acceptance, perhaps even a becalming joy, with a sense of love for others — for humanity, in all its imperfection. Watanabe, like Iván Ilych, is an exemplar of the emptiness that we can occupy, the shallowness of ambitions, and the comfortable numbness of conformity that characterize the unexamined life; but, simultaneously, Kanji Watanabe, like Iván Ilych, represents the exact opposite: the successful struggle for meaning, the actualization of significant change, and the serenity, joy, and purpose that Tolstoy believes is found in spiritual faith and that Kurosawa believes can be found in humanistic conduct.

While Kurosawa's films, often based on original screenplays, depict the extreme horrors of human conduct in its many manifestations and permutations, his films always involve an implied or overt plea for humanism and an optimistic faith that meaningful change is possible, even if it occurs in only one person at a time. We see these strains running through all of his movies, including such novel-based films as: *The Idiot* (1951), novel by Fyodor Dostoyevski; *High and Low* (1963), novel by Edward McBain; and *Red Beard* (1965), novel (*Akahige Shinryotan*) by Shugoro Yamamoto. Kurosawa's literature-based films (he has worked with plays and short stories, also) unfailingly demonstrate prodigious skill at retaining and communicating what is essential in the source literature while making the film uniquely and fully his own, independent work of art.

Like Akira Kurosawa, director Stanley Kubrick consistently demonstrates a mastery at preserving what is integral from the original novels while simultaneously creating films that exploit the literature in such a way that a self-reliant, but related, aesthetic work emerges. All eleven of Kubrick's feature films are based on literary sources, with each of them, except the short-story based *2001: A Space Odyssey*, being translations of novels. (See Table 9.)

Table 9.
Stanley Kubrick's Novel-based Films:

Movie/Year	Book	Author
The Killing (1956)	*Clean Break*	Lionel White
Paths of Glory (1957)	same title	Humphrey Cobb
Spartacus (1960)	same title	Howard Fast
Lolita (1961)	same title	Vladimir Nabokov
Dr. Strangelove (1963)	*Red Alert*	Peter George
A Clockwork Orange (1971)	same title	Anthony Burgess
Barry Lyndon (1975)	same title	William Makepeace Thackeray
The Shining (1980)	same title	Stephen King
Full Metal Jacket (1987)	*The Short-Timers*	Gustav Hasford
Eyes Wide Shut (1999)	*Traumnovelle/ Rhapsody: A Dream Novel*	Arthur Schnitzler

Kubrick does not associate himself with any one literary or film genre. His narrative range includes science fiction, crime, war, comedy, picaresque, psychological horror, satire, surrealism, and erotic suspense. His films follow no consistent translation methodology, with *Paths of Glory* made as a traditional translation of Humphrey Cobb's novel and *The Shining* functioning as a literal translation of the first fifty pages of Stephen King's book, only to metamorphose into a radical translation of King's work. However, like Kurosawa's literature-based films, Kubrick's films are interpretive translations of the source texts, which explicate, comment upon, and clarify the complexities of the parent literature, while simultaneously emerging as independent and distinctive works on their own.

A film that fails in this crucial way is *The Age of Innocence* (1993), director Martin Scorsese's literal translation of the Pulitzer Prize–winning novel of the same title by Edith Wharton. Scorsese's film never really breaks away from Wharton's text into its own self-reliant text and it never moves beyond a polite synopsis of Wharton's story. The film depends, in large part, on the repeated practice of culling and truncating lines from Wharton's novel — lines which, instead of being incorporated into the acting-script, are delivered via Joanne Woodward's voice-over narration. The narration diminishes the film's dramatic potency. Essentially, Wharton's writing ends up doing much of the movie's work, and the actors, mute and muted, are reduced to a pantomimesque performance. They are visual inserts, writ large, much like the sign-language performers who translate a television show for the hearing impaired. Each time that Woodward speaks, we are pulled away from the movie and back to the book. We are reminded of just how good Wharton's writing is. And, each time this happens, we temporarily exit the world of the film. As a result, the film fades in consequence of its own ill-chosen narrative device.

The voice-overs remind us that Wharton's writing throughout *The Age of Innocence* is masterful, and, that while the novel is about restraint, Wharton's prose never approaches a repressed writing style. Her writing, while always exquisite, is assertive and vigorous — even playful, at times, and, at times, irreverently humorous and richly insinuative. Scorsese seems to confuse the discourse with the methodology. His film is restrained, tamed — repressed into vacuity. Consequently, it never becomes what we longed for it to be: the prodigious offspring of the prodigious parent.

The film never articulates definite ideas regarding the integral meaning of Wharton's novel. In interview after interview Scorsese claims that the novel is about unfulfilled love; he remarks: "What attracted me to the book was the ... love story, and a love between two people, whether successful or unsuccessful, is common to everyone" ("Production Notes," 3).

If, indeed, the *primary* theme of *The Age of Innocence* is love (for many readers, it is not), the film, unlike the novel, never makes clear what, exactly, provoked the fervid love of Ellen Olenska (Michelle Pfeiffer) and Newland Archer (Daniel Day-Lewis). While the movie should be able to stand as a thing apart from the novel, those who see Scorsese's film, never having read Wharton's book, in all likelihood will be confused over why, exactly, Ellen and Archer love so ardently and so genuinely. This vagueness is a consequence of Scorsese's treatment of the novel's early crucial scene, Newland's plea that Ellen abandon her plans for divorce.

In Wharton's text, Newland, as a lawyer and a family member, is asked to convince Ellen that she should abandon her plans for divorce, since her divorce, no matter how warranted, would prove an embarrassment to her family and a violation of the social codes of wealthy New York society. In the course of his professional conversation with Ellen, Newland loses his positional surety. He grows baffled about the extent to which he believes in the very cause that he has been asked to promote. His argument, i.e., that Ellen should conform to the customs of their genteel tribe, strikes him as a composite of "stock phrases." His contact with her causes Newland to understand, in a way that he simply never did before, the horror that can result from blind compliance to social rules. Simultaneously, Newland also realizes the exact opposite, what Wharton terms "the ugly reality": the cold fact that, on occasion, an individual's happiness must be subjugated to the more compelling interest of others, that individual needs and desires, on occasion, must be sacrificed to the greater collective needs.

In Wharton's book, Newland's newly awakened ambivalence is his agony. Normally prepossessed and complacently sure of life's way, he loses his footing here and enters a torment of confusion over what is ethically right. Ellen, married to a profligate, grows to love Newland for the rarity and sincerity of the rectitude that he exhibits; and, he comes to love her for forcing him to think, for subtly insisting that he examine his life, and for inspiring him to venture a look behind the social veil. Archer's and Ellen's *raisons d'amor* begin in this crucial scene where he raises the subject of her divorce.

For some reason, Scorsese did not consider the scene critical. The sequence in the film is made less consequential; it is there as a device to get Ellen and Archer alone in a room so that we can *feel* how powerfully drawn each is to the other. What they actually discuss seems secondary to the natural attraction that is ignited here. Scorsese's Archer, indeed, looks awkward delivering society's "stock phrases," as he appeals to Ellen to forgo her divorce; but his discomfort grows from his feelings of embarrassment for having to defend such unsophisticated social values to the worldly and beautiful Ellen. So, instead, Day-Lewis flirts with Pfeiffer; head modestly down, he repeatedly looks up at her through his long dark eyelashes. His inflections tell her that he is only delivering the family line.

In removing Newland's ambivalence, Scorsese removes the platform on which the love between Ellen and Archer is constructed. The only way left to make sense of their love is to recognize that *The Age of Innocence* has been transformed into a Hollywood romantic paradigm, the first assumption of which is that the two romantic leads will, of course, fall in love with each other. Under this model, reasons are immaterial.

However, light years away from this facile Hollywood model, *The Age of Innocence* is Wharton's most complex and slippery work. It is an open puzzle that begins with the title. To one extent we see that Wharton is mercilessly ironic in referring to this age as innocent; to the other extreme, we, like her, cherish that time of innocent adherence to morals that that age professed to believe. The novel is a puzzlement.

In *The Age of Innocence*, manners are understood to be more than superficial acts, meant to demonstrate polite conduct. The novel asserts that the customs and the manners we absorb from our world form, in part, who we are; they help define the Self. When a person sheds customs, he invariably sheds a part of his own skin. This is necessary to do at times (as Wharton's own divorce and her emigration to France illustrate). *The Age of Innocence* reminds us that, while we are always free to change customs, and in certain cases have a moral responsibility to do so, when making any changes, we should be fully cognizant and heedful of the effects our choices have, not only on others, but also on the revising of Self. *The Age of Innocence* dramatizes the struggles and the effects on two characters, Ellen Olenska and Newland Archer, who are mindful of the results of such choices. In consequence, they opt to restrain their passion. Thus, the phrase "forbidden love," while an attempt at a provocative "hook" in the film's trailers, at best, trivializes Ellen and Archer's struggle.

Scorsese's failure at converting Wharton's novel into his film comes as quite a surprise if we consider that some of his best work is literature-based: *The Last Temptation of Christ* (1988) is his passionate reworking of Nikos Kazantzakis's book of the same name. In that film Scorsese splashes his religious turmoil, ambivalence, and uncertainty up there on the screen for all to see, and he does so with such probative fervor, that it leaves us infected with ideas. *Life Lessons*, Scorsese's contribution to the anthology film *New York Stories* (1989), and, arguably, one of the best contributions to an anthology in all of film history, is based on Dostoyevsky's autobiographical novella, *The Gambler*. And *Taxi Driver* (1976), Scorsese's monumental signature piece, is a radical reworking of Dostoyevsky's novella, *Notes from Underground*. These films document the great pendulum of human nature: the swing between stasis and action, between conformity and rebellion, between the violence of repression and the repression of violence, or, in short, Scorsese's films map the very vacillation that is the pith of Edith Wharton's *The Age of Innocence*.

Thus, it comes as no surprise that Scorsese's two best scenes in *The Age of Innocence*, the scenes that make us tingle because they remind us that we are, after all, watching a master at work, are suffused with a tension born of this swing between great repression and great violence.

The first of these is a brief, but chilling moment: May Welland's (Winona Ryder) success at an archery trial. For the first time, May lets us peek behind the mask of girlish, unthinking sweetness that she constantly assumes. She raises her bow (somehow Ryder looks taller in this scene), and straight-backed, fully self-assured, and unflinchingly, she aims straight for the heart of the target and pierces it through. May is the real archer in the family; when the trial demands it, unflinchingly, she nails hearts. This scene, beautiful in its brevity and potent in its sudden burst of violence from the seemingly docile May, is a moment of formidable filmmaking. Up to this point, Scorsese has held Ryder back — repressed her performance. (Ryder describes her acting in this movie as "minimalist" and claims that throughout the filming Scorsese kept asking her to "give less.") But, in this scene all stops are pulled, and we see that Winona Ryder, the actress, and her character May Welland seem to share a wicked delight in having fooled us up until then. Here they make us realize that there is more to both of these ladies, more layers upon layers of dark complexity, than we ever dreamed.

The second of these two successful scenes is May's farewell dinner to Ellen. This dinner (which, by sequencing the same series of images that we saw earlier at the van der Luydens' dinner, asks that we compare the two events) becomes a "quiet conspiracy" of assassins. The Family, we see, benevolently protects those who pledge loyalty (the point of the van der Luyden dinner), but annihilates any member who is disloyal. The assassination, done with smiles, is as violent as anything Scorsese has filmed. But these masterful Scorsese moments are rare in this film.

Perhaps it is reverence for Wharton's *The Age of Innocence* that makes Scorsese go soft. Something — an outsider's awkwardness before the excesses of refinement — something — seems to have short-circuited (restrained) Scorsese's efforts to transform Wharton's great novel into his great movie. The sequences, themselves, are beautifully composed; the craftsmanship is mesmerizing. There are clever and pure cinematic moments: a soft left/right wipe that closes like a curtain foreshadows Archer's comment that May is like a closed curtain; an eerie, abruptly inserted matte shot of Mrs. Mingott's mansion off Central Park visualizes how alien this "inaccessible wilderness" felt to New York society of the 1870s; and intentionally disruptive editing implies that art should not always be predictable. Thus, when Sillerton Jackson looks through his opera-glass to see Ellen Olenska, we expect the camera to show us Ellen,

The Age of Innocence (1993): May Welland (Winona Ryder) at an archery trial. Behind the mask of girlish sweetness that May assumes lies a deceptively formidable force.

as he sees her. Instead, Scorsese cuts to a long shot of the stage, followed by a three-quarters shot of Ellen's opera box, as viewed from the stage.

The film also has moments of haunting poignancy: the undulating mass of bowler hats, persisting against wind and rain — an image which somehow suggests that beneath this homogenized surface, each man's sad face is different; the resignation to despair often apparent in Pfeiffer's eyes; and the image of Archer and his grown son, products of very different ages, who, nonetheless, wear the same basic polka-dot tie, but somehow wear it differently.

Punctilious attention to detail went into the making of this film. The china, the food, the costumes, and the etiquette were each overseen by an expert in each of these fields. A dialogue coach helped the actors achieve the right articulated sounds. (Pfeiffer preferred to train by listening to recordings of Louis Auchincloss.) Mary Beth Hurt (Mrs. Beaufort), Alexis Smith (Mrs. van der Luyden), and Miriam Margoles (Mrs. Mingott) even had their portraits painted so that their likenesses would hang in their cinematic homes. Locations were rigorously scouted, and this rigor was rewarded. The Pi Kappa Phi fraternity house in Troy, N.Y., that served as Mrs. Mingott's home and the current Philadelphia Academy of Music which served as the old New York Academy of Music are both remarkably similar to Wharton's descriptions of the story's settings. Perhaps most effective of all is Scorsese's redressed interiors of the Tilden House on Gramercy Park (now the National Arts Club), which became the Beauforts' house and ballroom, a recreation that feels so authentic that my reaction was: So, *that's* what the Beaufort place *really* looked like.

But those moments when we believe in the cinematic reality of Scorsese's *The Age of Innocence* are rare. The movie — clever, attentive to detail, and handsomely manufactured — lacks ideas, audacity ... vision. As we watch *The Age of Innocence*, we want to look through the screen — or, at the least, feed on every single frame; but in the end this feast of images really does not add up to anything very substantial, perhaps because Scorsese's picture, ultimately, is polite. It is consciously artsy.

☞ *A successful novel-based film will demonstrate the capacity to translate what is most integral in the source text, while simultaneously emerging as a distinctive and independent work in its own right. This quality in a novel-based film may best be seen by comparison and contrast. With this standard in mind, watch multiple film versions of one novel that you have read. (For example, there are, at least, ten different versions of Alexandre Dumas's* The Three Musketeers; *nine different versions of Mary Shelley's* Frankenstein; *eight different versions of Bram Stoker's* Dracula; *five different versions of Nathaniel Hawthorne's* The Scarlet Letter; *four different versions of Dashiell Hammett's* The Maltese Falcon; *three different versions of F. Scott Fitzgerald's* The Great Gatsby; *two different versions of Franz Kafka's*

Metamorphosis, and two versions of Edith Wharton's The Age of
Innocence.*) As you watch the films, think of them intertextually, the
films in relationship to the novel and the films in relationship to one
another. In what specific ways is each successful or not in translating
what is integral from the novel, while asserting itself as a distinctively
independent work?*

While a novel-based film should emerge as an independent work, the
film *should not be so self-governing as to be completely independent of or antithetical to the source material,* as the fourth element of this rubric states.
Mildred Pierce (1945) is an example of a film whose representation of character and themes is so self-governing as to be fully contradictory to its
source novel.

The novel *Mildred Pierce* (published in 1941) was written by James
M. Cain, who also wrote *The Postman Always Rings Twice* (published in
1934), and *Double Indemnity* (published in 1943), both of which were
made into highly-regarded films.* Cain's work is characterized by a social
realism that depicts a dark world, filled with world-hardened characters
whose only dependable quality is that they will ever-act in violence and
vice, hoodwinking whatever poor soul is fool enough to care about them.
Cain's work is a significant contribution to the "Hard Boiled School" of
fiction which includes such writers as Raymond Chandler, Ross MacDon-
ald (Kenneth Millar), and Carroll John Daly.

This literary genre explores, in unrelentingly realistic detail, the flaws
of human nature (usually through plots thick with all of the seven deadly
sins) and the failures of American economic, political, and social structures. The Hard-Boiled School of fiction depicts what Raymond Chandler famously describes in *The Simple Art of Murder* as "a world gone
wrong," one with "streets that were dark with something more than night."
The unrelenting, harsh realism of this fiction is most frequently translated
to film through the conventions of *film noir,* a masterful example of which
is the 1941 film version of Dashiell Hammett's *The Maltese Falcon,* directed
by John Huston. A far less masterful example of this genre is the 1945
film, *Mildred Pierce,* based on James M. Cain's 1941 novel.

The novel *Mildred Pierce* probes the underbelly of character and
graphically exposes the defects of human nature and society. Set during
the depression, the novel *Mildred Pierce* is a dark satire of American bourgeois values, of social facades, and of a society that compels characters to

*Double Indemnity, *1944 (rather than the 1973 version), dir. Billy Wilder;* The Postman
Always Rings Twice, *1946 (rather than the 1981 version), dir. Tay Garnett*

grow tougher than their environment. An indictment of social ambition and the destruction that attends such rapaciousness, the book vividly casts Mildred Pierce and her older daughter, Veda, as vulgar social climbers, longing to live a more prestigious life than their middle-class town of Glendale, California, can ever offer them.

Early in Cain's story, when Mildred grows tired of financially supporting her unemployed husband, Bert, and even more tired of his philandering (the last straw is the affair he is having with a neighbor who rents shanties to poor Mexican families), she orders Bert to pack his bags and leave. Mildred, struggling to support herself and her two daughters, Veda and Ray, is rejected by employment agencies, whose companies unabashedly declare that they hire "No Jews ... [and] No women." When the job market fails her, Mildred uses her sexuality. She pursues Bert's former business partner, Wally Fay, and seduces him, in the hopes that he will be a means of financial guidance and support, possibly even agree to marry her. When that does not work out, Mildred starts her own business, first by selling pies, and later by opening a restaurant in which the largest source of profit comes from the post–Prohibition alcohol that Mildred serves. Selling alcohol, during the depression, provides such a financial boon that Mildred to is able to open other restaurants, in tonier Beverly Hills and Laguna Beach.

Her money attracts the handsome, once-rich playboy Monty Beragon, whom Mildred eventually marries, only to discover that he is having an affair with her very own daughter, Veda, the book's greedy and grasping girl-without-a-conscience. Finding Monty and Veda together in bed, Mildred attempts to strangle her own daughter. The story's loose ends are tied up as Monty swindles Mildred out of her business and her money; Ray, Mildred's sweet, younger daughter, dies; Veda abandons Mildred for a singing career in New York; and the once beautiful and sensual Mildred Pierce becomes an unregenerate alcoholic, who ages into "a dumpy thing."

There is an open sexuality and promiscuity to Cain's Mildred and an odd wrinkle to her obsessive love for her daughter, Veda, a love rendered peculiarly complex in Cain's book, as when Mildred "took the lovely creature [Veda] in her arms and kissed her, hard, on the mouth" (268). It is a book of distorted souls. Cain's fictional world is one in which striving after the American dream corrupts, rather than ennobles, a character; and society is largely made up of unprincipled beings who lay to waste any vestige of innocence. The rags-to-riches journey of Cain's *Mildred Pierce* is a descent into a moral abyss of fools, victims, and villains.

Mildred Pierce (1941): In this Warner Bros. sanitized film version of James M. Cain's novel of a dark, unrelentingly harsh, and thoroughly corrupt world, a re-envisioned Mildred Pierce (Joan Crawford) emerges as a virtuous, honest, and long-suffering mother dedicated to her daughter Veda (Ann Blyth), as Wally Fay (Jack Carson) looks on.

The Warner Bros. film version of *Mildred Pierce* stands counter to the novel's point; and it obliterates many of the characteristics of the literary genre in the process, converting Cain's hard boiled fiction into probity-filled, long-suffering-woman melodrama. While Cain's work is a raw indictment of human vulgarity and vice and a critique of the American society that breeds such human corruption, the movie was made as a star vehicle for Joan Crawford. As such, the character of Mildred Pierce is sanitized and transformed into a 1940s icon of female virtue: beautiful, self-assured, well-spoken, and well-heeled, an ever-sacrificing mother of inexhaustible energy.

In altering character, the film also necessarily alters the plot of Cain's novel. In a departure from the book, Veda (Ann Blyth) coldly kills Monty (Zachary Scott); and Mildred, out of abiding, vehement, and unconditional love for her daughter, falsely confesses to the police that she was the one who committed the murder.

Throughout the film, we may judge Mildred's lion-fierce love for her daughter, Veda, to be excessive, as we do in the book; but, in a way vastly different from the novel, we see her as noble throughout the movie. She is long-suffering, self-sacrificial, and, above all, moral. Joan Crawford's Mildred does not yell the coarse things at her daughter that the book's Mildred does, she does not make her fortune through the sale of alcohol to depression clientele, and she does not use her sexuality solely to gain social and financial footing. Joan Crawford's Mildred Pierce betters herself through American true grit: grueling hard work, persistence, ingenuity, and determination. She is depicted as a role model of intelligent and elegant female strength, virtue, and fortitude. In heroicizing Mildred, the film *Mildred Pierce* stands diametrically opposed to the ideas, themes, and ethos that Cain's work embodies. In this important way, it is a seriously flawed film translation of a novel.*

The film *Mildred Pierce* is historically important, however, since Joan Crawford's Mildred stands as an exemplar of spirited, but constrained, femininity, whose dark and curious masculine appearance emerges as far more provocative than conventional feminine beauty, whose restrained surface hints at deep yearnings, and who always has to maneuver within the corseted restrictions of her society. As such, the movie *Mildred Pierce* expresses a part of the American *zeitgeist* that found articulation in the genre known as American "women's films" of the late 1930s and 1940s and is historically significant for this reason.

While many of the films in this genre were based on stage plays, there were significant novel-based films that stand as exemplary "women's films" of the late 1930s and early 1940s. See Table 10 for examples.

Novel-based films must strike the right balance. They must exercise an independence from the book that enables them to stand as meaningful works of art on their own, while avoiding being so fully self-governing as to have an in-name-only relationship to the source book. The greatest novel-based films are able to exist apart from the book because they are films, not just filmed-books. Such movies maximize the very elements that are distinctively inherent to film, while preserving the essential features of the literary text, as we see evident in the novel-based film *The English Patient*.

For a thorough analysis of this novel and film and the specific ways in which the movie Mildred Pierce *consciously imitates the film* Citizen Kane, *please see James W. Welsh's "Mildred Pierce" in* The Encyclopedia of Novels into Movies *(Facts on File, Inc., 1998).*

Table 10.
Novel-based Women's Films of the 1930s and 1940s

Film Title	Director	Novel Title	Author
Camille (1936)	George Cukor	La Dame aux Camelias	Alexandre Dumas fils
The Good Earth (1937)	Sidney Franklin	same title	Pearl S. Buck
Stella Dallas (1937)	King Vidor	same title	Olive Higgins Prouty
The Old Maid (1939)	Edmund Goulding	same title	Edith Wharton
Wuthering Heights (1939)	William Wyler	same title	Emily Brontë
Gone with the Wind (1939)	Victor Fleming (also George Cukor and Sam Wood)	same title	Margaret Mitchell
Ninotchka (1939)	Ernst Lubitsch	same title	Melchior Lengyel
All This, and Heaven, Too (1940)	Anatole Litvak	same title	Rachel Lyman Field
Now, Voyager (1942)	Irving Rapper	same title	Olive Higgins Prouty
Mrs. Miniver (1942)	William Wyler	same title	Jan Struther
Above Suspicion (1943)	Richard Thorpe	same title	Helen MacInnes
Letter from an Unknown Woman (1948)	Max Ophuls	same title	Stefan Zweig

Case Study: The English Patient

What makes *The English Patient* especially interesting to study is that both the novel and the film can stand alone as paradigms of their genres, the modern novel and the non-linear narrative film respectively. Each utilizes the specific tools of its medium to create equally memorable, rhapsodic and compassionate disquietudes on love in the time of war. The two works are so self-reliant that each can be effectively explored, fully independent of each other. Yet, when the novel and the film are examined side by side, an interplay emerges that produces insights into each individual work that studying the novel *The English Patient* or the film in isolation might not produce. Additionally, the film *The English Patient* provides a clear illustration of the successful employment of each of the four points of the aesthetic rubric.

Michael Ondaatje's Novel, *The English Patient* (1992)

Winner of the prestigious Booker Prize (1992), *The English Patient* was written by poet and novelist Michael Ondaatje. Ondaatje's sense of verse is apparent in the lyrical style of *The English Patient*, and the novel's principal themes are continuations of themes that appeared in two of his earlier poetic works: *The Dainty Monsters* (1967) and *The Collected Works of Billy the Kid: Left-Handed Poems* (1970). Like those two works, *The English Patient* explores love, memory, exile, the conflicted sense of national identity, the political and moral danger of complicity with the ruling elite, the fiery intensity of sexual passion, the postmodernist sense of history as a function of perspective, the tension between creative and destructive energy, and, above all, the many manifestations of the outsider — the isolato. Stylistic conventions that emerge in *The English Patient* appeared first in Ondaatje's poetry: fragmentation, action that moves backward and forward in time, interruptions of and intrusions on the story, subversion of any notion of linear narration, shifting narrative points of view, and the blending of genres.

The English Patient is a continuation of an earlier Ondaatje novel, *In the Skin of a Lion* (1987), which first introduces David Caravaggio, the Italian-Canadian thief, and Patrick Lewis, Hana's stepfather, who dies of burns in *The English Patient*.

The English Patient opens in Tuscany, twenty miles outside of Florence, at the Villa San Girolamo, where Hana, a French-Canadian nurse, is caring for a single patient, so badly burned in an airplane crash that neither his identity nor nationality is ascertainable. He is believed to be English. However, not English at all, the patient is the Hungarian, Count Laszlo de Almásy, a member of the Royal Geographical Society, a group of cartographers who create maps of the North African desert shortly before the outbreak of World War II.

Hana's spirit and her faith have been near fully destroyed by the vast human destruction she has witnessed as a nurse during combat and by the specific war-related deaths of her unborn child, her fiancé, and her stepfather. Just twenty years old, she remembers soldiers "coming in with just bits of their bodies, falling in love with [her] for an hour and then dying." As the war nears its end, Hana welcomes the solace she finds in taking care of one dying man in the relative peace of the Italian countryside. In the quiet and remove of the Tuscan villa, Hana's "English" patient slowly tells her his story. Affected by the large doses of morphine that he takes for the pain, his narration is intermittent, fragmented, non-linear, and often dream-like. Its qualities define not only Almásy's narration, but the narrative structure of the entire book, also. The novel, which spans seven years, is assembled from ever-shifting, multiple points of view, Almásy's being only one of several consciousnesses that we enter.

Almásy's memory carries him back to the pre-war Sahara Desert, where he is working on a map-making expedition in northern Africa. (Ondaatje's use of maps, geography, and cartography work as metaphors for people, for their particular contours, and for our need to explore and to know — to *map*— the intricate terrain of those we love.) Almásy's routinized life is radically disrupted when a newlywed couple — Katharine Clifton, an English woman, and her pilot husband, Geoffrey Clifton — joins the cartography expedition. Against their reason and will, Almásy and Katharine fall in love. Their affair, the description of which is delayed for one hundred and thirty pages, begins in Cairo in 1938 and is tempestuous — fiery — with a blaze that deeply and irreparably damages their own lives and the lives of others.

The novel weaves together the lives of several characters: Count Laszlo de Almásy (the "English" patient); Katharine Clifton, Almásy's married lover; Hana, his nurse; Kip, the kind and gentle Sikh, who falls in love with Hana while serving as a British Army lieutenant in a bomb disposal squad; David Caravaggio, Hana's childhood friend and a morphine addict, who carries a personal vendetta against Almásy and who turns up one day at the villa; and Geoffrey Clifton, Katharine's husband.

The English Patient explores the uncertainty and indeterminacy of identity and nationalism and the extent to which politics constructs selfhood. As such, the novel provides fertile ground for exploration in postcolonial theory. Kirpal Singh, from the Punjab of India, renamed the more–Anglicized "Kip" by an English military officer, stands both apart from and assimilated by British imperial culture. Kip is the paradox of one person who is both an Anglophile and an anti-colonial. Geoffrey Clifton, the outwardly easy-going, apolitical aristocrat, is actually working for British Intelligence on the African expedition; the Hungarian, Count Laszlo de Almásy, incorrectly labeled "English," is believed to be a

Gestapo spy, though the truth of this is never determined*; and the Italian-Canadian David Caravaggio, believed to be a spy for the Allies, is tortured (his thumbs are amputated) by order of an Italian, Ranuccio Tommasoni, working for the Germans.

Issues of identity and post-colonial theory are also insinuated in the novel's love relationships — all of which fail: Katharine and Almásy's, Katharine and Geoffrey's, Caravaggio and Giannetta's, Hana and her fiancé's, and Hana and Kip's. While Katharine and Almásy's love is marked by the tropes of fire — its potency to give and take life — and desert sand, with its unstable, ever-shifting, threatening, and mystifying nature, Kip and Hana's love is lyricized through the tropes of art and explosives, both of which Kip understands deeply and intuitively. Hana is soul-weary of the explosions upon explosions, and the capricious deaths without warning that characterize life as a combat nurse; and Kip, a sapper, has been trained to recognize explosives and to detonate them before they can cause harm. Hana, young and innocent, never expects the hidden explosives that take their toll on all around her, while Kip cannot look upon a field, a room, a roadway, or a church — anything — without seeing the threat of a hidden bomb's existence. Kip knows that bombs are often secreted in the most benign locales: the spines of books, the trunks of flowering fruit trees, and the wires within a piano. He meets Hana by warning her away from the piano that she innocently is about to play in the villa, and later he saves her life when she strolls, unknowingly and unmindfully, into a field of grass filled with random, active mines. Hana needs Kip to live, and he needs her, too, the truth of which is poeticized by his needing "a third hand," which Hana provides, to defuse the live wires of a bomb.

In their brief time at the villa, Kip tells Hana of the glorious Italian statuary that he has come across in his war-time travels through Italy and how he slept beside a "grieving angel ... that he found beautiful." He brings her to a partially bombed-out church filled with numbingly beautiful frescoes. He understands humankind's potent capacity to level great destruction, but also to create prodigious beauty, and in the church, alone

---

Caravaggio tells Hana a rumor, the veracity of which is never determined. Caravaggio claims that Almásy sided with the Germans during the war by carrying out Rommel's request to guide the Nazi spy, Eppler, safely across the desert and into Cairo. In the novel, the truth of this rumor, as well as Almásy's political ties, are kept vague and indeterminate. However, the historical, real-life "Almásy" clearly did work for the Germans. James M. Welsh explains: "As revealed to The Washington Post by Elizabeth Salett (December 4, 1996), the fictional character was based on an actual Nazi spy who later became an aide-de-camp to Field Marshal Erwin Rommel of the German African Corps" (Tibbetts and Welsh, Novels, 114).

with Kip, Hana comes to understand it, too. Kip, a product of colonial India, falls in love with Hana, from Canada, a country also once a colony of England. The two love deeply and sweetly and genuinely, yet cultural codes prohibit their marrying, and, ultimately, Kip returns to India to assume the role his family expects of him as a second son. He becomes a doctor, marries, and has children. Both exiles of sorts brought together in Italy through war, Kip and Hana return to their own countries, where they live "in their customs and habits," while feeling ever as outsiders.

The English Patient explores the complexities of emotional, political, national, and personal displacement. It examines the tangle of love and duty, Self and Other; and it does so with a poetic delicacy and a visual alertness that elevates literature to something more than just fiction.

☞ *1. Read* The English Patient. *How would you describe Ondaatje's writing style? Think of the narrative structure of the work, of the visual elements he incorporates. In what specific structural and visual ways does the novel resemble a film or lend itself to the qualities of film? What structural and visual elements might make the novel difficult to translate to the screen?*

☞ *2. The novel* The English Patient *makes reference to many other literary, historical, and artistic works, each of which is chosen for the intertextual relationship that it creates with Ondaatje's novel. These works referenced in the novel include: Caravaggio's paintings, Herodotus's* Histories, *Tacitus's* Annales, *William Shakespeare's* The Tempest, *Stendhal's* The Charterhouse of Parma, *Herman Melville's* Pierre, *Leo Tolstoy's* Anna Karenina, *James Fenimore Cooper's* The Last of the Mohicans, *and Rudyard Kipling's* Kim. *Choose any one work and explore its intertextual significance to* The English Patient.

The Traditional Film Translation of *The English Patient* (1996)

The film *The English Patient* communicates definite ideas concerning the *integral* meaning and value of Ondaatje's literary text. When director/screenwriter Anthony Minghella brought Michael Ondaatje's novel to the screen, he understood that fundamental to the work were the stylistic conventions employed throughout the novel. As such, Minghella creates in film the equivalents of Ondaatje's fragmentation, his action that moves backward and forward in time, his interruptions of and intrusions on the story, his subversion of any notion of linear narration, his shifting narrative points of view, and his blending of genres — in this case film genres, as the movie functions as an art film, a woman's picture, an action-adventure story, and an experimental study in the structuring of narration.

Minghella understood that how a story is told affects what is being expressed, and, as such, his non-linear structuring gets at fundamental ideas inherent in Ondaatje's novel: that human memory does not operate in accord with tight linear structures; that life does not adhere to causal logic and rational linear sequences; and that history, personal and multinational, to varying degrees, is a function of perception.

The film functions as a traditional translation of Ondaatje's novel by maintaining the overall traits of the novel (its plot, settings, themes, and stylistic conventions), but revamping details in ways that are seen as necessary and fitting. The time constraints of a feature-length film were a consideration (the movie is kept to 160 minutes); and, in the interest of time, Minghella omitted portions of the 300-plus-page book, the most significant alteration of which was to diminish the Hana (Juliette Binoche) and Kip (Naveen Andrews) love story and to focus more specifically on Katharine (Kristin Scott Thomas) and Almásy's (Ralph Fiennes) story, with the plots involving David Caravaggio (Willem Dafoe) and Geoffrey Clifton (Colin Firth) made more incidental. In the process of concentrating on the English Patient's love story, however, the film romanticizes Almásy's character in ways that the book does not. He is made younger (in the novel he is fifteen years older than Katharine), and his compliance with the Nazis is no longer ambiguous. In fact, his cooperation with them is made clear, and even somewhat virtuous. Almásy agrees to guide a Nazi spy across the desert and back to Cairo in exchange for the Germans' assistance in transporting him back to the Cave of the Swimmers, where a grievously injured Katharine lies waiting for rescue. As James Welsh explains, "Minghella's film, more than Ondaatje's novel, romanticizes this committed Nazi collaborator by transforming him into a heroic lover who collaborates with the Germans only to save the woman he loves" (*Novels*, 114).

Much as the novel creates a complex of intertextual meanings (see ☞ 2. above), the film references some of these same works, with the same effect. Especially strong is the visual re-creation and employment of Almásy's memorabilia-filled, battered copy of Herodotus's *Histories*. Herodotus's historical accounts were culled from oral stories that he heard as he traveled from oasis to oasis, much as we cull the history of Almásy, Katharine, Kip, and Hana from the piecemeal stories that we are told on

The English Patient (1996): Count Laszlo de Almásy (Ralph Fiennes) and Katharine Clifton (Kristin Scott Thomas). Their emerging relationship explores the complexities of emotional, ethical, political, national, and personal displacement.

the screen. While the film does a commendable job of incorporating Ondaatje's use of Herodotus as intertext, the film also dislodges itself sufficiently from Ondaatje's novel to stands as an independent work of art which creates intertextual relationships of its own. Most interestingly is the subtle series of thematic references to Alain Resnais's *Hiroshima, Mon Amour*, and the visual mannerisms of Resnais's film (its particular rhythms, textures, editing practices, and camera placement) that Minghella employs in similar ways.

☞   *Watch both* The English Patient *and* Hiroshima, Mon Amour. *What specific visual ideas has Minghella taken from Resnais's film? What thematic similarities exist? In the novel Kip and his brother debate Hiroshima. What is the relationship of their debate to the questions posed within* Hiroshima, Mon Amour? *What parallels exist between*

the stories? Between characters? Between such themes as the relation-
ship of past to present, of subjective time, of personal and national
anguish, and of interracial love?

The film *The English Patient* exhibits a collaboration of filmmaking skills that tells a beautiful story beautifully. The film employs the strengths of Walter Murch's editing, Gabriel Yared's score, Stuart Craig's production design, and John Seale's cinematography to create a graceful, fluid film that shifts from the realistic to the dreamlike, from the past to present, from one pairing of lovers to another, and from the curiously beautiful contours of the desert to the equally curious and lovely contours of the human body. Sound is used simply, yet effectively, as when the western song "Jelly Roll Blues" blends in with Arabic chatter, when the simple sound of a car horn carries Almásy back to his memories of Cairo, and when visual edits are accomplished through overlapping sound, as when a piano playing in the background while Katharine is in the African desert becomes the music that Hana is playing on the piano at the Italian villa in the sequence following immediately.

The film *The English Patient* demonstrates the audacity to create a work that stands as a world apart from the novel. In keeping with the values of pure cinema, the movie relates its story largely through visual images, rather than through dialogue taken from the novel. Much as the novel creates a distinctive, poetic, and lyrical style, the film creates a distinctive, highly evocative, and similarly lyrical style largely through its memorable images. Examples of this include Hana swinging in pure joy and abandon as Kip raises her up on a rope hoist to see the church frescoes; the solitary biplane soaring leisurely over a contour of desert dunes shot to look like a woman's body and later replicated in the shot of Katharine's bare back; the magical and mystical Cave of the Swimmers; Almásy carrying Katharine's dead body wrapped in a pure white silk parachute against the golds and reds of the desert; Hana's simple reflection in a basin of water; fragments of mirrors, glass, and shells catching the reflection of the fragmented Hana and her broken-apart world; and the simple beauty of Kip removing his turban and setting free his long dark silky hair, which he washes unaware of the depth and effect of this simple act.

The novel *The English Patient* was the recipient of the prestigious Booker Prize; the film, analogously, was the winner of nine Academy awards, including Best Picture of 1996. Both the novel and the film have been honored, appropriately, as worthy examples of their own art forms.

One especially challenging way in which the film equals an achievement of the novel is in its rendering of the interior life of its characters. While novels are inherently disposed to presenting interiority, this same task, that is, depicting the internal life of a character, presents a particular challenge for film. Prose allows direct description of a character's inner thoughts, feelings, and responses in ways that film does not. Literature can use the devices of words, such as interior monologues, verbal narration, and lengthy descriptive passage, to explain, often in subtle detail, the complexities of a character's innermost perceptions and thought processes. Prose is not limited to the outside view of a character in the way that a camera is. The camera must find its own methods of communicating the inner workings of character.

One interesting example of a film which finds its own modes of expressing the inner operations of character is *Last Tango in Paris* (1972), director/screenwriter Bernardo Bertolucci's traditional film translation of Robert Alley's novel. Bertolucci's film not only depicts the inner life of its characters; but also, and even more challenging for film, conveys complex emotional and psychological matters that the characters, themselves, do not quite understand. Film critic Pauline Kael considered *Last Tango in Paris* to be "a landmark in movie history," and throughout her praise-filled review of the movie, she describes the impact of this film as one "that has made the strongest impression on [her] in almost twenty years of reviewing" (*For Keeps*, 450, 456).

Like Alley's novel, Bertolucci's film is deeply revelatory about the most private inner regions of its two principal characters, Paul (Marlon Brando) and Jeanne (Maria Schneider)—and as deeply disturbing. The novel is a stark treatise on existentialism, as is the movie. The film *Last Tango in Paris* uses the resources of cinema—lighting, angles, color, movement/stasis, sound, editing, and acting—to bring us into the characters' inner lives that Alley's book captures so effectively. Both the novel and the film are about two strangers: Paul, an American living in Paris, and Jeanne, a much younger, engaged, Parisian woman, who meet and have a brief, torrid affair in an empty Parisian apartment. Paul insists that the two know as little as possible about one other, not even each another's names; and while we are shown details of Paul's and Jeanne's lives outside of their tryst, the two know only of each other what they experience in the Parisian flat.

Jeanne does not know that just prior to their having met, Paul lost his wife to suicide; and, in response to the acute depression, guilt, and anger that her death has brought on, he uses sex as a conduit for human

Last Tango in Paris (1972): Paul (Marlon Brando) and Jeanne (Maria Schneider) in the Paris apartment they share. Cinematographer Vittorio Storaro's intimate camera records the poetic rawness of the performances by Brando and Schneider and their portrayals of the emotional cores of their characters.

connection, and, contrarily, as proof of one's acute isolation from all intimate human contact. Also an expression of his aggression, the sexual
exchanges of Paul and Jeanne are often brutal — impolite and impersonal —
and, yet, there is an attending tenderness that comes through in Brando's
performance. In the stark barbarity and bravura of Paul's sexual demands
on Jeanne, we see just how vulnerable and needy he is, how deeply he craves
the touch of intimacy, validation, and understanding, and how profoundly
he is grieving the human condition. Paul can only express his soulful needs
in crude, cruel, and debasing acts of sexuality; and in the alarming stark-
ness of it all, we see the complex inner working of Paul and of Jeanne, the
colonel's daughter who is energized by her older lover's naughty sexual
orders.

Cinematographer Vittorio Storaro's unflinchingly intimate camera
records the poetic rawness of the performances by Brando and Schneider
and the emotional core of the characters that they somehow release. However, when *Last Tango in Paris* first opened, many mainstream theaters, as
well as art houses, refused to book it because of the film's frank treatment
of sexuality, which by current standards seems somewhat less shocking
than it seemed in 1972.

Last Tango in Paris is, of course, by American standards, a foreign
film. Foreign films that are based on novels often generate the bonus of
introducing us to the literature of other nations. Because we have seen the
film, we become interested in reading the novel upon which it has been
based. This has given rise to the publishing phenomenon of novels that
were popular in their native countries becoming more popular internationally after the release of a successful film. Table 11 lists examples of novels that were popular in their native countries, but specifically gained
English language readership in the aftermath of their film's success.

There are countless film translations of novels, and there is an ever-
growing number of novelizations of movies, i.e., books written subse-
quent to the film's release and done with the intent of capitalizing
financially on the popularity of a given movie. These are novels based on
the screenplay and include works as varied in taste as *Pretty in Pink* (by
H. B. Gilmour from screenplay by John Hughes), *Top Gun* (by Mike
Cogan from screenplay by Jim Cash and Jack Epps, Jr.), *2001: A Space
Odyssey* (by Arthur C. Clarke from screenplay by Stanley Kubrick and
Arthur C. Clarke), and *Dirty Harry* (by Phillip Rock from screenplay by
Harry Julian Fink and R. M. Fink). While these novels remain faithful to
the details of the screenplay's story, they lack the style, complexity, sub-
tlety, and inventiveness of literary excellence.

Table 11.
International Novels Popularized by Their Film's Success

Book	Author	Country of Film Production	Film Title & Year of Release	Director
The Four Horsemen of the Apocalypse	Vicente Blasco Ibáñez	Spain	same title 1921	Rex Ingram
(*Los Cuatro Jinetes del Apocalipsis*)			1961	Vincent Minelli
Devdas	Saratchandra Chatto-padhyay	India	same title 1928	Naresh Chandra Mitra
			1935 (two different films, with different casts; one in Hindi, the other in Bengali)	P. C. Barua
			1955 (in Hindi)	Bimal Roy
			2002 (in Hindi)	Sanjay Leela Bhansali
			2002 (in Bengali)	Shakti Samanta
Tale of the Genji (*Genji Monogatari*)	Murasaki Shikibu	Japan	same title 1952	Kosaburo Yoshimura
		Japan	1966	Kon Ichikawa
		USA	1987	Gisaburo Sugii
Pather Panchali and *Aparajito*	Bibhuti Bhusan Banerjee	India	*The Apu Trilogy* 1956–1959	Satyajit Ray
Two Women (*La ciociara*)	Alberto Moravia	Italy	same title 1960	Vittorio De Sica
Macunaima	Mario De Andrade	Brazil	same title 1969	Joaquim Pedro de Andrade

→

Book	Author	Country of Film Production	Film Title & Year of Release	Director
The Garden of Finzi-Continis (Il giardino dei Finzi-Contini)	Giorgio Bassani	Italy	same title 1971	Vittorio De Sica
Xala	Ousmane Sembene	Senegal	same title 1975	Ousmane Sembene
The Woman and the Puppet	Pierre Louys	Spain	That Obscure Object of Desire 1977	Luis Buñuel
Red Sorghum Family	Mo Yan	China	Red Sorghum 1987	Zhang Yimou
Kitchen	Mahoko "Banana" Yoshimoto	Japan	same title 1989	Morita Yoshimitsu
Goodbye Tsugumi	Mahoko "Banana" Yoshimoto	Japan	Tsugumi 1990	Jun Ichikawa
Wives and Concubines (Quiqie Chenggun)	Su Tong	China	Raise the Red Lantern 1991	Zhang Yimou
Farewell, My Concubine	Lilian Lee	China/Hong Kong	Ba wang bie ji 1993	Kaige Chen
Central Station	Joao Emauel Caineiro	Brazil/France	Central do Brasil 1998	Walter Salles
The Mystic Masseur	V. S. Naipaul	India/ Trinidad/ Tobago	same title 2001	Ismail Merchant

Curiously, there is not one, single, sustained literary novel that functions as a translation of a film, that reconfigures and transforms the original cinematic material into the writer's notion of the integral meaning
and value of the film text. While there are many novelizations of screenplays, there is no novel that translates a film in such a way that the liter-

ature emerges as a self-reliant text, an accomplished and individualistic offspring of the movie. To date, there is no *film-based* novel that attempts a direct and conscious translation — a literal, traditional, or radical translation — of a film from the language of cinema into the language of literature. Simply put and curiously, in the case of the novel, there is no existing literature that attempts to do with film what film has done with literature.

CHAPTER V

Plays into Film

In many ways, the stage play is the literary medium most similar to the motion pictures. Both forms integrate like elements of performance.* Like a movie, a stage play engages actors in dramatic situations who incorporate the directives of written dialogue and body movement into their work. The actors' presence in the play or film raises issues of intertextuality as their performances are often not isolated events, but, instead, exist within the context of past roles they have played, their degree of popularity at the moment, and their real-life situations to which the audience is privy. The actors' past histories cause the current performances to resonate in both obvious ways and in unmappably complex ways in each viewer's response, affecting, to varying degrees, each spectator's reception of the entire play or film.

Like a movie, a play utilizes sets, sound effects, lighting, costumes, directors, and producers all working in cooperative service to create a seamless whole. Both forms invariably rely upon visual composition. However, unlike other visual art forms, painting or sculpture, for example, films and plays are temporal. They move through time; and the construction of each, thus, implements temporal compositional elements, i.e.,

---

*The practice of reading plays is a modern usage, with its origins, arguably, in the writing of such modern dramatists as Henrik Ibsen and August Strindberg, who consciously made even their stage directions (which would never be heard by an audience) more literate and literary, with the awareness that their plays would be read as a thing apart from any performance. The custom of making the stage play concurrently a reader's text is apparent in the writing practices of contemporary playwrights as diverse as Tennessee Williams, David Mamet, and Sam Sheppard.
    More recently, a wider, popular interest in reading screenplays has emerged; and in response to the growing interest, many more screenplays are being published and even posted on the Internet (in all stages of completion), with writer/director Kevin Smith often generously making his shooting script available on his web site.

those various transitional devices that move the audience from one scene or sequence to another (please see the discussion of literary and film "transitions" in Chapter I).

Plays and films are constructed from an ever-shifting series of *mise-en-scène*-the arrangement of all the visual components occurring at any given moment on the stage or the screen. The term *mise-en-scène*, frequently used in film discussions, originated in theater where it was employed to describe the specific elements of staging determined for a given play. In plays and in film, the arrangement of the visual elements — the composite of all the objects, people, lighting, and color — is very similar. However, unlike staging, filming can incorporate camera movement, distance, and angles to shape its *mise-en-scène*; and, unlike filming, staging can employ creative ways of utilizing its very real three dimensions, a quality that the two dimensions of film can only simulate.

Movies and plays are performed to an audience of viewers who react both individually and collectively to what they experience, and who sit in a theater in a fixed position in relation to, and at an approximately equal distance from, the screen or the stage. The point of view for the theater audience remains static, delineated by the focal field of the stage. Film, in contrast, has the ability to overcome the confines of the proscenium. It can shift audience perspective and create the illusion that the constancy of distance between performer and spectator is shifting. Both theater and film have their distinct ways of calling the audience's attention, at any given moment, to specific visual detail. Film accomplishes this largely through camera placement. Theater, instead, relies on the actor, aided, perhaps by effects of lighting and sound, to compel the audience to look at chosen elements on stage.

The running time of a feature film approximates the performance time of a standard play, and the movie screen in a theater (with an aspect ration of 1.85 to 1 for standard-wide or 2.35 to 1 for wide-screen) is shaped like a proscenium stage, so much so that for "a long time the medium of the motion picture was regarded as a 'new proscenium'" (Tibbetts, *The American Theatrical Film*, 1).

But, ironically, it is the inherent compatibilies of the two forms that, also, ironically, present the greatest difficulties for the transition of a play to the screen, as the filmmakers must find the means of making the movie something more than simply a filmed stage play. The movie must negotiate specific ways of eliminating the stagy feeling that would seem disruptive and discrepant in a film.

Early movie versions of plays were often simply "filmed theater," where a stationary camera was situated to record a performance occurring on a stage. In the earliest years of film production, it was a desirable quality for a movie to replicate the proscenium stage, creating the illusion that the movie-goers were in a legitimate theater, watching a play or attending a popular vaudeville show. By 1920, theoretical disputes arose regarding the nature, value, and function of film and its relationship to theater. The debate is embodied in the divergent views of David Belasco and Hugo Munsterberg.

Theater's much-admired director/producer/playwright David Belasco (1853–1931) maintained that film is an offshoot of theater, and a somewhat inferior art form, at that. David Belasco's stage work falls into three genres: historical spectacle, melodrama, and domestic narratives. No matter the genre, however, the same abiding aesthetic value permeates all his work: a driving insistence that the world being depicted be suffused with accurate, and, at times, spectacular, visual details — costumes, props, sets, and lighting — that recreate, as realistically as possible, the "intimate details of daily life" of the milieu being represented (Vardac, 121). Thus, Belasco's name has become synonymous with the "Drama of Realism."* According to Belasco, a film is strongest when it replicates the aesthetic values of the stage. Whether stage or screen, Belasco would value the creation of a viewing experience that would approximate the real experience of the narrative. In the case of film, the camera should function as a recorder, with the signature (the distinguishing stylistic qualities) of the filmmaker kept unobtrusive.

To the other extreme, the experimental psychologist and theorist Hugo Munsterberg (1863–1916) asserted that film is a self-reliant art form and was to become nothing less than *the* art form of the twentieth century. In 1916, Hugo Munsterberg published *The Photoplay: A Psychological Study*. The work, written without any intellectual antecedent on the topic, was the first theoretical treatment of film. *The Photoplay* considers cinema in terms of three distinct topics: first, the history of film (its genesis and technological developments, its initial dependence on the "stage play," and its eventual emancipation from theater); second, the psycho-sociological aspects of film; and third, the aesthetics of film.

Munsterberg's aesthetic theory asserts that art is its own context. Not the conduit for other experiences, art must submit to its own aesthetic criteria. In championing film as an aesthetic medium, Munsterberg cautioned that the function of movies is not to attempt replication of our expe-

---

For a discussion of "Belasco and the Drama of Intimate Realism," see Vardac, pp. 129–135.

riences of the natural or the theatrical world, but to utilize those spatial, temporal, and causal relationships that are unique to filmmaking.

Early filmmakers were divided on this debate between film as an offshoot of theater versus film as an independent art form. D. W. Griffith operated much more in Munsterberg's tradition by exploring, discovering, and exploiting those qualities and effects that are unique to film. In contrast, Cecil B. DeMille operated in accord with Belasco's tradition, working much more in the mainstream of cinematic representation. DeMille endowed his movies with the *theatrical* values established by Belasco: proscenium composition, pageantry, spectacle, pictorial realism, and painstakingly authentic staging details. To this day, play-based films invariably will favor one of these two major, divergent traditions.

☞ *Watch a film by Cecil B. DeMille (examples include* The Cheat *[1915]*, Joan the Woman *[1917]*, The Ten Commandments *[1923]*, King of Kings *[1927]*, *or* Cleopatra *[1934]*). *Watch the film in terms of Belasco's staging ideas: the look of the mise-en-scène as composed on a proscenium stage and the integration of pageantry, spectacle, pictorial realism, and precise, authentic staging details (props, lighting, set design, and costumes). Under these aesthetic values, the camera and the editing should be unobtrusive, with the camera inconspicuously recording the action and the editing invisibly stitching together the shots. Watch a DeMille film in terms of these camera and editing protocols.*

Watch a film by D. W. Griffith (examples include The Avenging Conscience *[1914]*, The Birth of a Nation *[1915]*, Intolerance *[1916]*, Broken Blossoms *[1919]*, Way Down East *[1920] or* Orphans of the Storm *[1921]*). *Watch the film in terms of Griffith's attempts to break with stage traditions, the very quality that Munsterberg's film aesthetics advocates. Look at the cinematic values in Griffith's film — the things that Griffith shows us a movie can do that the stage cannot; for example, his particular use of close-ups and mid-shots, camera movement, rhythmic editing, and the effects that film can create through lighting. For Munsterberg, film editing is a distinct and defining element of cinema's aesthetics. Editing allows a movie to shift effortlessly in time and in locale, and, in doing so, parallels the workings of the human mind, which shifts effortlessly in these same ways. Notice the particular ways in which the Griffith film that you watch is cut.*

Belasco's overall aesthetic values are at work in 1999 film version of *The Winslow Boy*, a traditional translation of Terence Rattigan's 1946 play

of the same title. Rattigan based *The Winslow Boy* on the real 1910 case of
George Archer-Shee ("cadet Ronald 'Ronnie' Arthur Winslow" in the film),
a schoolboy, expelled from a British naval academy for the alleged theft
of a five-shilling postal order. His father, believing in his son's innocence,
decided to clear the family's name by fighting the expulsion openly in
court. When Sir Robert Morton, the solicitor who argued the "gross inde-
cency" case against Oscar Wilde, agreed to defend young Archer-Shee,
the case became high-profile, sparking nation-wide interest throughout
Edwardian England, much in the same way as the O. J. Simpson trial
became front-page news in 1995 America and the Monica Lewinsky/Bill
Clinton ordeal distracted the American people, not to mention their Congress, in 1998.

In addition to this 1999 movie, *The Winslow Boy* has been translated
to film four other times, with three television productions (1958, 1977,
and 1990) and one earlier theatrical-release film, the 1948 movie directed
by Anthony Asquith and starring Robert Donat (Sir Robert Morton),
Cedric Hardwicke (Arthur Winslow), and Margaret Leighton (Catherine
Winslow). The 1948 film underscores the external agencies that become
involved in the Winslow case. With swift shifts of locale which cinema
can implement but the stage cannot, the 1948 film transports us to
Osborne, England, and the Royal Naval Academy there, to inside the
offices of both the First Sea Lord and the Second Sea Lord of the Admi-
ralty, and to the lofty corridors of Parliament, the floor of the House of
Commons, and the trial before the Lord Chief Justice. In addition, the
movie shows a Sunday church service, multiple rooms in the Winslow family house, an evening at the theater with them (which suddenly incorporates a song and dance number: the mildly risqué "Whom Were You with
Last Night"), and the city streets, complete with an organ grinder and
monkey.

In contrast to the 1948 movie of *The Winslow Boy*, the 1999 film
largely contains the action within the stage-bound setting that Terence
Rattigan constructed.* With this restricted setting, the movie could have
been filmed theater, a method of stage to screen translation which records
the performance as a stage piece, enacting the play as written and restricting the *mise-en-scène* to exactly what a theatrical audience might see were
they looking at the stage; but it is not filmed theater. To remind us of this

*The cast includes Jeremy Northam (Sir Robert Morton); Nigel Hawthorne (Arthur Winslow);
director David Mamet's wife, Rebecca Pidgeon (Catherine Winslow); and Pidgeon's real-life
brother, Matthew Pidgeon, playing Catherine's brother Dickie Winslow.

distinction, the 1999 *The Winslow Boy* cuts, occasionally, to remote locales (a newspaper office, the House of Commons, and the Horse Guards), but these cuts are kept infrequent and brief. Incorporating cinematic techniques (location shooting, editing, camera placement and movement), the film simultaneously privileges the values of theater promoted by David Belasco. The 1999 film structures the look of the *mise-en-scène* in ways that resemble visual composition on a proscenium stage. It accentuates stage acting through the actors' speech, movements, and gesticulations; and it integrates a preference for pictorial realism, dramatic spectacle, and precise, authentic staging details (props, lighting, set design, and costumes). The Winslow house was shot on location in a home in Clapham, a section of south London; the costumes were constructed in scrupulous accord with historical accuracy; and props (newspapers, cartoons, souvenir cups, sheet music, post cards, and pencils), accurate to the time, were used throughout the film.

A traditional film translation of Rattigan's play, the 1999 *The Winslow Boy* was directed by David Mamet, who is, himself, a playwright best known for such intricate, twisting dramatic works as *Sexual Perversity in Chicago,** *American Buffalo, Glengarry Glen Ross, Oleanna, House of Games,* and *The Spanish Prisoner,* all of which are stage plays which have been made into films. Mamet's plays, in form and style, employ discontinuity, disjointedness, dislocation, eclecticism, and "the grammatical chaos of ordinary conversation" (Dean, 22). In contrast to the modern tones and compositional values of Mamet's plays, the narrative structure of *The Winslow Boy* is classical. It adheres to compositional values of a clean, balanced, well-ordered narrative line, one which employs symmetry, clarity, decorum, proportion, unity, and logic. However different in style and structure the play may be from Mamet's own writing, *The Winslow Boy* is concerned with essential themes that occupy Mamet's plays: language that often conceals emotion rather than expresses it; human behavior (including modes of speaking) as a construct of manners — societal rules and norms; appearance versus reality; the effects of alienation; and the value of drama not as "an attempt to depict something which is real in the external world but rather an attempt to depict something which is real in an internal world" (Mamet, quoted in Dean, 18).

In keeping with the original stage play (which takes place entirely in the Winslow home) and in accord with Mamet's own dramatic values, his

---

*About Last Night ... *(1986, dir. Edward Zwick) is the film version of Mamet's play* Sexual Perversity in Chicago.

film of *The Winslow Boy* contains the action almost entirely within Rattigan's interior settings because the containment focuses our attention on the effect that the very public lawsuit has on the internal world of the Winslow family, their friends, and their associates. The story of the Winslow boy is not about the debates raging within the British House of Commons or even about the decisions of Osborne's Royal Naval Academy, Mamet's film tell us. *The Winslow Boy* is about the inner life of the Winslow family, a life that is going on in the confined region behind the closed doors of the family's South Kensington home. Rattigan's stage play laid open that interior world. By restricting the action largely to Rattigan's stage space, Mamet's film translates not only the specific intent of the play, but also, and more largely, David Belasco's belief in the power and value of the focalizing, circumscribing, delimitating space of the stage.

☞ *Read Terence Rattigan's play* The Winslow Boy. *Watch the three distinctly different film translations of it: the 1948 movie, which employs the devices of cinema to open up the stage space; the 1990 television production, which conforms largely to the values of filmed theater*; and the 1999 film, which privileges the conventions of the stage while utilizing cinematic conventions. Watch the movies in terms of David Belasco's values. Assess the merits of one of the films by evaluating it according the four points of the aesthetic rubric introduced in Chapter IV and available in Appendix A.*

Plays rely largely on dialogue. Words — the actors' lines — move the narrative forward and reveal developments in character. A difficulty with the Belasco tradition of translating a stage play to film is that the movie can become mostly talk, an example of which is *Closer* (2004), Mike Nichols's literal film translation of Patrick Marber's play of the same title.

In contrast to Belasco's tradition, play-based films that follow Munsterberg's tradition will utilize modes of representation that are distinctly cinematic; images, for example, will accomplish what words do in a play. Diverse examples of a stage-to-screen translation made in this tradition include *Casablanca* (1942, dir. Michael Curtiz from the play *Everybody Comes to Rick's* by Murray Burnett and Joan Alison); *The Lower Depths* (1957, dir. Akira Kurosawa, playwright Maxim Gorky); *Stalag 17* (1953, dir. Billy Wilder, playwrights Donald Bevan and Edmund Trzcinski); *Oedipus Rex* (1967, dir. Pier Paolo Pasolini, playwright Sophocles); *Chimes*

---

*The cast includes Ian Richardson (Sir Robert Morton), Gordon Jackson (Arthur Winslow), and Emma Thompson (Catherine Winslow).

at Midnight (1967, dir. Orson Welles, from William Shakespeare's *Henry* plays); *The Elephant Man* (1980, dir. David Lynch, playwright Bernard Pomerance); and *Death and the Maiden* (1994, dir. Roman Polanski, playwright Ariel Dorfman).

Munsterberg's valuation of film as a distinct art form with its own unique and fundamental qualities found expression in films that came to be termed "pure cinema" (see Chapter I). In contrast to David Belasco's view (i.e., that film was a related, but inferior, medium to theater), "pure cinema" (or *film d'art*) asserts that cinema has it own distinctive language, techniques, and aesthetic values and that a film exists in its purest form and is most aesthetically successful when it most fully employs those qualities exclusive to *its* art. In the particular case of play-based films, under the values of *film d'art*, a play translated to the movie screen was most successfully rendered when it employed those techniques inherent to cinema.

In terms of its relation to theater, pure cinema strutted the fact that a movie could do things that theater simply could not do, i.e., shift instantaneously between set and location shots; change the audience's perspective by moving and repositioning the camera; manipulate emotional responses through such devices as extreme close-ups, high angles, and editing; and create more subtlety of performance through the small gestures and facial movements that the camera can record, but which would be lost on the stage. An early and valuable example of pure cinema and, more specifically, of a film which makes a strong statement about the specific ways in which cinema is an art form distinct from theater is Ernst Lubitsch's silent-film version of Oscar Wilde's stage play *Lady Windermere's Fan* (1892).

When Lubitsch decided to make a *silent* film (1925) of Oscar Wilde's *Lady Windermere's Fan*, he took up the challenge of a play whose distinctive worth resides in the witty interplay of words. Wilde's *Lady Windermere's Fan* is an operation of rhetoric, of spoken language. The play's wit, its energy, its plot, characters, and meaning all rely on verbal exchanges, rather than dramatic development, visual codes, and non-verbal actions. With very little dramatic activity occurring in the play, *Lady Windermere's Fan* is Wilde's experiment in structure and rhetoric, his rebellion against the aesthetic protocol of late nineteenth-century theater. In direct contrast to the prevailing conventions in which emerging plot and character development drove the drama, or melodrama, Wilde's play offers a very thin plot, flat characters who never develop, a minimum of dramatic suspense, and limited emotional range.

In *Lady Windermere's Fan*, an engaging story and complex, developing characters which were the prevailing dramatic conventions of the late nineteenth-century, are reduced to trifles. Instead, the play anticipates the values, themes, and conventions of what later would evolve into the twentieth century's absurdist theater.*

Theater of the absurd fundamentally holds that existence lacks a coherent, meaningful design. Life is devoid of a given purpose. Existence lacks reason, order, and meaning. Life is illogical, ridiculous, meaningless ... absurd. Absurdist theater fundamentally challenges even the capacity of language to mean. Under the conventions of theater of the absurd, thus, dialogue is often flagrantly illogical, consisting of repeating patterns of words. Language and action often conform to minimalist standards. Plot structure lacks psychological intricacy and is often kept to a minimum, with little actually happening in regard to story development. (It is said that in *Waiting for Godot*, Samuel Beckett's two-act absurdist play, "nothing happens twice.") In absurdist drama, actions are often repetitive and inconsistent with the dialogue. Time is skewed or there is an indifference to any sense of time.

In theater of the absurd, characters lack strong, distinguishing qualities and, as such, are, arguably, interchangeable. They are not strongly individuated by what they do or what they say. Void of the psychological complexity and depth that we see, for example, in classical theater, they are flat, often humorously so; and while the characters may occupy the same stage space, they do not connect with one another in any substantial or significant way. Their attempts at communication with one another are, ultimately, thin, meaningless, and superfluous — manifesting the playwright's existential comment on the absurdity of all human attempts at meaningful connection.

☞ *Read any one of Oscar Wilde's plays (examples include* Lady Windermere's Fan *[1892],* A Woman of No Importance *[1893],* An Ideal Husband *[1895], and* The Importance of Being Earnest *[1895]). Think of the conventions of theater of the absurd. In what specific ways, does the Wilde play that you have read anticipate the conventions, values, and themes of absurdist theater?*

The earliest of these plays, *Lady Windermere's Fan*, defied the prevailing conventions of nineteenth-century European theater and replaced these with absurdist values. The plot of the play is thin. Lady Windermere

---

For a thorough discussion of this theatrical convention see Martin Esslin's The Theater of the Absurd.

believes that her husband is having an affair with the disreputable Mrs. Erlynne. This is, of course, a misunderstanding further complicated by Lord Darlington's own declarations of love for Lady Windermere, Mrs. Erlynne's mysterious influence over Lord Windermere, the gossip of the Duchess of Berwick, and an ornate fan. Often considered a comedy of manners, *Lady Windermere's Fan* is existential in theme and epigrammatic in style, conventions more in keeping with absurdist theater than the comedy of manners. Wilde's meaningless society is populated with shallow people made more absurd through absurd inconsistencies of character. His most sincere, love-torn romantic, Lord Darlington, is also the character who speaks the epigrammatic line, "I can resist everything except temptation" (Act I, scene 1).

As in the absurdist tradition, Wilde's play devalues individuation of characters. His cast is a collection of social chatterers who speak a language so free of substance that their utterances are often interchangeable. Dumby happens to be the character who explains that "Experience is the name everyone gives to their mistakes" (Act II, scene 1), but the comment could have been appropriately uttered by any character in the play, as could Mrs. Erlynne's Act IV comment about London fog and serious people.* The words the characters speak (as distinguished from the aggregate language of the play) are meaningless. As in the absurdist tradition, meaningful communication is impossible, even humorously preposterous in Wilde's case. While this early Wilde play incorporates some of the prevailing characteristics of theatrical melodrama — a sensational plot, an excessive appeal to emotion, and a denouement that leaves the audience gratifyingly tear-filled — *Lady Windermere's Fan* ends in a vacancy of resolution among characters, an absurdist convention in itself. Deceptions continue. No meaningful communication has occurred between the mother and the daughter or between husbands and wives, because the characters benefit from, and prefer, illusion, a theme central to the absurdist manifesto.

Wilde's fiercest critics at the time indicted his work as facile, even frivolous. (Henry James called the opening night performance of *Lady Windermere's Fan* "infantine.") What his critics failed to realize is that in *Lady Windermere's Fan* the beginnings of a new stage convention were being forged. However, film director Ernst Lubitsch seems to have rec-

---

*"London is too full of fogs and — serious people, Lord Windermere. Whether the fog produces the serious people or whether the serious people produce the fogs, I don't know, but the whole thing rather gets on my nerves, and so I'm leaving this afternoon by the Club Train" (Act IV, scene 1).

ognized in Wilde a shared impulse: that desire to push at the boundaries
that defined both men's art.

In Wilde's play, *Lady Windermere's Fan*, it is the words, the workings
of language, that become the motivating energy and the theme of the play.
However, Lubitsch's movie, *Lady Windermere's Fan*, is, ironically and dar-
ingly, a *silent* film in which Lubitsch replaces Wilde's language, an aesthetic of words antithetical to the aesthetics of silent film, with cinematic
language. This is constructed in accord with what has come to be known
as "the Lubitsch touch": a cheeky, adroit, and sophisticated visual wit, in
this case, equal to Wilde's wit of words.

The film is infused with a maverick's delight to prove that Wilde's
words are quite unnecessary and extraneous to Lubitsch's visual translation of them. Composed according to the values of pure cinema, the film
all but empties Wilde's play of its words. Lubitsch's camera supplants
Wilde's pen in a film in which Lubitsch at once pays homage to Wilde's
play while simultaneously winking a naughty eye at his audience as he lets
us in on his secret: Wilde's wit is not the only form of witty language.

Thus, we have Wilde's epigrammatic equivalents in Lubitsch's visual
witticisms: Our first view of Mrs. Erlynne (Irene Rich), richly dressed and
artfully painted, cinematically quips that she is "like an *edition de luxe* of
a wicked French novel, meant especially for the French market" (Act II).
In another example, the movie's society women, who wear proper frocks
and sit properly in straight-back chairs, are the visual analogue to Wilde's
"None of us ... look what we really are" (Act II). And, in another example, a scene at the racetrack, refracted through several shifting points of
view, is a humorous, extended visual metaphor for "My own business
always bores me to death. I prefer other people's" (Act III).

Largely by utilizing the moving camera's spatial versatility, Lubitsch
demonstrates that film possesses capacities that theater does not. He does
this though his use of insert shots, close-ups, and long shots, through the
opening up of space, the shifting of perspectives, and the extended use of
oblique shots, as in the protracted sequence involving Lord Augustus Lor-
ton's ringing of Mrs. Erlynne's doorbell.

The four basic and constitutive qualities, the characteristics, that contribute to the success of any literature-based film (detailed in Chapter IV)
operate, for the most part, successfully in Lubitsch's radical film translation of Wilde's play. In accord with the first of these characteristics, the
film communicates definite ideas concerning the integral meaning and
value of Wilde's *Lady Windermere's Fan*, as Lubitsch interprets it and as
can be legitimized by the written text, itself. For Lubitsch, the integral

meaning of the play resides in its wit, in its absurdity, and in its cheekiness at redefining the boundaries of its medium; as such, those integral qualities are what the film translation most respects and most successfully communicates. However, this film does not explore the darker textures of Wilde's play, his indictment of the repressive, hollow *fin de siècle* mentality of the wealthy, that many readers of Wilde's play may judge as absolutely central to its meaning.

The second of these characteristics asserts that the film must exhibit a collaboration of filmmaking skills. Lubitsch's film, *Lady Windermere's Fan*, does this through its smooth integration of elegantly composed *mise-en-scène* often comprising tightly composed frames, its lighting, editing, set designs (rich, yet sparse), and the acting, most notably that of Irene Rich, Ronald Colman, and Bert Lytell.

In its adroitness at making a silent screen version of Wilde's word-witty play, the movie demonstrates an audacity to create a work that stands as a world apart from the play and that successfully exploits the dramatic literature in such a way that a self-reliant, but related, aesthetic offspring is born, the third characteristic of a successful literature-based film. In its willingness to tamper with the sanctity of Wilde's verbal wit, Lubitsch's film demonstrates a different kind of respect for and understanding of *Lady Windermere's Fan*. Just as the play is a wonderfully iconoclastic departure from nineteenth-century theater, so Lubitsch's silent film is an iconoclastic departure from cinema's early twentieth-century proclivity to reproduce, with the strictest fidelity, the action, dialogue, and theatrical mode of the original play. As Wilde's play comments on the evolution of theater, Lubitsch's film comments on the evolution of play-based films. No longer simply a vehicle for recording a stage work, cinema was asserting its differences from theater. The movie is a thought-filled comment on Wilde's play that asserts a certain independence for the film, dislodging it from Wilde's work, while simultaneously replicating what, for Lubitsch, is crucial in Wilde's text: its iconoclasm. The film compels us to think about the bold theatrical innovations in Wilde's play, while its own cinematic boldness, simultaneously, compels us to consider the extent of responsibility that a play-based film might owe to its original source material.

The silent film, *Lady Windermere's Fan*, is a radical translation of the source text. However, Lubitsch replicates, in his own fashion, the play's characters, basic story, central themes, and driving wit in a manner that, arguably, is not fully self-governing or antithetical to Wilde's play, the fourth characteristic of the aesthetic rubric.

Dialogue is crucial to all of Wilde's dramatic works. Since verbal discourse, rather than a story that can be told through visual sequencing, is particularly central to all of Wilde's plays, it is especially interesting to observe how film translations of his stage work get around — to the extent that they do — the static quality that can attend the filming of lengthy verbal exchanges among characters. To this end, reading a Wilde play, watching a film translation of it, and scrutinizing the specific ways in which the movie eludes a stasis of dialogue affords a wonderful opportunity to see the particular modes cinema employs in translating a stage play into film. Oscar Wilde's plays are a source of film material internationally. As such, his work is additionally interesting to explore in terms of cinema's capacity to render, visually, multicultural approaches to the same text. Table 12 lists a sampling of multi-national film translations of Wilde's plays.

Table 12.
Some Film Translations of the Plays of Oscar Wilde

Wilde Play	Movie Title	Year Released	Director
An Ideal Husband			
	Ein Idealer Gatte	1935 (Germany)	Herbert Selpin
	An Ideal Husband	1947 (U.K.)	Alexander Korda
	Ein Idealer Gatte	1965 (West Germany for television)	Detlof Krüger
	Idealnyj muzh	1980 (Soviet Union)	Viktor Georgiyev
	An Ideal Husband	1998 (U.K.)	William Cartlidge
	An Ideal Husband	1999 (U.K.)	Oliver Parker
	Ideální manzel	2002 (Czech Republic for television)	Zdenek Zelenka
The Importance of Being Earnest			
	The Importance of Being Earnest	1952 (U.K.)	Anthony Asquith
	The Importance	1981	Michael Atten-

→

Wilde Play	Movie Title	Year Released	Director
	of Being Earnest	(U.K. for television)	borough and Michael Lindsay-Hogg
	The Importance of Being Earnest	1992 (Australia for television)	
	The Importance of Being Earnest	1992 (USA for television)	Kurt Baker
	The Importance of Being Earnest	2002 (USA/U.K./France)	Oliver Parker
Lady Windermere's Fan			
	Lady Windermere's Fan	1916 (U.K.)	Fred Paul
	Lady Windermere's Fan	1925 (USA)	Ernst Lubitsch
	Lady Windermeres Fächer	1935 (Germany)	Heinz Hilpert
	El Abanico de Lady Windermere	1944 (Mexico)	Juan José Ortega
	The Fan	1949 (U.K.)	Otto Preminger
	Lady Windermere's Fan	1972 (U.K. for television)	Rudolph Cartier
	Lady Windermere's Fan	1985 (U.K. for television)	Tony Smith
A Woman of No Importance			
	A Woman of No Importance	1921 (U.K.)	Denison Clift
	Eine Frau ohne Bedeutung	1936 (Germany)	Hans Steinhoff
	Una Mujer sin importancia	1945 (Argentina)	Luis Bayón Herrera
	A Woman of No Importance	1982 (U.K. for television)	Giles Foster

For issues that are arguably even more involved than those posed by Oscar Wilde's plays, William Shakespeare's plays present a most complex example of the particular challenges encountered in translating into film a play whose most significant trait is its use of words, a quality antithetical to the non-verbal strengths inherent to film. The task of cinematic translation is additionally complicated by Shakespeare's frequent use of blank verse, the cadences of which suffer from editing a Shakespearean play to suit the time constraints of a feature-length film. Any film translation of Shakespeare's work must, thus, negotiate carefully the preeminence of his words with the preeminently non-verbal, visual quality of film. (See Appendix B for a list of Shakespeare plays translated into film.) What is so interesting in the study of Shakespearean texts that have been reconstituted into cinematic texts, beyond the topic itself, is that such a study provides ample and excellent examples of four approaches filmmakers take in bringing the stage to the screen.

The first approach is filmed theater. Filmed theater stays as closely as possible to Shakespeare's word for word text, adhering to the play, as written. The movie's running time approximates the stage's performance time, with film-time literally replicating stage-time. Filmed-stage is the most hospitable approach to providing the complete text of a Shakespeare play on screen, since little cutting of lines from the play is required to serve the time constraints faced by a more cinematic, less stage-bound film, one that might consume screen time with expansive tracking shots of battles, lingering close-ups of characters in thought, or sweeping pans of a magical, mid-summer forest.

John Gielgud's *Hamlet* (1964), Tony Richardson's *Hamlet* (1969), Edwin Sherin's/Joseph Papp's *King Lear* (1977), and Norman Campbell's *Romeo and Juliet* (1993) are examples of filmed-theater. The overall values of filmed-theater abide in the British Broadcasting Company's productions of all thirty-seven of Shakespeare's plays.

In addition to filmed-stage, three distinct tacks have emerged in translating Shakespeare's plays into film. These three approaches are best represented by the work of Laurence Olivier, Akira Kurosawa, and Franco Zeffirelli. Each of these three adheres to significantly different concepts in rendering Shakespeare's plays into film, and each director can stand as representative of a foundational mode of translating Shakespeare to cinema. Zeffirelli employs a populist approach that is sympathetic to the Shakespeare-shy and phobic. Kurosawa engages in a radical approach that, at once, proclaims both the universality of Shakespeare's work and the non-verbal means by which cinema can translate the potency, complexity, and beauty of Shakespeare's words. Olivier prefers a dialogic approach in which cinematic elements (camera movement and placement; rapid shifting of locales and perspectives; large spatial expanses; reaction shots; cross-cutting; and dissolves) engage in a parlay with theatrical elements (prosce-nium blocking, constricted space, theatrical acting, painted backdrops, moving dioramas, and a static camera placed at a distance approximate to the distance of one watching the performance from an orchestra seat). Thus, in his approach to bringing Shakespeare to the screen, Olivier cre-ates a dialogue between the essential values of David Belasco and those of Hugo Munsterberg, as discussed earlier in this chapter.

Olivier directed film versions of three of Shakespeare's plays: *Henry V* (1944), *Hamlet* (1948), and *Richard III* (1955). As is the case in the majority of film versions of Shakespeare's plays, each of the three Olivier films is a traditional translation of Shakespeare's work in which the film stays close to Shakespeare's primary text, while shifting, eliminating, or adding scenes and/or lines in ways that the filmmaker (Olivier, in this case) saw as necessary and fitting for his feature-length films and his modern audiences. The first of the plays that he directed, *Henry V*, is a gifted example of the life of the play, as a stage piece, encountering the forces of cinema.

Henry V is primarily focused on the values and qualities that char-acterize an ideal king, with King Henry representing all that is finest in English royalty. The play is the third in Shakespeare's Henry trilogy, with the two earlier plays (*1 Henry IV*, *2 Henry IV*) presenting Henry as the young Prince Hal. Riotous and tavern-brawling, Prince Hal experiences an unruly, yet very humanizing, education under the influence of Sir John Falstaff. His education is an odd kingly preparation that yields, in *Henry V*, heroism tempered by that nature of humility and human understand-ing necessary to great rulers. Shakespeare wrote the play at a moment when England, facing the prospect of an escalating war, was experiencing a mounting patriotism.*

The play clearly expresses an Anglo-Saxon idealism and Shakespeare's pride in things English. Much as the writing of the play was timed to inter-sect with the rise of England's patriotic zeal, the film — if something short of propaganda — was consciously produced to rally national enthusiasm for World War II England.† Olivier, at the time, was "approached by Jack

---

In 1599, the English army, under the leadership of the Earl of Essex, fought in Ireland to sup-press the rebellion led by the Earl of Tyrone. Henry V (1600) makes direct reference to Essex, "from Ireland coming/Bringing rebellion broachèd on his sword" (V, i, 31–32).

†*See Gorman Beauchamp's essay, "Henry V: Myth, Movie, Play," for a thorough*   →

Beddington of [England's] Ministry of Information and given a budget that would allow him to make a spectacular film in Technicolor"; and the movie was "financed as part of the war effort to bolster morale and the spirit of the English people, then under siege by air and sea by Germany during World War II" (Welsh, Tibbetts and Welsh, *Stage Plays*, 373).

With the generous budget that he was allocated, Olivier was free to give us the multi-layered, complex *Henry* that he understood. In translating the play to film, he opted for the best of Technicolor meeting the best of theatrical staging. His *Henry V* operates as a strong, traditional rendition of Shakespeare's work, largely retaining the play, intact, but complementing it through cinema's close-ups and sweeping pans, its cross-cutting and reaction shots, and its multi-layered soundtrack and heightening tinctures of Technicolor. Concurrently, the film works as a thing apart from the heroic story of King Henry and the patriotic *esprit de corps* it was promulgating. Olivier's *Henry V* explores a concept that Shakespeare raises in the play's Prologue: the very nature of theater and the crucial role the audience's imagination must assume throughout a performance:

> ... But pardon, gentles all,
> The flat unraisèd spirits that hath dared
> On this unworthy scaffold to bring forth
> So great an object. Can this cock-pit hold
> The vasty fields of France? Or may we cram
> Within this wooden O the very casques
> That did affright the air at Agincourt?
> O, pardon: Since a crookèd figure may
> Arrest in little place a million;
> And let us, ciphers to this great account,
> On your imaginary forces work.
> Suppose within the girdle of these walls
> Are now confined two mighty monarchies,
> Whose high uprearèd and abutting fronts
> The perilous narrow ocean parts usunder.
> Piece out our imperfections with your thoughts:
> Into a thousand parts divide one man,
> And make imaginary puissance.
> Think, when we talk of horses, that you see them,
> Printing their proud hoofs i'th' receiving earth;
> For 'tis your thoughts that now must deck our kings...
> —*Henry V,* I, i, 8–28

analysis of the ways in which the film distorted Shakespeare's play in order to rally support in England's World War II audience.

The Prologue explains that the stage performance needs the cooperation of the audience — their imaginations and thoughts — to witness the sweep of events about to unfold in the theater. Mindful of the need for audience complicity, Olivier positions his movie audience at the Globe Theatre, 1600, where *Henry V* is being performed. Shakespeare's play becomes a play performed within a movie. The film opens at the Globe, with the theater's attendees searching for seats. The sequence is filmed in such a way that we, the movie audience, seem to walk in the footprints of the moving camera, as seventeenth-century London Globe patrons, getting situated to see *Henry V.* The camera next takes us behind the curtain to see the Globe actors as they are about to enter the stage. The play within the film begins and the movie sequences that follow are classic filmed-theater, as the camera records the performance occurring on stage at London's Globe Theatre. The actors' make-up and attire assume the particular features of stage costumes, the backdrops are painted, the acoustics are stage-like, the acting is theatrical, and the spatial confines of a stage fill the movie screen.

In the course of the film, however, Oliver moves Shakespeare's play off the Globe Theatre stage and into the vaster, outdoor expanses possible in film, where he explores theater's antithesis by showing on screen the very things that the Prologue tells us cannot be shown on stage: the "vasty fields of France," the two mighty monarchies abutting fronts, and the thundering horses in battle. Throughout the film, expanses of space and armies of actors are set against confined spaces and limited numbers of performers; natural landscape is contrasted to theatrical artifice; and ever-shifting perspective is apposed to fixed point of view.

Thus, throughout Olivier's *Henry V,* film is contrasted to stage, as Olivier explores the staging and cinematic modes that "On your imaginary force work" and that "piece out our imperfections with your thoughts." There is no seamless integration of the theatrical and the cinematic modes in Olivier's film, nor is there meant to be, but rather a very mindful intent to create a repartee between stage and screen, the elements of one countering the other, each asserting a preeminence of form. In creating the exchanges that occur between the capacities of stage and of film, Olivier is not asking which form, stage-play or film-play, is superior, but rather what particular forces, capabilities, methods, and techniques in each medium activate deep and creative responses in the audience.

In his film translation of *Henry V* (1989), Kenneth Branagh follows in Olivier's tradition, while expanding upon it. Both films, Olivier's and Branagh's, are traditional translations of Shakespeare's play, which retain much of the play, as written, while eliminating or adding scenes and lines as deemed necessary. (Both movies, for example, include lines from *1 Henry IV* and *2 Henry IV*.) Like Olivier's *Henry V*, Branagh's film version is largely dialogic, if more subtly so, as cinematic elements engage in a parlay with theatrical elements.

Like Olivier's film, Branagh's *Henry V* opens backstage, but instead of being taken behind the curtain in a theater, we are taken behind the set of a movie, amid the clutter of contraptions needed in film production. Laurence Olivier's backstage reminder that theater relies on artifice becomes Kenneth Branagh's rejoinder: film, too, is constructed from artifice. In Branagh's film, Derek Jacobi, an accomplished *stage* actor, delivers the Prologue. Speaking from the back-reaches of the movie set, he appears outside of the diegesis, the world of the play's story. Standing on a movie set within a movie set and being filmed by a camera with an extraordinary capacity to record the recreation of the sweeping expanses of Shakespeare's setting (the English and French courts, the battlefields), Jacobi apologizes for the limitations of the "unworthy scaffold to bring forth/So great an object"; and, while Shakespeare's Prologue offers an apology for the limitations of the stage, Jacobi's sweep-of-his-hand reference to the movie set asks to what extent film, also, is a medium "unworthy" to render so "great an object" as the nature of King Henry and, implicitly, the glorious mysteries of Shakespeare's writing.

While Branagh's *Henry V* employs less theatricality and more realism in the form of costumes, lighting, acting, and locales than Olivier's film — wanting clearly to dislodge *his* movie from the other one* — Branagh's film, like Olivier's, is exploring the very questions raised by the Prologue: What are the limitations and strengths inherent in theater — and, by implication, in film — and what part does the audience play in the reception of a performed work?

Even as both the set and the location shots look less stage-bound and more realistic than in Olivier's *Henry V*, Branagh frequently restricts the film space in ways that mimic the confines of a stage. He closets action in small spaces, which suggest, as the stage does, that more expansive regions lie beyond the scope of view, but are never shown. Filmed sequences frequently follow stage blocking. For example, as characters exit a scene, the camera does not follow them out, but instead, remains behind,

---

Free of the World War II circumstances that prompted Olivier's more idealized interpretation of Henry V, Branagh constructs an equally strong, but somewhat less perfect, King Henry, one arguably more in keeping with Shakespeare's view.

Henry V (1989): Kenneth Branagh's *Henry V* employs less theatricality and more realism in the form of costumes, lighting, acting, and locales than Laurence Olivier's earlier *Henry V* (1944) did.

the film audience left fixed on the vacated space much as the stage audience is.

Branagh takes his camera into vast, natural settings, then, within the natural setting, uses tight framing which returns us to the stage's spatial context. Throughout Branagh's *Henry V*, the reconstruction of historical realism through cinema's virtually unlimited capabilities to recreate and to record historical moments — complete with vast battlefields alive with cannons shooting, flying arrows, campfires blazing, and Henry galloping atop a white horse (a wink to Olivier's white horse in *Henry V*) — is set beside the stage's capacity to have us imagine those same scenes. The glorious vastness of cinematic space is set beside the intensity of compression created by stage space; photography's capacity to move anywhere and to deliver realist detail, up and close (we witness Bardolph's execution for robbing a church from shifting perspectives) is set beside the perspectival advantages of theatrical distance and point of view consistency; and the camera's ability to traverse all enclosures and to reconstitute historical locale is set beside theater's capacity to activate our "imaginary forces" in order to see what lies "within the girdle of these walls."

Olivier's and Branagh's *Henry V* films make statements about the unique strengths and limitations of both theater and cinema, and they do so in a way that insists that we be aware — remain conscious and mindful — of their explorations. This quality is operative in Olivier's film translation of *Hamlet* (1948), a Freudian interpretation of Shakespeare's play and, arguably, a movie that now may seem "mannered and stylistically overdone, far too conscious of its attempt to be 'cinematic'" (Welsh, Tibbetts and Welsh, *Stage Plays into Film*, 364). The volley between theatrical and cinematic qualities also operates in Kenneth Branagh's *Hamlet*. Running over four hours, Branagh's *Hamlet* is the first full-text film translation of the play and one that is unusually strong in demonstrating the differences between theatrical spectacle and cinematic spectacle.

Olivier's and Branagh's films of *Henry V* and *Hamlet* engage a dialogue between theater and film — at times, a stage/screen fencing match of sorts and, at others, a *pas de deux*. These two directors, both of whom also wrote the screenplays for their films, want their audiences to think about what is occurring on the screen. The dynamic each creates between theater and cinema is presented in a manner that, to varying degrees and at various points, clearly calls attention to itself, and, in doing so, disrupts our escape into the illusion created by cinema.

We cannot be caught up in the illusion of film and be aware of it, as a film, at the same time. In contrast to Olivier's and Branagh's practice of having the film announce itself as film, making the audience mindful, at points, that they are watching a movie, Franco Zeffirelli, operating in a populist mode, aspires to have the audience members lose themselves in the film's reality and be absorbed fully in an empathic relationship with the world of the cinematic present. In his traditional film translations of Shakespeare's plays, Zeffirelli's approach aims to have the viewers be caught up and swept away in the cinematic *reality*— or the illusion of reality — of the Shakespearean worlds that he creates on screen.

The desire to regress into the cinematic illusion is, according to Jean-Louis Baudry, the desire to return to an early stage of development "in which the separation between one's own body and the exterior world is not well defined." It "artificially leads back to an anterior phase of ... development," similar to the dream state (313). With a passion, quiet, but fierce, many film-goers desire — crave — the transcendent experience cinema promises to provide. The craving is dangerous. In order to satisfy it, we viewers are willing to give ourselves over to the "hallucinatory psychosis of desire," i.e., a state in which the illusion becomes reality (Freud, quoted in Baudry, 309). In our desire to lose ourselves fully in the illusion of cinema, we willingly invite the disappearance, the subsuming, of our own personhood.

Populist cinema, Zeffirelli's included, succeeds to the extent that we are borne away to and swept up in the reality of the movie. We escape into it; we are subsumed by it; and, for the time, the cinematic illusions, on a very deep level actually, become our only functioning reality. When someone rustles a candy wrapper or talks during the film, it ruptures our relationship to the screen, shattering the cinematic reality, and reminding us that we are, after all, really only in a movie theater. We grow annoyed by the disruption in direct proportion to the degree to which we have entered the film's reality. This simple feature, the capacity to be swept up in the cinematic illusions, is the key to the success of populist cinema — not just Zeffirelli's movies, but also Schwarzenegger, samurai, and SWAT films.

While Zeffirelli's films — his films of Shakespeare and of opera (*Pagliacci, Carmen, La Traviata*) — have origins more highly thought of, perhaps, than most action/adventure fare, the cinematic ethos that drives them is the same: the desire to make the movie's subject matter — in Zeffirelli's case, the *art*— more accessible to a popular audience, who will become fully absorbed in the experience of it. A populist film approach uses the prevailing cultural codes of its audience, i.e., those visual and verbal styles that are most readily understood. It creates strong audience identification because, regardless of its setting, the populist approach uses the dominant values, tropes, humor, manners, mannerisms, and codes of masculine and feminine beauty of the expected audience's immediate world. It is particularly appropriate that Shakespeare be translated via a populist approach, as Shakespeare, himself, was a very *à la mode* writer. When Jacobean theater was popular, he wrote *King Lear*, where Gloucester's eyes are gouged out on stage in full view of the audience; and when the masque was popular, Shakespeare wrote *The Tempest*.

Zeffirelli directed three feature films of Shakespeare's plays: *The Taming of the Shrew* (1966), *Romeo and Juliet* (1968), and *Hamlet* (1990).* Each of the three films attempts the theatrical realism valued by David Belasco, as all three "present a solid and believable world of dimension and sub-

Zeffirelli also co-directed with Alan Cooke a U.K. television production of Much Ado About Nothing *(1967).*

stance" (Vela in Welsh, Vela, Tibbetts, *Shakespeare*, 81). Also in keeping with Belasco's tradition, each of Zeffirelli's Shakespeare films incorporates pageantry, spectacle, pictorial realism, and painstakingly authentic staging details. Consistent with a populist mode of representation, each of the screenplays makes cuts to Shakespeare's text that reduce complications of character and story. Thus, Zeffirelli's *The Taming of the Shrew* fully dispenses with the Christopher Sly "Induction"; *Romeo and Juliet* omits Romeo's crucial scenes with the Apothecary and with Paris at the Capulets' crypt; and *Hamlet* cuts the play's entire first scene and much of the second, omits Hamlet's fourth soliloquy, while, overall, "transposing lines capriciously and removing whole scenes that are necessary for contextualizing the action" (Welsh and Vela, Welsh, Vela, Tibbetts, *Shakespeare*, 23).

Zeffirelli's three Shakespeare films, beautifully photographed and staged, are important in their ability to make Shakespeare accessible, even popular, with a mass audience. Much of the films' popularity had to do with casting decisions. In determining what actors would appear in the feature roles two guiding principles prevailed: current codes of masculine and feminine beauty and box-office draw. Thus, *The Taming of the Shrew* featured Hollywood's most amorous and bawdy married couple, Elizabeth Taylor and Richard Burton, as Shakespeare's own amorous and bawdy, real-life married couple. *Romeo and Juliet* cast, as the young star-crossed lovers, actors Olivia Hussey, then sixteen years old, as Juliet, and Leonard Whiting, then seventeen, as Romeo, both of whom were actors closer in age to Shakespeare's characters than any previous movie had dared attempt and who figured on the screen as icons of teenage beauty. *Hamlet* featured action/adventure Aussie superstar Mel Gibson, cast, interestingly against type, as Shakespeare's pendulously tentative Danish prince.

Each of these three Shakespearean plays that Zeffirelli made into a populist film can also be seen in one additional populist film translation: *Hamlet* (2000, dir. Michael Almereyda); *Romeo and Juliet* as *Panic Button* (1964, dir. George Sherman), and *The Taming of the Shrew* as the film *10 Things I Hate about You* (1999, dir. Gil Junger).

A teen-movie variation on *The Taming of the Shrew*, *10 Things I Hate about You* is overlaid with 1990s frankness and 1980s New Wave music. Set at Padua High School, *10 Things* depicts Kat Stafford (Julia Stiles), Shakespeare's fiery Katharina, in terms of an outsider who reads Sylvia Plath, listens to Joan Jett, gets drunk, and vomits on Patrick (Heath Ledger), the Petruchio character, rendered, in this version, as little else than a cool, naughty teenage hunk. The two find love at the senior prom;

Kat articulates what she has learned in a sonnet, written for English class; and, hearing that, we are left craving any part of Shakespeare's verse or human understanding.

Panic Button turns the tragedy of *Romeo and Juliet* into a comedy as two unemployed and talent-challenged film stars are persuaded by mobsters to make a movie of *Romeo and Juliet*, though, unbeknownst to them, the mobsters expect it to be so badly made as to be a sure flop. (The movie must lose money for income tax purposes.) Instead, their outlandish *Romeo and Juliet* is a huge success, winning the prestigious Venice Film award. The over-the-top performances of Maurice Chevalier as Phillippe Fontaine/Romeo, Jane Mansfield as Louise Harris/Juliet, and Michael Connors as the producer, Frank Pagano, add to the good-natured, if un–Shakespearean, ludicrous charm of the film. *Panic Button* is the forerunner to Mel Brooks's *The Producers*, a work which, rather than moving from stage to screen, moved in reverse: from screen (1968) to Broadway stage (April 2001).

Michael Almereyda's *Hamlet* casts Ethan Hawke as Shakespeare's prince in a film that runs only 114 minutes (compared to Olivier's *Hamlet* at 158 minutes and Branagh's full-text *Hamlet* at over four hours). Retaining some, but editing out much of Shakespeare's text, the movie is set in contemporary New York City, with King Claudius as the CEO of "The Denmark Corporation," and Hamlet intoning "To be or not to be" at a Blockbuster video store, where his speech of indecision is recited in the action/adventure section of the store, a gratuitous sight gag that works.

Very different from the populist approach that characterizes Zeffirelli's Shakespeare films and from the stage/screen dialogics that characterizes Olivier's and Branagh's work, Akira Kurosawa engages a radical translation mode in his films of Shakespeare's works. Kurosawa has directed three film versions of Shakespearean plays: *Throne of Blood* (1957) from *Macbeth*, *The Bad Sleep Well* (1960) from *Hamlet*, and *Ran* (1985) from *King Lear*.

Case Study: King Lear *and* Ran

William Shakespeare's *King Lear* and Akira Kurosawa's *Ran* can stand, self-sufficiently, as paradigms of their particular forms, with each of the two works, respectively, creating enduringly powerful — complex, beautiful, and compassionate — meditations on good and evil, youth and old age, love and hate, loyalty and betrayal, peace and war, and self-knowledge and self-delusion. The two works are so self-standing that each, the play and the film, can be effectively experienced and explored, fully independent of each other. However, Shakespeare's *King Lear* and Kurosawa's *Ran* are unusually complex works and the intertextual linking of them can effect insights that studying the play and the film in isolation might not produce. Additionally, *Ran* provides a clear illustration of the successful employment of each of the four points of the aesthetic rubric.

William Shakespeare's Play *King Lear*

Shakespeare based *King Lear* on a mythical king, well known in British lore. The first written account of King Lear appeared in Geoffrey of Monmouth's *Historia Regum Britanniae* (1136), where Lear and his three daughters are cited as "rulers of ancient Britain" (Harbage, 1060). Composed sometime between 1605 and 1606, *King Lear* belongs to Shakespeare's compositional phase that also includes *Macbeth*. Both works explore the mutability of fortune, the corrupting influences of worldly power, the conflict of good and evil, the rewards to be found in virtue, and the wisdom attained only by passing through self-horror, degradation, isolation, and despair.

King Lear (1605) is Shakespeare's study of a king whose anguished fall from worldly power results in his acute enlightenment. At the beginning of the play, Lear, weary of the work of rule and wanting to "shake all cares and business from our age" (I: i: 39), decides to divide his kingdom among his three daughters, Goneril, Regan, and Cordelia. He announces that he will base his division of the wealth and power on each daughter's public proclamation of the depth of her love for her father. Words serve Goneril and Regan well, as each, in an adeptness of rhetoric, indulges her father's whim with grandiose articulations of filial love. The youngest of the three daughters, Cordelia, refuses to condescend to such tricks of rhetoric, attempting to explain to her father that such oratory displays are not proof of devotion and that "my love's/More ponderous than my tongue" (I: i: 77–8). Arrogantly foolish, Lear disowns Cordelia, announcing: "Here I disclaim all my parental care,/Propinquity and property of blood,/And as a stranger to my heart and me" (I: i: 113–15). He divides his realm between Goneril and Regan, who fully betray and abandon him and turn Lear's once-unified kingdom into two hostile factions, warring for dominance.

Lear destroys what he loves best: his kingdom, his rank, his reputation, his privilege, and his daughter. It is only at the darkest moment of his loss and despair, bitterly crowned by the death of Cordelia, that Lear understands the depth of his folly and the authenticity of Cordelia's love, loyalty, and goodness. His enlightenment, coming so late in his life as to be piteous and so integral and replete as to be hopeful to us all, invokes an abiding pathos in those who witness and engage Lear's tragedy. In its parallel structuring of plot (Lear's story with Gloucester's) and in its parallel structuring of character (Edgar with Edmund, Cordelia and Kent with Regan and Goneril, the fool with Oswald, Lear with Gloucester), *King Lear* has been described as a play that says its truths powerfully — and says them twice.

Akira Kurosawa's *Ran*: A Radical Film Translation of *King Lear*

The concurrence of piteous tragedy and abiding hope present in Shakespeare's play is also present in Akira Kurosawa's *Ran*, his radical film translation of *King Lear*. *Ran* reminds us how universal Shakespeare's play is. Kurosawa said, "When I look at Japanese history — or the history of the world for that matter — what I see is how man repeats himself over and over again" (Richie, 115). Instead of being set in first-century B.C. Britain, *Ran* (the Japanese word for "chaos") takes place in sixteenth-century feudal Japan, where Shakespeare's king is refashioned as the warlord, Lord Hidetora Ichimonji (Tatsuya Nakadai), and where Hidetora is given a personal history that Shakespeare's play does not provide, a ruthless ascendancy to royal power. Throughout *Ran*, one cannot help but feel an eastern sense of karma at work as Hidetora's past abuses are returned to him in the abuses he suffers from his two sons and his daughter-in-law, Taro's wife, the breathtakingly evil Lady Kaede (Mieko Harada). Reflecting on *Ran*, Kurosawa commented:

> The character of Hidetora is one that begins at the pinnacle of worldly power and confidence — a result of having carried out unspeakable deeds throughout his life to attain it. What happens in the course of the film is that he is forced to pay for these unspeakable deeds. It is only at the point where he has fallen to the depths of misery and desperation and has been treated not like a great warrior but like a beggar, that he arrives at his first understanding of what is important in life. Through his downfall he attains a kind of purity and his first glimpse of clear, blue, sky when he realizes that all he really needs is the love and understanding of one son. So his destiny to me is the most pitiful and, at the same time, the most magnificent that I have been able to conceive in my films [Oumano 79–80].

Ran (1985): Akira Kurosawa's radical translation of Shakespeare's *King Lear*. Lord Hidetora [Lear] (Tatsuya Nakadai) shares a rare moment of lucid revelation with his loyal companion, Kyoami (Peter) [the Fool].

In Hidetora, Kurosawa creates a character who, he states, "starts out at the point where the Macbeth character finishes." Kurosawa explains: "Macbeth begins as a fairly good person, and over the course of the play, with the intensification of his ambition, he becomes a very evil person" (Oumano, 80). Thus, in *Ran*, Kurosawa is creating an intentional intertextuality among four works: Shakespeare's *Macbeth* and *King Lear*, and his own films, *Ran* and *Throne of Blood*, the latter as his radical translation of *Macbeth*. In *Ran*, the character of Hidetora is, thus, both the logical outcome of Macbeth and King Lear operating under the codes of feudal Japan.

In keeping with feudal Japan's dictate that the line of descent must always pass to a male heir, Lear's daughters are made Hidetora's sons: Taro (So Terao), Jiro (Jinpachi Nezu), and Saburo (Daisuke Ryu). Adhering to the contours of Shakespeare's story, in *Ran* the youngest and most virtuous child, Saburo, is misjudged and disinherited, while the remaining sons, Taro and Jiro, violently betray their father by attacking Hidetora in his stronghold, massacring his retinue, and burning his castle. While Hidetora escapes the mayhem, he is incapable of making sense of the horror his own sons have committed. He wanders in despair, dazed and confused, through the wilderness with only one attendee, his fool Kyoami ("Peter"/Shinnosuke Ikehata). In a departure from Shakespeare's literal text, Hidetora's despair is not only caused by his children's betrayal of him and the dawning self-awareness of his own destructive foolishness, but, also, in part, by the painful confrontation with his past, of his facing the odious deeds and folly of choices he made throughout his life of insatiable ambition and over-vaunting ego.

In *Ran*, Kurosawa's world is one of cause and effect, where the chaos of existence is directly traceable to the inhumanity of human conduct. In contrast, *King Lear* does not create a context — a personal history — for the character of Lear, and Shakespeare's play, thus, abides more in the painful zone of a man "more sinned against than sinning," one whose greatest fault, as far as we know, is not a treacherous corruption of ambition, but a foolish pride and grandiosity that dulled Lear's ability to discern the false from the true — Lear's tragic blindness.

In the radical ways in which Kurosawa's film retells the story of King Lear, and, more specifically, in its inclusion of a personal history of Hidetora, which, arguably, changes the character of Lear in ways antithetical to Shakespeare's view, *Ran* could be faulted for being so self-governing as to be too independent of Shakespeare's source material, the fourth characteristic of the aesthetic rubric. In *Ran*, however, the alterations of story ultimately hover on the surface of a film in which Kurosawa's Hidetora undergoes the same basic arc of experiences — the foolish choices, destructive outcomes, filial treachery, insanity, and despair — that yields the very same agony of understanding that Shakespeare's Lear undergoes. Each man realizes how negligible he is in the universe; how present, real, and intractable evil is; how his fatuous judgments have destructively affected good people; how indifferent the universe can be to justice; and how degrading and self-annihilating the process of aging can be.

As is necessary to a strong literature-to-screen translation, *Ran* gets at the integral meanings of Shakespeare's play and, in doing so, it demonstrates a collaboration of cinematic skills that yields a forceful and beautiful film. In his review of the movie for *The New York Times*, Vincent Canby stated that "One would have to be willfully blind" not to recognize "the grandeur of Akira Kurosawa's *Ran*." Kurosawa's depictions of battles are masterfully photographed and edited together — sweeping and overpowering, in a way that would be impossible to depict on stage. Epic in scale, with warriors totaling over twelve hundred, dressed in full medieval costumes, the battle sequences are spectacularly staged and designed, with their startling blood reds and royal golds and legions of warriors. However, the expected dialogue and sound effects of battle are, instead, unexpectedly replaced by a sound track comprising only music.

The visual success of the entire movie is aided by Kurosawa's decision to film each shot as one scene and one take, but with three cameras working simultaneously, each set at different positions and engaging in different movements. The footage from all three cameras was then edited together. The film maintains a beautiful, static visual quality, an effect created largely by the camera moving only when the actors do. As well, the film integrates close-ups sparingly and judiciously. The use of three, simultaneously recording cameras helped Kurosawa in his method of filming close-ups. As Kurosawa explains, "The problem with closeups is that if the actor is aware that the camera is only going on his face, he tends to act only with his face. So when I do closeups, I do them in a way that the actor doesn't know that only his face is getting into the frame. For me it is extremely important that he act with his whole body and his whole soul" (Oumano, 80).

Ran integrates cross-cultural traditions: samurai legend with Shakespearean text, eastern music with western music, the Buddhist sensibilities of Lady Sue with the Machiavellian-like values of Lady Kaede, and classical Japanese Noh (No) Theater (the high theatricality of the acting and make-up) with western cinema (most specifically the influence of directors John Ford, Howard Hawks, and George Stevens).

In his radical translation of Shakespeare's *King Lear*, Kurosawa fully reworks the setting, genders, language, style, and medium of the play and embraces a cross-cultural approach to Shakespeare's text. In doing so, Kurosawa gets at secondary meaning that is integral to Shakespeare's work: how ageless and timeless, how trans-cultural and universal the figure of Lear is. As Shakespearean scholar Alfred Harbage explains: Shakespeare's *King Lear* is in "the tradition" of a "symbolic figure," sometimes "called *King* as well as *Mankind, Everyman, Genus Humanum,* and the like" (1062). In *Ran* Kurosawa continues and enlarges upon this tradition.

This tradition is also enlarged upon by two other trans-cultural, radical film translations of Shakespeare's play: Jocelyn Moorhouse's *A Thousand Acres* and Jean-Luc Godard's *King Lear. A Thousand Acres* came from Jane Smiley's American novel of Lear living in Iowa's farmlands and was made into the 1997 film, directed by Moorhouse. French filmmaker Jean-Luc Godard's 1987 film, *King Lear,* fully reworks the setting, style, language, and medium of the Shakespeare's play, placing his *King Lear* in "a bizarre, contemporary punk-apocalyptic setting," with alterations of

Shakespeare's characters that include Woody Allen as a film editor, Peter Sellers as William Shakespeare, Norman Mailer as himself, and Jean-Luc Godard as a professor (Yates, 382). However, most critics agree that Godard's *Lear* fails to communicate his integral ideas regarding Shakespeare's text in conjunction with faults of composition, editing, and sound.

☞ *Sometimes we learn the most about cinema by studying mistakes. To this end, read William Shakespeare's play,* King Lear, *then watch Godard's radical translation of the play. Referring to the concepts described in "The Language of Film" (Chapter II) and to the four points of the aesthetic rubric (Appendix A), analyze the specific ways in which Godard's film is successful and not successful as a radical translation of Shakespeare's play. Is it, as most critics contend, a mistake? Godard's approach to film translation of literature is consciously cavalier. He does not regard "fidelity" to the source text as a value of film translations of literature. Instead, he praises cinematic originality. Evaluate Godard's* King Lear *according to its own standard: originality. Is the film gimmick or greatness or something else?*

Shakespeare's plays have been the source for many radical translations — on the stage and the screen. Two notable examples of radical film translations of Shakespeare's *Henry* plays include Orson Welles's *Chimes at Midnight* (1967) and Gus Van Sant's *My Own Private Idaho* (1991), both made from a combination of Shakespeare's *1 Henry IV* and *2 Henry IV.*

In addition to the *Henry IV* plays, *Chimes at Midnight* integrates elements of Falstaff's appearance in three other Shakespearean plays: *Richard II, Henry V,* and *The Merry Wives of Windsor.* Working largely with *1 Henry IV* and *2 Henry IV,* though, the film moves the principal focus away from Prince Hal and onto Sir John (Jack) Falstaff, the figure that Welles called "perhaps the only purely good character Shakespeare ever wrote." *Chimes at Midnight* shows the shifts that occur in the relationship between the boisterously jovial Falstaff and the young Hal, the future king of England. Their relationship, deep at its roots, culminates in Hal's abrupt decision to abandon Falstaff, the association with whom, the prince comes to believe, threatens the integrity of the British monarchy. Hal leaves Falstaff behind, dismissing his importance as little more than a deliberate mask of frivolity, taken up in his youth, which he throws off in maturity. Welles's performance captures the integrally profound sorrow that Jack Falstaff, having loved Hal as a son, knows — the prevailing and the abject loss that any father would feel. While harsh budgetary limitations resulted in obvious flaws in the movie, the most pronounced of which is the muddled soundtrack, the failings are subdued by the film's synergy of skill: its beauty of composition, its distinctive use of lighting, its insightful screenplay, and its depth of performances, notably, Orson Welles as Jack Falstaff, Keith Baxter as Prince Hal, and John Gielgud as King Henry IV. *Chimes at Midnight* is understood, also, as an autobiographical statement by Orson Welles, with Hal's ungrateful abandonment of Falstaff paralleling Welles's own treatment by Hollywood studio moguls, who, by 1967, had dismissed his worth to them, indifferently tossing Welles aside to scrounge for independent financing of his film projects.

Like *Chimes at Midnight*, *My Own Private Idaho* is a radical translation of the *Henry IV* plays. Set in contemporary Portland, Oregon, the film reconstitutes Shakespeare's text to focus on two young hustlers: Scott Favor (Keanu Reeves), the Hal character, and Mike Waters (River Phoenix), an amalgam of Prince John (Hal's brother) and Ned Poins (his friend). The two meet, form a brotherly alliance, and for a time affect each other's lives during a crucial time of personal change. They join up with Bob Pigeon (William Richert), who, like Falstaff, is the head of a band of merry thieves. (Unlike quick-witted Falstaff, however, Bob Pigeon speaks in a garbled mixture of Elizabethan English and American street slang, the one pronounced flaw in the film.) Mike is a gay prostitute, who suffers from poverty and narcolepsy. Scott is the son of privilege and elevated station (his very wealthy father is the mayor of the city). Both young men are adrift, abandoned by their parents (Mike, literally, and Scott by parental lack of interest); and both are searching for a way back home. For Mike, this search manifests itself in his narcoleptic dreams which reveal his longing to be reunited with his mother, his memory's embodiment of life's last and only abiding gentleness. For Scott, the search is translated into riotous, refractory behavior, targeted to get his father's attention. Seeming far afield of Shakespeare's *Henry* plays, *My Own Private Idaho*, instead, is Gus Van Sant's insightful meditation on Shakespeare's penetration into the brokers of power, into the very nature of those who rise and maintain ascendancy, authority, and wealth. Much like *Chimes at Midnight*, *My Own Private Idaho* looks into the core of Prince Henry, into his *necessary betrayal*. With an understated, malingering beauty and with a radical style that translates Shakespeare into the tones of American cowboy music and the images of flattened Midwestern landscapes, Gus Van Sant creates a curious, thought-filled, and bold translation of Shakespeare's *Henry IV* plays.

☞ *After reading Shakespeare's* 1 Henry IV *and* 2 Henry IV, *watch* Chimes at Midnight *or* My Own Private Idaho; *or after reading*

King Lear, *watch* Ran. *All of these films are best understood when considered to be products of "visual thinking," i.e., a self-conscious use of the visual, rather than the verbal, as the mode of expression and an insistence that what is most crucial to the film is there, in the images.* Shakespeare's work, in contrast, represents the pinnacle of "verbal thinking," and, thus,* Ran, Chimes at Midnight, *and* My Own Private Idaho *are most radical, not in the particular ways in which they reconstitute Shakespeare's story and characters, but in their translating from the verbal mode into the visual. Study any one of these films closely in terms of how it employs the language of film to translate Shakespeare's language of words into a visual medium.*

Shakespeare's plays have been made into a number of radical film translations which, in all manner of ways, reshape Shakespeare's work in extreme or revolutionary ways. These films are listed in Table 13.

Table 13.
Radical Film Translations of Shakespeare Plays

Shakespeare Play	Movie Title	Year Released	Director
The Comedy of Errors (1594)			
	The Boys from Syracuse (musical)	1940 (USA)	A. Edward Sutherland
	The Merry Wives of Windsor (opera)	1952 (Germany)	Georg Wildhagen
Hamlet (1602)			
	[The Mystery of] Hamlet (silent)	1920 (Germany)	
	Der Rest Ist Schweigen (The Rest Is Silence)	1960 (Germany)	Helmut Kautner
	The Bad Sleep Well	1960 (Japan)	Akira Kurosawa

→

**For an elaboration of this concept see Rudolph Arnheim's essay, "Visual Thinking."*

Shakespeare Play	Movie Title	Year Released	Director
1 Henry IV (1597)			
2 Henry IV (1598)			
	Chimes at Midnight	1967 (Spain/ Switzerland)	Orson Welles
	My Own Private Idaho	1991 (USA)	Gus Van Sant
King Lear (1606)			
	Ran	1985 (Japan)	Akira Kurosawa
	King Lear	1987 (France)	Jean-Luc Godard
Macbeth (1606)			
	Scotland PA	2002 (USA)	Billy Morrissette
	Joe Macbeth	1955 (U.K.)	Ken Hughes
	The Throne of Blood	1957 (Japan)	Akira Kurosawa
	Macbeth	1972 (U.K.)	Roman Polanski
	Men of Respect	1990 (USA)	William Reilly
Othello (1604)			
	Men Are Not Gods	1937 (U.K.)	Walter Reisch
	A Double Life	1947 (USA)	George Cukor
	Il Peccato di Anna (Anna's Sin)	1953 (Italy)	Camillo Mastrocinque
	Othello (ballet)	1960 (USSR)	Vakhtang Chabukiani

→

Shakespeare Play	Movie Title	Year Released	Director
	All Night Long	1962 (U.K.)	Basil Dearden
	Catch My Soul (rock opera)	1973 (USA)	Patrick McGoohan
	O	2001 (USA)	Tim Blake Nelson
Richard III (1592)			
	Tower of London	1939 (USA)	Rowland V. Lee
	Tower of London	1962 (USA)	Roger Corman
	Looking for Richard	1996 (USA)	Al Pacino
Romeo and Juliet (1595)			
	Romeo and Juliet	1944 (Mexico)	Miguel Delgado
	Carry on Teacher	1959 (U.K.)	Peter Rogers
	Romeo, Julie a tma (Sweet Light in a Dark Room)	1960 (Czechoslovakia)	Moris Ergas
	Romanoff and Juliet	1961 (USA)	Peter Ustinov
	West Side Story (musical)	1961 (USA)	Robert Wise and Jerome Robbins
	Panic Button	1964 (USA)	George Sherman
	Los Tarantos	1964 (Spain)	Rovira-Beleta
	China Girl	1987 (USA)	Abel Ferrara
	Zebrahead	1992 (USA)	Anthony Drazan
The Taming of the Shrew (1593)			

Shakespeare Play	Movie Title	Year Released	Director
	Kiss Me Kate (musical)	1953 (USA)	George Sidney
	10 Things I Hate About You	1999 (USA)	Gil Junger
The Tempest (1611)			
	The Tempest (silent)	1908 (U.K.)	Percy Stow
	Forbidden Planet	1956 (USA)	Fred McLeod
	The Tempest: by William Shake-speare, as seen through the eyes of Derek Jarman	1980 (U.K.)	Derek Jarman
	Tempest	1982 (USA)	Paul Mazursky
	Prospero's Books	1991 (U.K./France)	Peter Greenaway

Among the radical translations of Shakespeare are three musical theater versions of his plays: *The Boys from Syracuse*, *Kiss Me Kate* and *West Side Story*. Each of these Shakespeare-based musicals adheres to the most popular musical theater scenario: boy meets girl.

This boy-meets-girl tradition is given an entirely new perspective, however, in the dramatic musical, *Hedwig and the Angry Inch*. Written by and starring John Cameron Mitchell with music and lyrics by Stephen Trask,* *Hedwig* opened off–Broadway (1998 at the Squeezebox), and after a successful run, moved uptown to the James Street Theater in New York, where it became a Broadway hit. The play was brought to the screen in 2002.

Hedwig and the Angry Inch tells the story of a neo-glam, transsexual rock performer, born in East Berlin (prior to unification) as a male named Hansel. Hansel, the transsexual, falls in love with Sgt. Luther Robinson, an American GI stationed there, has a sex-change operation which is

---

Stephen Trask has his film debut as "Angry Inch" band member, Skszp, in the movie Hedwig.

botched (creating the "angry inch" of the title), and marries Luther, only to be abandoned by him. Renaming herself "Hedwig," she is a songwriter/singer, who performs her material with the puffed confidence of a star. Hedwig's vaunt, theatricality, glamour, and anti-social behavior — her vulnerability and acerbic complexity — are alluring to young Tommy Gnosis, who is living under the domineering control of his military father. Hedwig and Tommy fall in love, but Tommy betrays Hedwig by stealing and performing her songs, which catapult Tommy Gnosis to the rock stardom that Hedwig has dreamed of.

Hedwig and the Angry Inch is a non-normative text, concerning itself, as it does, with a subject matter that is marginalized or not widely accepted as normal. However, at its core, the play abides in the most prolific and universal of musical theater themes: love. Hedwig, whose longing for fame and for human love is really the search for self-identity and self-acceptance, believes that love is nothing less than the union with her soul mate, her other half. In this belief, she articulates the same concept that Aristophanes professes in Plato's dialogue, "Symposium." The genders, Aristophanes explains, were not two, as they are now, but originally three genders in one composite form:

> [T]here was man, woman, and the union of the two, having a name corresponding to this double nature, which had once had a real existence, but now is lost.... [T]he primeval man was round, his back and sides forming a circle; and he had four hands and four feet, one head with two faces.... Terrible was their might and strength, and the thoughts in their hearts were great, and they made an attack on the gods.... Zeus discovered a way ... [to] humiliate their pride and improve their manners. He said, "men shall continue to exist, but I will cut them in two and then they will be diminished in strength.... They shall walk upright on two legs." After the division the two parts of man, each desiring his other half, came together, and throwing their arms about one another, entwined in mutual embraces, longing to grow into one another.... Thus, man is always looking for his other half.... And when one of them meets his other half, ... the pair are lost in an amazement of love and friendship and intimacy [Plato, 144–46].

The lyrics of Hedwig's song, "The Origin of Love," recount, almost verbatim, Aristophanes's disquietude on love from "The Symposium." Later in the rock musical, in "Hedwig's Lament," she reinforces the idea of the "origin of love" as "a sad story/How we became/Lonely two-legged creatures." Like Aristophanes, Hedwig concludes, "So we wrapped our arms around each other/Trying to shove ourselves back together." "The Origins of Love" and "Hedwig's Lament" maintain that we spend our lives searching for the soul who completes us, our other half, whom Hedwig believed she had found in Tommy Gnosis.

However, unlike Aristophanes's parable, *Hedwig and the Angry Inch* concludes that the attainment of personal completion must come from within and not from without. Hedwig is Plato's primeval man. He is a composite of three genders: Hansel, the male; Hansel, the female; and Hedwig, the third gender, neither male nor female, but somehow a unity of both — the "double nature" gender that Plato describes. Thus, Hedwig contains unity within him/herself. Ken Triwush, who played the role of Hedwig on stage, explains, "John [Cameron Mitchell] is saying that you have to find the completion within yourself first, before you can go finding anybody else. Toward the end of the play, Hedwig realizes this. He has a catharsis where he strips himself of everything external, pulling off his clothing and wig."*

The theatrical production of *Hedwig* locates all the action in a single setting, on the stage of a small theater where Hedwig is performing that evening. (The actual stage that the actor is playing on, the James Street Theater, for example, is mentioned by name in the course of Hedwig's monologue, which can be changed to accommodate any change of venue.) Concurrent with Hedwig's performance and nearby at a much larger venue (across the river at Giants Stadium, for example), mega-star Tommy Gnosis is performing, snatches of which we hear, but never see. (Intermittently, Hedwig opens a door on the stage and listens to the ovations Tommy elicits from the stadium crowd.) Tommy's ascendancy represents all that Hedwig has lost.

With the exception of one role (Yitzak), all the roles in the stage production (including Luther, Hedwig's mother, and Tommy Gnosis) are performed by Hedwig, as she reenacts all the places and people triggered by her memory. While Hedwig's band, The Angry Inch, appears on stage, the play is very nearly a one-person show, placing great claims on the Hedwig actor to virtually carry the play. The film is a different matter.

In the film, the actor playing Hedwig (John Cameron Mitchell) only plays Hedwig. The other roles are performed by other actors. Dislodging itself from the stage, the film constructs multiple settings. The camera journeys easily from East Berlin to Kansas, showing the locales that Hedwig only describes on stage. In the theater, it is difficult to show a literal journey, a real landscape, or a chain of Bilgewater restaurants, as this film does. It is equally difficult for theater to show the opposite, the small details:

Ken Triwush, personal interview, 17 September 2003.

Hedwig and the Angry Inch (2002). John Cameron Mitchell as Hedwig. Based on the play written by and starring Cameron Mitchell with music and lyrics by Stephen Trask, *Hedwig* tells the story of a neo-glam, transsexual rock performer. Non-traditional in its story, the film is concerned with traditional, fundamental musical theater themes: girl meets boy (in variation), love, loss, and the search for identity.

the play of feeling that crosses the eyes, the vulnerable expression of anxious hands, or the acerbic lifting of an eyebrow that the film *Hedwig and the Angry Inch* shows so intimately.

Produced on a six-million-dollar budget (against *Moulin Rouge*'s 50-million-dollar budget, for example), the film *Hedwig* stands wonderfully apart from its stage play origins, as a self-reliant work that employs the distinct practices of cinema to translate the most integral meanings of the stage work to the screen. In its stage-to-screen transition, *Hedwig and the Angry Inch* adroitly employs cinematic usages to overcome the stagy feeling that would seem intrusive in a film. This same cinematic adroitness is evident in the movie musical *Chicago* (2002, dir. Rob Marshall).

Based on an amalgam of true crime stories, the original play, *Chicago* (1926), recounts the quasi-true story of a vaudeville showgirl, Roxie Hart, who cold-bloodedly shoots her lover. Roxie becomes the accommodating and enterprising accomplice to Chicago's infamous yellow journalism, which, willing to write almost anything that sells papers, prints sensational, entertainingly tawdry, but untrue, stories about Roxie that feed their gossip-delighted readership. *Chicago* was written by Maurine Dallas Watkins, who, herself, was a journalist at the Chicago *Tribune*.

Watkins's play was made as a silent film (*Chicago*, 1927), directed by Frank Urson and starring Phyllis Haver (Roxie Hart) and Robert Edeson (Billy Flynn). In 1942, *Chicago*, retitled *Roxie Hart*, was brought to the screen a second time in a movie that was radically affected by the demands of Hollywood's Production Code.

The Motion Picture Production Code (also referred to as the "Hays Code") was a uniform standard of "decency" imposed upon Hollywood film studios by the Motion Pictures Producers and Distributors Association, the MPPDA, later called the Motion Picture Association of America or the MPAA.

The Production Code clearly specified the subjects, language, and behavior that were forbidden to be brought to the American screen.* Instituted in March 1930 and implemented rigorously for the next twenty years, the Production Code was enforced by the PCA (Production Code Administration), headed first by Will Hays and later (July 1934) by Joseph Breen. Initially instituted to keep the movie industry independent of all United States government censorship, the PCA was a self-regulating agency which saw as its duty the implementation of moral authority and the setting of defined standards of decency that all major motion pictures shown in the United States were required to follow. The dictates of the Code spilled over into the private lives of the filmmakers, who were held to the same moral standards that their films were. If a film failed to secure the approval of Hays's or Breen's office, the consequences were ruinous. The project would be shelved, since without the Administrative approval, anyone producing, distributing, or exhibiting the movie would be fined significantly. Theater owners, understandably, were not willing to accrue such fines (as high as $25,000 per screening of an unapproved movie), and without an exhibition venue, the film could never be distributed. The

---

*The Production Code, with only minor revisions, remained, though not strictly enforced, until 1968, when the film industry adopted the system of ratings that we know today. The gradual collapse of the studio system in the 1950s weakened the authority of the Code, opening the way for breakthrough films like Otto Preminger's The Moon Is Blue (1953) and Howard Hughes's French Line (1954) to be released by MPAA member companies (RKO and UA respectively) without the PCA seal of approval.

code exercised a fundamental effect on American movies of the time, including the movie *Roxie Hart*, the 1942 film of *Chicago*.

The dictates of the Production Code Administration dominated Hollywood filmmaking in 1942, and, consequently, Maurine Watkins's cynical comedy, *Chicago*, had to be reworked to conform to the strict moral codes of Joseph Breen's office. Watkins's play clearly centers on Roxie Hart as an unregenerate adulteress, an unrepentant murderess, and an unabashed showgirl who would do anything for publicity. She not only, without qualm, murders her lover, but also attempts to have her husband take the blame for the shooting. When she cannot escape indictment for murder, Roxie hires flashy attorney Billy Flynn, who turns all notions of legal justice into flagrant, yet successful, photo opportunities that catapult Roxie just where she wants to be, in the limelight.

The play *Chicago* was fully antithetical to the moral values demanded by the Motion Picture Production Code, which held among its "General Principles" that *Law, natural or human, shall not be ridiculed* and that *the sympathy of the audience should never be thrown to the side of crime, wrongdoing, evil, or sin.* To be made into a film in Hollywood 1942, *Chicago* had to be rewritten and sanitized before the Breen office would authorize its production.

With a newly-turned screenplay by Nunnally Johnson, *Roxie Hart* tells the more polite story of a 1920s showgirl (Ginger Rogers) who agrees to confess to a murder that she did not commit. (In this version, her husband actually did it.) Though innocent, Roxie tells police that she pulled the trigger, killing a burglar in their apartment. She agrees to the false confession because a theatrical agent, Mr. Lynne Overman (Jake Callahan), convinces Roxie that the publicity would be good for her career. It is. With the help of Overman, Roxie's legal peril gets the sympathetic interest of the press, affording Roxie — and Ginger Rogers — the opportunity to preen and dance before the reporters who are covering her trial. Directed by William Wellman from Nunnally Johnson's adroit script, *Roxie Hart* has a subtle subtext, which, despite (or in *spite* of) the demands and constraints of the PCA, nonetheless manages to imply that nothing about Roxie is quite as innocent or naive as it appears, and that the man shot by her husband in their apartment was something *more* than just a chance burglar.

Chicago was reworked and rewritten yet again, this time as a musical. With a book by Fred Ebb and Bob Fosse, lyrics by Fred Ebb, and music by John Kander, *Chicago* opened in 1975 to a successful run on Broadway and underwent two subsequent successful Broadway revivals. While much of the original story and language of Watkins's play was retained, Ebb, Kander, and Fosse's *Chicago* added songs and dance numbers and enlarged the part of Velma Kelly to a co-starring role. The musical *Chicago* does a strong job of understanding and communicating definite ideas concerning the integral meaning and values of the original play.

In a press response to Maurine Watkins's play, *Chicago* is sardonically and humorously said to be "dedicated to all the beautiful women in the world who have shot their husbands full of holes out of pique" (Halliwell, "*Roxie Hart*"). The musical *Chicago* opens with "All That Jazz," a song in which Kander and Ebb provide their musical translation of that dedication. Like the dedication, their opening song is a cynical comment on the willingness of humans — of the press, of lawyers, of husbands, of wives, and of ordinary people — to act solely, simply, and unremorsefully in their own best interest and to think of such conduct as merely what one has to do to get by, to accept it as *all that jazz* that just comes with life.

After multiple attempts to bring the stage musical to the screen (the most persistent efforts of which considered Madonna and John Travolta in the starring roles), the film *Chicago* was produced and released by Miramax in 2002. While the movie demonstrates an exceptional collaboration of filmmaking skill in its acting, directing, choreography, cinematography, and editing, it can be faulted for missing the integral meaning of the original play, that deeply dark and cynical attitude toward the press, toward legal justice, toward the means by which one secures professional success, and, in general, toward human nature, that Maurine Watkins's wickedly entertaining play conveys and that the stage musical maintained.

In the film *Chicago*, we have a very different Roxie Hart (Renée Zellweger) and Velma Kelly (Catherine Zeta-Jones), a difference created through performance and through changes made to the text of the play and the musical. (In the film, song lyrics, for example, largely Roxie's, are edited, with the turn in phrases turning the character, too.) Both Zellweger, as the steely, self-serving, cute blond, and Zeta-Jones, as the viciously lethal, dark vamp, are breathtakingly beautiful and oddly charming — quite likeable, even — but they lack the brittle edges and the inner venom that the characters in Watkins's play have and that the Broadway legends, Gwen Verdon (as Roxie) and Chita Rivera (as Velma), created.* Zellweger and Zeta-Jones are not deficient in their portrayals, just different.

The dance sequences throughout *Chicago* are rapidly cut and often inter-spliced with tight shots of the dancers' attenuated arms, long legs,

---

*Chita Rivera makes a cameo appearance in the film, as a tough-talking, cigarette-smoking inmate, who chats with Roxie when she first arrives at prison.

and painted faces; but these sequences are so the product of their editing that the choreography seems to be as much the work of Martin Walsh, the film editor, as of Rob Marshall, the director/choreographer. The rapid editing creates a dizzying, flashy energy in keeping with the flashy nature of the characters, the film's tone, and the play's themes. However, missing from *Chicago*'s dance sequences are the sustained wide shots and the lengthy, uninterrupted takes of single dance sequences that mark great film dancers at the top of their form (Fred Astaire, Ginger Rogers, Gene Kelly, Cyd Charisse, and Gwen Verdon). The dance sequences in the movie *Chicago* point to a significant feature separating a stage musical from a movie musical: film editing, which can splice together different takes of the same dance routine, creating the illusion that the actors rose to the rigors of the role and danced the entire number, perfectly, just as we see it on the screen. Theater's live performance, in contrast, compels the actors to actually complete the dance in the single, uninterrupted execution that the stage performance requires, and to do so with unflagging energy, each evening of the play's run.

Not unique to dance sequences, the same is true of the acting in both media. The stage performance requires that the actor get it right, in full, for each performance. Acting in film, however, like dancing, can benefit from cinema's given: the editor's capacity to select and integrate into the movie the best take or even the best parts of different takes of the same shot.

We need only to look at the film *Chicago*, a movie wonderful in all the cinematic devices it deploys, to understand why it is generally held that stage is fundamentally an actor's medium and film is fundamentally a director's/editor's.

CHAPTER VI

Short Stories into Film

The task of translating a literary work to the screen takes a curious turn when the film's parent text is a short story. In other literary genres (novels and plays in particular), the filmmakers normally must find ways of abbreviating or even omitting passages contained in the literature. A film translation of a short story, however, presents a different problem. Rather than requiring that the filmmakers decide what to omit from the literature, the short story's inherent brevity usually asks that they expand upon the material that the story provides. The study of a short story's translation into a film must include the provocative exploration of the reasons, the methods, and the means by which the movie extends the original literary source.

A short story, by definition, is a brief narrative, composed in prose and including no more than 2,000 words, although definitions of "long short stories" allow the length to extend to as many as 20,000 words. The impulse to storytelling is as old as language itself, with the specific oral traditions of legends, folk tales, fables, and myths having existed throughout all of human history and in all cultures. Carl Jung's conclusion that there is a story-creating or myth-creating impulse common to all people in all known cultures is, he believes, a function of the psychological process common to all humans. Jung holds that myths and their attending rituals have their origins "so far buried in the mystery of the past that they seem to have no human source," but are "collective representations emanating from primeval dreams and creative fantasies" (42–43). Central to these cross-cultural stories is the "hero myth," which, Jung holds, always refers to a "powerful man or god-man who vanquishes evil ... and who liberates his people from destruction and death" (68). Oral traditions and written texts are replete, Jung demonstrates, with hero-myths centering also on god-women.

With the development of cuneiform writing in Mesopotamia and hieroglyphic writing in Egypt (both c. 3,000 B.C.E.), the first written stories appeared.* Often abiding in the sacred and providing religious and ethical guidance, these early prose narratives were followed by the middle period of writing (100 C.E.–1450). During this period, prose interest shifted from the sacred to the secular in such representative works as *The Thousand and One Nights/The Arabian Nights* (anonymous, c. 850, Arabia), the *Decameron* (by Giovanni Boccaccio, c.1353, Italy), and *Makura no Soshi/The Pillow Book* (by Sei Shonagon, c. 996–1012, Japan).

☞ *Among the stories in* The Thousand and One Nights *are those of Ali Baba and the Forty Thieves, Aladdin, and Sinbad. As* The Bedford Anthology of World Literature *asserts (with a certain hyperbole), these stories "have been made into movies by Hollywood studios on almost an annual basis" (Davis, 435). The* Decameron *has been translated to film at least ten times, with the most successful work being that of Pier Paolo Pasolini's* Il Decameron *(1971), based on nine of Boccaccio's stories. Makura no Soshi/The Pillow Book has been translated into film by Peter Greenaway (1996). Choose any one of these Middle Period literary works. Read it. Watch any one film translation of the story/stories. Evaluate the film in terms of the fours points of the aesthetic rubric (Appendix A).*

In considering the long and rich history of the short story, it seems misleading, at best, to credit its founding to any one age, culture, or individual. Yet, we refer to Balzac or Poe or O. Henry as the father of the short story. In the nineteenth century, writers emerged who *consciously* considered the aesthetics particular to the short story genre, wrote about these particular aesthetics, and based their compositional strategies on those specific concepts. Those short story writers include Prosper Mérimée

---

The first written reference to storytelling appears on Egyptian papyri, dating back as far as 3,000 B.C.E., where there occurs an account of the "sons of Cheops" having entertained their father by narrating stories. The Descent of Inanna (c. 2,000 B.C.E.), written in cuneiform on clay tablet, is a series of tales all relating to the hero-goddess Inanna. While much of early writing consists of a series of brief narratives, these works are often composed in verse, not prose. Examples include: The Epic of Creation (c. 1,800 B.C.E., Mesopotamia), Hymn to Osiris (c. 1,520 B.C.E., Egypt), Rig Veda (c. 1,000 B.C.E., India), The Book of Songs (c. 1,000–600 B.C.E., China), The Iliad and The Odyssey (c. 800 B.C.E.), and the Dao De Jing/Tao Te Ching (c. 600–300 B.C.E.). However, prose narrations recounting a series of brief, separate episodes (stories) appear in such early writing as The Epic of Gilgamesh (c. 700–600 B.C.E., Mesopotamia), Shu Jing/Book of History (c. 800 B.C.E., China), Upanishads (c. 900–100 B.C.E., India), and Hebrew Scripture (examples: the "Book of Genesis" and the "Book of Exodus," c. 900–500 B.C.E., Israel).

in France, E. T. A. Hoffman in Germany, and Edgar Allan Poe in America.

In "The Philosophy of Composition," Edgar Allan Poe establishes his short story criteria, which he also applies to poetry. His philosophy provides a blueprint for composition, which he arrives at by considering the "*modus operandi*" by which some of his own works were "put together." Poe explains that writing proceeds not from an inspired bolt from his subconscious or a visitation from his muse, but rather "step by step, to its completion, with the precision and rigid consequence of a mathematical problem." Reflecting on this process, Poe holds three qualities to be basic, essential, constituent elements of a successful short story or poem. They are: brevity, single effect, and beauty.

By "brevity" Poe means a story or poem length capable of being read, in completion, in "one sitting" so that the "single effect" will not be diminished or destroyed by interruption. Poe's values of brevity and single effect are the very values assumed by most feature-length filmmakers, limiting, as they do, the movie's duration to that which an audience can comfortably consume in a single sitting so that the single effect of the film will not be lost. Thus, the driving principles of feature-length film production are most in keeping with the driving principles of the effective short story.

By "Beauty"—or the "poetical"—Poe means that which elicits "the excitement or pleasurable elevation of the soul." Poe adds that "the death then of a beautiful woman is unquestionably the most poetical topic in the world" ("Philosophy of Composition," *Essays*, 19). Poe explores the theme of the death of a beautiful woman in *The Fall of the House of Usher*, a story concerned with the disintegration of Roderick Usher, the bereaved lover (filial or otherwise, it is intimated) of his twin sister Madeline, whom he has buried alive. Poe's complex of psychology and symbolism was translated in a fascinating manner by directors Luis Buñel and Jean Epstein. Their film, *Fall of the House of Usher* (1928), is a radical translation of Edgar Allan Poe's short story, a film in which story narration is incidental to depicting what the filmmakers see as most integral to Poe's story: psychological state. Thus, the movie intimates rather than demonstrates that Roderick buried his sister alive. (His reason for doing so is never made clear. He may or may not have misjudged her catatonic state for death.) She escapes from her vault and is instrumental in setting the family mansion ablaze. A silent film, the work incorporates very few inter-titles, and those that are included are largely sentence fragments incorporated in a manner that deemphasizes the importance of Poe's words in relation to

Buñel and Epstein's images. Lighting, angles, and camera movement are used to represent deteriorating mental states in this movie, impressionistic in style and psychological in tenor. Buñel and Epstein employ a fast moving, animated camera that records matters from unusual angles. They integrate slow motion; incorporate double, even triple exposures; and reconstitute spatial and temporal properties. All of these techniques become expressions of Roderick Usher's psychological state. Throughout Buñel and Epstein's film, objects (examples: curtains, clocks) take on human qualities as the movie endows the inanimate with life and celebrates the power of cinema to perform such godlike tasks. Crucially, Buñel and Epstein understand — and are able to translate to the screen — Poe's *logic*, a "logic entirely divorced from reality, and seeming to arise superior to reality" (Quinn, 31).

Poe's "logic" informs his short stories, his poetry, and his treatises. In "The Poetic Principle" he theorizes about superior reality — the absolute ideal of beauty — and in his tales and poems Poe's protagonists, often alone and always alienated, progress toward this ethereal ideal. They do not succeed in their aspirations, however, because Poe did not seem to believe that the phenomenal world could actually be transcended, the numen apprehended. In *Eureka* Poe writes "as an individual, I may be permitted to say that I *cannot* conceive Infinity, and am convinced that no human being can" (21). Yet Poe's characters try, again and again, to comprehend infinity, to experience numinous beauty, to perceive "Original Unity" (*Eureka*, 2). Single-mindedly committed to this pursuit, they are lured by their longings for beauty and subsequently betrayed when their encounters become horrific.*

Poe has considerable ambivalence toward his questers. He often mocks their attempts, satirizes the vast hubris implied in their efforts to transcend the phenomenal world, while he simultaneously lauds their tenacious, single-minded pursuit of "*la idée.*" Their pursuits are the acts of madmen, but the alternative, Poe implies, is the humdrum existence of life led as the business of trivialities. Again and again Poe sets up the conundrum: His madmen are visionaries, but their "visions" are only the dubious apparitions of truly mad men.

Poe's ambivalence, his simultaneous mocking and elevating of his

---

There is a sizeable body of criticism that argues that in their experience of horror, Poe's characters resultingly experience a certain numinous beauty; and, consequently, his madmen are true, transcendental visionaries. No doubt, Poe's short stories provoke and intrigue the full gamut of readers, from the most modest sixth grader through the most sophisticated scholar — and the full gamut of filmmakers, too.

protagonists, is an integral quality of his writing for producer/director Roger Corman, who has made seven movies based on Poe's work. While somewhat less subtle in his burlesque of, and acclaim for, the protagonist than Poe is, Corman achieves the same mocking/lauding effect by heightening absolutely everything in his films: the mercurial, eerie sound effects; the claustrophobic atmospheres; the ever-lingering mist; the dim, shadowy, cobwebbed, labyrinthian Gothic mansions; the shock-cuts; the flamboyantly lit storms; and the larger-than-life performances of his actors, notably Vincent Price,* Ray Milland,† Peter Lorre,§ and Basil Rathbone.** Corman's exaggeration, the emphasis and underscoring of the sounds and images in his films, creates a cinematic equivalent of Poe's madly dispersed dashes, exclamation points, and italicized foreign phrases. Corman sees a great, tormented soul, driven to madness in each of the central characters of his Poe films, and he has his actors play the characters in that broadstroke way. While his Poe films often are radical translations of the stories, the films unfailingly translate the integral and intricate nature of Poe's protagonists: they are educated, cultivated, intelligent, and sensitive, but their minds operate in realms so horrific and weird as to suggest the comical.

☞   *Director Tim Burton claims that Roger Corman had a lasting influence on his own style of filmmaking and that Corman's Vincent Price/Edgar Allan Poe films of the 1960s were very much on his mind when he made* Sleepy Hollow *(1999). Watch* Sleepy Hollow. *Try to see the imprint of Roger Corman in Burton's cinematic hyperbole: the eerie, Gothic surroundings; the monochromatic color scheme shocked with red blood; the arched acting (notably, Christopher Walken as the Headless Horseman); the gruesome information (murder by decapitation), the intermittent comical tone, and the oddities of character. Read Washington Irving's short story, "The Legend of Sleepy Hollow." Scrutinize the film's Cormanesque, free-ranging method of translating Irving's narrative structure, plot, and characters (example, Irving's Ichabod Crane, schoolmaster, as Johnny Depp's Ichabod Crane, Private Investigator). After considering all these aspects, critique* Sleepy Hollow *in the terms provided by the aesthetic rubric (Appendix A).*

*The Fall of the House of Usher, The Pit and the Pendulum, Black Cat, "Morella" and "The Black Cat" in Tales of Terror, The Raven, The Masque of the Red Death, and The Tomb of Ligeia.
    †The Premature Burial.
    § "The Black Cat" in Tales of Terror.
    ** "The Facts in the Case of M. Valdemar" in Tales of Terror.

The Pit and the Pendulum (1961): The set of the infamous torture chamber during the Spanish Inquisition. The film is a radical translation of Poe's story, as its plot involves an adulterous wife (Barbara Steele) who has faked her own death and is trying to drive her husband (Vincent Price) crazy. Writer/producer/director Roger Corman's style is apparent throughout the film: eerie sound effects; ever-present cobwebs and gloomy mist; dark, shadowy, and labyrinthian mansions; and larger-than-life performances.

Like Poe stories, Corman's Poe films are simultaneously Gothic and mock–Gothic because, like Poe, Corman has a fascination for the very horror that he derides. When asked about the tone of his movies in general and about *The Premature Burial* (1962), in particular, Corman remarked: "There is a very fine line between horror and humor." Horror and humor are, he held, "two sides of the same coin" (Frank, 100). He further adds, "My theories about comedy are that comedy is serious and that the actors or, or should I put it another way, the characters, must never be funny" (105). Filled with proto–Gothic mannerisms, the performances Corman solicits from his actors are remarkably unrestrained, and, as in Poe, it is the very lack of restraint that makes the protagonists somehow deeply magnificent and deeply comical.

   Corman's seven Poe films translate ten of Poe's works. (*Tales of Terror* is an anthology film which incorporates four of Poe's short stories.)* However, Poe's influence on Corman extends well beyond the specific movies that he made. As Alan Frank argues, Corman read Poe voraciously and Poe's works "were to serve as the basis for [Corman's] seminal series of Sixties horror movies" (7). His film translations of Poe's stories are B-grade movies, ostensibly concentrating on the Gothic terror that is clearly a constituting element of much of Poe's fiction; but they also encode things that are more complex: the tenuous relationship of horror and humor and the Freudian elements present in Poe's writing. Departing from his previous tradition of working in black and white, standard gauge film and on a very restricted budget, Corman's Poe films are shot in color, in CinemaScope or Panavision, and on a much larger budget than he previously was allotted. Consistent with his manner of filming, his shooting schedule was always kept tight (*Usher*, for example, was filmed in fifteen days).† Also congruous with the length of Poe's short stories, Corman's films, though theatrical features, were kept quite short, often just eighty minutes.

☞   *Read any one of Edgar Allan Poe's short stories that have been made into a film by Roger Corman (see Table 14). Study the film translation in terms of what the movie retained, deleted, and/or added to the plot of the story. Look at the elongated screen space that CinemaScope or Panavision provided. In what specific ways and for what specific reason does Corman utilize the visual opportunities that Scope allows? Suspense is heightened often when space is constricted, the exact opposite of the spatial expansion of CinemaScope and Panavision. Does Corman's use of Cinemascopic space inhibit or intensify the movie's suspense? Is any Freudian imagery or are any Freudian themes apparent in the film? Does your experience of Corman's humor add to or miss the point of Poe's work?*

   While Corman's films deploy a heightened use of cinematic practices to translate what he finds most integral in the writing, particularly to accent that thin line that separates horror and humor, his movies, arguably,

---

*The Haunted Palace (1963), starring Vincent Price and Lon Chaney Jr., takes its title from Poe's poem, but it is based on H. P. Lovecraft's The Strange Case of Charles Dexter Ward.
   †Notorious for his tight shooting schedules, Corman filmed his favorite movie, Creature from the Haunted Sea (1968), in only a day and a half. In his autobiography, How I Made a Hundred Movies in Hollywood and Never Lost a Dime, Corman explains that Creature is his personal favorite because it is the only one of his movies in which the monster wins.

Table 14.
Roger Corman Film Translations of
Edgar Allan Poe Short Stories and Poetry

Title of Poe Work	Title of Film	Year/Country of Release	Format	Duration
"The Fall of the House of Usher"	The Fall of the House of Usher	1960 USA	color CinemaScope	79 mins.
"The Pit and the Pendulum"	The Pit and the Pendulum	1961 USA	color CinemaScope	85 mins.
"The Premature Burial"	The Premature Burial	1962 USA	color Panavision	81 mins.
"Morella" "The Black Cat" "The Cask of Amontillado" "The Facts in the Case of M. Valdemar"	Tales of Terror	1962 USA	color standard	120 mins.
"The Raven" (poem)	The Raven	1963 USA	color Panavision	86 mins.
"The Masque of the Red Death"	The Masque of the Red Death	1964 U.K.	color Panavision	86 mins.
"Ligeia"	The Tomb of Ligeia	1964 U.K.	color CinemaScope	81 mins.

fail to translate the profundity inherent in Poe's writing. But Eric Rohmer accomplishes this in *Bérénice* (1954), his fifteen minute long, radical film translation of Poe's short story "Berenice." In its use of shadows, claustrophobic distortions, and graceful, poetic photography, *Bérénice* shows the influence of Rohmer's favorite director, F. W. Murnau, about whose film *Faust*, Rohmer wrote a book.* Like Murnau (in his 1926 film, *Faust*, for example), Rohmer helps us see the humor in the vast hubris of the protagonist; however, Rohmer's humor is subtle in contrast to Corman's.

Perhaps in no other short story of Poe's is a character's hubris and the pendulum of derision and fascination that Poe holds for him more apparent than in "Berenice." The story centers on the mad narrator, Egeus,

*Eric Rohmer, *L'organisation de l'espace dans le Faust de Murnau, Paris: Union générale d'éditions, 1977.

who explains, in an inflated tone, that he is descended from a noble, time-honored "race of visionaries" (*Works*, Vol. V, 14). Zealously contemplative and always alone — even when in the presence of others — Egeus passes his time in a brooding contemplation of minutiae. He is shaken from these more common observations by the wondrous hint of what he perceives to be transcendent beauty: his cousin/fiancée Berenice, or, more specifically, Berenice's excessively white teeth, which exert a "strange and irresistible influence" over Egeus. In consequence, all "other matters and all different interests [become] absorbed in their single contemplation" (*Works*, Vol. V, 23). Egeus tells us that "*que toutes ses dents etaient des idées. Des idées!*" (*Works*, Vol. V, 24); and monomaniacally he persists in his observations and meditations upon Berenice's "thirty-two small, white and ivory-looking substances" (*Works*, Vol. V, 27). Action usurps contemplation as Egeus, anxious to possess "the Idea," removes the teeth from the mouth of the entombed, yet alive, Berenice.

Egeus's obsession, which he narrates in passionate, highblown language, is Poe's satirical assault against men like Egeus and their macabre attempts to possess the Idea. The story is wickedly ghoulish, even for Poe. It is also unusually droll. We follow, stunned with incredulous amusement, at Egeus's attempts at experiencing supernal beauty via a woman's teeth, his efforts to possess *la idée*, to possess it literally.

Despite his barbed derailing of Egeus's efforts, however, Poe reverences the impulses that motivated his character: the desire to establish contact with the spiritual, to transcend the common, and to reach the perfect exhilaration of Beauty perceived. These same impulses motivate many of Poe's characters, who, in their pursuit, are necessarily alone. They engage in activities that alienate them from society and from the riotous distractions of everyday life. Solitude becomes their means of transcendence; and there is considerable romance in their self-elected alienation, in their Faustian effort to reach beyond mortal knowledge. They fail, always. But, their failure resounds with the mad, romantic glory of a reach that exceeds the actual grasp.

Poe's characters are gloomy, romantic, isolated figures who shun social involvement in order to pursue something they believe to be far more meaningful. We see this pattern again and again in Poe's short stories. His protagonists often disdain contact with others. They consider the world outside an incipient distraction, and their actions repeatedly advance the impression that Poe's heroes cannot be swayed by society's admonishments. They listen to their own hearts and want to silence the beating of any other heart that dares to intrude upon their solitary pursuits. Poe's protagonists adhere to Emerson's famous maxim: *Trust thyself.* Their hearts beat (in misanthropic solitude) to that iron string; and although Poe may often mock his characters' mad extremes, their aspirations are the impulses he commends most solemnly in "The Poetic Principle." Inspired by "an ecstatic prescience of the glories beyond the grave," Poe's solitary characters are following an "immortal instinct, deep within the spirit of man" (*Works,* Vol. IX, 143).

In their "wild effort to reach the Beauty above," Poe's narrators invariably sequester themselves from the world (*Works,* Vol. IX, 144). We see this in his stories such as "Liegia," "The Fall of the House of Usher," "Morella," "The Tell-Tale Heart," "The Oval Portrait," "A Descent into the Maelström," and "The Premature Burial," all of which have been made into films. It is a theme which recurs in Poe's poems: "The Raven," "Alone," "The Lake: To —" and "Silence — A Sonnet." Even Poe's detective fiction implies that truth can only be discerned in solitude. In solving his cases, C. Auguste Dupin works alone. Dupin is successful not because he pieces together minute details, but because he searches out the "beauty of the greater scheme of which the facts are only small details" (Levine, 164). Truth comes to him as Poe believed it comes to any artist, through a burst of insight (the writing down of truth for Poe — i.e., poetic composition — is another matter entirely); and although Dupin cannot be said to achieve transcendental truth, he does succeed at perceiving a brief portion of the pattern, a fragment of the overall design.

Poe's image has become a popular one: the dejected artist, alone and misunderstood, who braves the pains of alienation so that he might pursue a higher calling, which the world clearly judges as mad. For Poe, essentially a romantic, the individual's vision must prevail over all other considerations. His images are vastly popular in film, as attested by the fact that well over 250 known movies worldwide have been made based on his short stories. As such, Edgar Allan Poe's work stands as one of the most frequently engaged sources, internationally, of film translations of the short story.

☞ *Watch any one film of an Edgar Allan Poe short story that you have read. (Internet movie data bases like imdb.com can provide suggestions.) What does the movie deem as integral to its translation of Poe? the terror? the complex relationship between humor and horror? the archetypic image of the alienated artist/visionary? the ambivalence Poe holds for his protagonist? the implied, curious sexuality (fetishism, necromancy, incest)? the romantic ideals? the single effect? the extrav-*

agant style and complex visual nature? the fascination with the strange, the supernatural, and the mystical? the tension between the sublime and the ridiculous? the psychological? What particular cinematic practices does the film employ to further what it sees as integral to Poe's writing? (See Chapter II, "The Language of Film," for ideas.) Is this collaboration of cinematic skills successfully executed in the movie?

Richard Wilbur describes Edgar Allan Poe as the "monarch of the domain of his own visions" (372), an appellation suited to the other *master of suspense,* Alfred Hitchcock. While director/screenwriter Alfred Hitchcock has never made a film based on a Poe work, he claims that Poe's writing exerted a persistent influence on him:

> At sixteen I discovered the work of Edgar Allan Poe. I happened to read first his biography, and the sadness of his life made quite an impression on me.... Very likely it's because I was so taken with the Poe stories that I later made suspense films. I don't want to seem immodest, but I can't help comparing what I've tried to put in my films with what Edgar Allan Poe put in his novels: a completely unbelievable story told to the readers with such spellbinding logic that you get the impression that the same thing could happen to you tomorrow [Hitchcock in Spoto, 39].

In addition to his ability to narrate "a completely unbelievable story" and to do so with "spellbinding logic," Hitchcock shares Poe's wickedly ghoulish and unusually droll sensibilities, his interest in human psychology, his innuendoes regarding the *wrinkles* in his protagonists' sexual tastes, and his framing of alienated anti-heroes, whose unorthodox behavior he finds amusingly odd and worthy of study. Such protagonists include Dr. Edwardes/John Ballentine (Gregory Peck) in *Spellbound* (1945); Devlin (Cary Grant) in *Notorious* (1946); Bruno Anthony (Robert Walker) in *Strangers on a Train* (1951); L. B. Jeffries (James Stewart) in *Rear Window* (1954), and John "Scottie" Ferguson (James Stewart) in *Vertigo* (1958). Furthering his identification with Poe, Hitchcock, himself, claims that "both Poe and I are prisoners of the suspense genre. If I had made *Cinderella* into a movie, everyone would look for a corpse. And if Poe had written *Sleeping Beauty* they'd be looking for a murderer!" (Hitchcock in Spoto, 40).

There is a Poe-presence in Hitchcock's films. "Truffaut, Rohmer and Chabrol, for example, briefly note that in *Strangers on a Train* related imagery connects Bruno [Anthony]'s Oedipal compulsions with Poe's fascination with Berenice's teeth" (Perry, 393). Hitchcock learned, "likely from Poe," to focus "attention on significant objects. The key in *Notori-*

ous, the glass of milk in *Suspicion*, the knife in *Sabotage* are for Hitchcock what the eye in 'The Tell-Tale Heart,' the letter in 'The Purloined Letter,' and the teeth in 'Berenice' are for Poe" (Perry, 394). Both Poe and Hitchcock explore the disintegration of sanity into madness (Poe's "William Wilson," "The Tell-Tale Heart," and "Ligeia" and Hitchcock's *Spellbound, Frenzy,* and *Psycho*), and both construct characters who are "obsessed with murder or love, often seeking to kill that which they love" (Perry 395). Examples include Poe's "The Assignation" and "Fall of the House of Usher" and Hitchcock's *Vertigo* and *Shadow of a Doubt.*

With a script written by playwright Thornton Wilder from a short story by Gordon McDonnell, *Shadow of a Doubt* (1943) features Joseph Cotten as Charlie Oakley—"Uncle Charlie"—a serial murderer who appears charmingly normal. Like Poe's Montresor in "The Cask of Amontillado," Charlie is malice incarnate, a cold killer who, feeling ever-superior, plays on the vanity of his victims (widows) and murders them in ruthless premeditation. Charlie is sane, suave, and entirely aware of his wrongdoing; yet, oddly, for a time, we are drawn to him and even root for him, as we do Montresor.

Poe and Hitchcock both explore character in terms of doppelgängers, both females and males. In Poe, we see this female doubling in Ligeia/Rowena in the short story "Ligeia" and in Hitchcock in Madeline/Judy in *Vertigo.* Both works center on the excessive love of a male (Ligeia's husband and Scottie) for his female ideal (Liegia and Madeline, respectively), who represents nothing less to him than beauty incarnate, the sublime, the conduit to the mystical and supernal—*la idée.* Both women die at approximately the same point in the narrative; and both narratives portray and probe the compulsive, bizarre behavior of the bereaved male lover, who, in his desire to resurrect and possess the dead woman whom he venerates, attempts to possess her living successor, whom he then inadvertently kills.

Male doppelgängers take the form of the two William Wilsons in Poe's short story "William Wilson," and Hitchcock's pair, the criminal and Manny, in *The Wrong Man* (1957), from Maxwell Andersen's story, "The True Story of Christopher Emmanuel Balestrero" and Herbert Brean's article, "The True Story," published in *Life* magazine and based on real events. In both "William Wilson" and *The Wrong Man,* the protagonist has a look-alike, eerily unrelated by any family ties, but so extraordinarily similar in features as to be taken for the other. Poe's protagonist, William Wilson, in describing his counterpart (who bears "the same Christian and surname as" he), clearly states: "Wilson was not, in the most remote degree, connected with my family. But assuredly if we *had* been brothers, we must have been twins" (*Works*, Vol. IV, 167). In *The Wrong Man*, Christopher Emmanuel "Manny" Balestrero (Henry Fonda) is accused of a crime he did not commit because the criminal, fully unrelated to him, looks identical enough to be mistaken for Manny. Both works can be deconstructed in terms of the Freudian dynamic of the ego and super-ego, which are rendered in terms of a malevolent, violent half who perpetrates a crime that victimizes the innocent half. Each work is manifestly psychological, exploring one man's conflict with his inner self, the conundrum of good and evil occupying the same visage, and the descent into dementia that results (for William Wilson and for Rose Balestrero, Manny's wife).

☞ *We know that Hitchcock, from age sixteen on, was widely read in and significantly influenced by Edgar Allan Poe. For example, in his essay, "Why I Am Afraid of the Dark," Hitchcock explains the specific effect that reading a collection of Poe's stories (published as* Tales of the Grotesque and Arabesque*) had on him (Gottlieb, 142–145). Included in this short story collection are: "The Tell-Tale Heart," "The Fall of the House of Usher," "Ligeia," "William Wilson," "The Cask of Amontillado," "The Masque of the Red Death," and "The Premature Burial." Read any number of Poe's stories; see any number of Hitchcock's films. What shared sensibilities, themes, and imagery do you see converging in the works of Poe and Hitchcock?*

In each and every one of their works, in major or minor strains, both Poe and Hitchcock demonstrate, often with chilling effect, the mordant truth that all things in nature change. When this is a dominant theme, the consequence of the change is that what was once known, deeply loved, and reverenced is *nevermore*, as in "Ligeia" and *Vertigo*. Both Poe and Hitchcock, curiously, make a bird an annunciator of this sorrowful and terrifying percept, Poe in "The Raven" and Hitchcock in *The Birds*.

Alfred Hitchcock's film *The Birds* (1963) is a traditional translation of Daphne du Maurier's short story. Du Maurier's story restricts all the action to one family (the Hockens) on one farm isolated by its location "at the far end of the peninsula, where the sea surrounded the farmland on either side" (du Maurier, "Birds," 7). Hitchcock retains what is essential in the original story, the slowly developing awareness of an irrational, but fundamental, disruption of the Natural Order, signified by the menacing and fatal attacks against people by innumerable, otherwise ordinary, birds. He enlarges upon the original plot, however, expanding the story's basic circumstances to include a romantic couple — Mitch (Rod Taylor) and Melanie (Tippi Hedren)— and the various inhabitants of a west-coast American seaside town named Bodega Bay, with its elderly and its small school children, all of whom are terrorized by the birds. While broadening the plot, Hitchcock maintains what is integral to du Maurier's story: that any concept of nature's Great Chain of Being, in which humans are second in authority only to God, is an illusion, and that, instead, a haphazard, arbitrary, perilous, and unpredictable world exists, which we would rather see as an ordered, predictable, just, and governable one. Du Maurier's story ends with the Hockens family hiding, but still vulnerable, in their boarded-up English coastal farm cottage, with its limited food supply, knowing the lethal assault of the birds is a worldwide phenomenon and wondering "Won't America do something? ... They've always been our allies, haven't they? Surely America will do something" (du Maurier, "Birds," 42). Hitchcock's film ends in an analogous way: Mitch and Melanie driving in a car, windows closed and doors locked (like the Hockens' cottage, the car is a constricted, claustrophobic space) amid legions of pernicious birds, threateningly asserting their power over humans. Hitchcock reconstructs du Maurier's nightmarish world in which all causal chains and all expectations of natural order and behavior have been dismantled. While the movie has been criticized for a lifeless screenplay, it is noted for its strong cinematic practices: its instances of eerie silence and its effectual absence of a musical score; for its meticulous editing, particularly its use of montage, as in the birds' attack on Melanie in Mitch's house; and for much of its camera work, including what is arguably Hitchcock's most famously ironic overhead shot: the "bird's eye view," occurring during the climatic fire scene. *The Birds* is one of eight films that Hitchcock made based on short stories. (See Table 15.)

François Truffaut maintains that Alfred Hitchcock "outranks the rest" of directors because "he is the most complete film-maker of all. He is not merely an expert at some specific aspects of cinema, but an all-round specialist, who excels at every image, each shot, and every scene" (Truffaut, 18). David Sterritt comments on Hitchcock's "compulsively precise camera" (Sterritt, 1); and James M. Welsh asserts that "Hitchcock *was* a genius ... recognized as the ultimate auteur director" (Leitch, viii).

Curiously, Hitchcock's movies have moments of glaring artificiality, when we pause and wonder why "the master of technique" did not choose to use the technology at hand to create a more realistic rendering of those shots which seem so very fake and so discordant within the visual realism that he creates. Compounding their artificiality, these shots occur within otherwise realistic-looking shot sequences. Hitchcock does this both at

Table 15.
Alfred Hitchcock Films Based on Short Stories

Movie Title	Short Story Title	Author	Hitchcock Cameo
Mr. and Mrs. Smith (1941)	"Mr. and Mrs. Smith"	Norman Krasna	on street, passing Robert Montgomery
Shadow of a Doubt (1943)	"Shadow of a Doubt"	Gordon McDonnell	on a train to Santa Rosa, playing cards and holding a full house
Lifeboat (1943)	"Lifeboat"	John Steinbeck	in the before and after photos in a newspaper ad for "Reduco Obesity Slayer"
Stage Fright (1950)	"Man Running" and "Outrun by the Constable"	Selwyn Jepson	in street, turning to see Jane Wyman who is disguised as Marlene Dietrich's maid
Rear Window (1954)	"It Had to Be Murder" (subsequently published as "Rear Window")	Cornell Woolrich	in songwriter's apartment, winding a clock
The Man Who Knew Too Much (1934 and 1956)	"The Man Who Knew Too Much"	Charles Bennett	in Moroccan marketplace, watching acrobats
The Wrong Man (1957)	"The True Story of Christopher Emmanuel Balestrero"	Maxwell Anderson	in the film's prologue, narrating
The Birds (1963)	"The Birds"	Daphne du Maurier	outside of a pet shop, walking two white terriers as Tippi Hedren enters

incidental and at crucial moments in his films. A random offering of these instances includes Alicia Huberman's (Ingrid Bergman) horse-riding in *Notorious*; Madeleine Elster's body falling off the tower in *Vertigo*; Melanie's piano-playing at Mitch's house in *The Birds*; and the imposing ship docked in the harbor near Bernice Edgar's (Louise Latham) house in *Marnie*. In each case, the intrusion of overtly artificial sequences, or components of sequences, seems counterproductive to the film's intent. It ruptures the story's reality and exposes the suspense for what it is — just movie-manufactured illusions. Just as quickly as these artificial shots appear, however, they are overtaken by classical movie-making, where all the cinematic techniques work as indiscernible threads that synthesize the shots and sounds into a credible, harmonious whole. Here, we willingly lose ourselves fully and once again in the cinematic illusions Hitchcock famously and adroitly creates.

This is Hitchcock's signature: God at play, directing us where his whim will.

Alfred Hitchcock's films demonstrate how fully and deeply cinema, in the hands of a master, can control our perceptions, our responses, and our sensibilities. We follow where and as it leads us. We enter and exit its reality at the master filmmaker's choosing, largely, in Hitchcock's specific case, by means of cinematic practices substantial in intent and conscious in deployment. The artifice is played with typical Hitchcockian guile and feigned innocence, but it is there, as surely as each of his cameo appearances is — innocent enough, puckish even, until we realize that each and every time we notice him, the *real* director, we are pulled from the film's reality, only to be returned again.*

Hitchcock's cameos and his deployment of artificiality have the effect and affirm (consciously or not) the values of distanciation, i.e., the separation or distancing of the audience from the world of the performance, a theory fundamental to playwright/director Berthold Brecht. Central to Brecht's theory of distanciation is the belief that people sitting in front of a theatrical stage or a movie screen must remain fully aware that they are in a theater, watching a performance. He insists that "one tribute we can pay to the audience is to treat it as thoroughly intelligent" (Brecht, "Conversations with Brecht," 14). No matter how much spectators may want to lose themselves in the illusion, Brecht holds that an intellectual distance must be maintained; the experience must be demystified; and theatrical or cinematic illusion, he insists, must always be identified as such, even while the emotionality of the work is maintained.

Where classical theater and classical film seek to maximize the engagement of the spectator with the performed or projected illusion, Brecht's theory of distanciation aspires to hinder all identification of the audience

---

*Hitchcock's cameo appearances began innocently enough in The Lodger (1926) where, in need of extras, he appeared in scenes himself: at an office (only his back) and in a crowd (at the arrest).

with the characters and events in the play or the film. The structure of Aristotelian theater and, by extension, classical cinema, is a structure that Brecht insists be revolutionized. Brecht's theory seeks to undermine — as do Hitchcock's cameos and his glaringly artificial shots — the fixed position of spectator/spectacle, which Brecht maintains is an unhealthy structure of representation, exchange, and identification.

No longer passive receivers of spectacle, no longer allowed to lose themselves in empathic identification with projected illusions, Brecht's spectators are pulled into conscious awareness of the performance. In Brecht's theory, theatrical or cinematic space (Brecht worked in Hollywood from 1941 to 1947, where he earned his living largely by writing movie scripts) must employ any manner of distancing techniques. In cinema, this could be accomplished by having the actor directly address the camera, by shaking the camera, or by creating any manner of stylistic disruptions and alienating effects, like Hitchcock's artificiality suddenly inserted into a realistic sequence. Any device of this sort makes spectators aware that they are in fixed seats, watching a performance.

For Brecht, the theater's fourth wall and the cinema's screen are exposed for the illusions that they are. There is no theatrical/cinematic world for us to enter, no fantastic portals for us to pass through. Brecht's aim is to break the hold of theatrical and cinematic illusion, to unseat the passive spectator. One manner in which this is accomplished is by reflexivity, where the play or the movie refers back to itself or to its own modes of construction, as occurs throughout Hitchcock's *Rear Window* (1954).

In *Rear Window*, L. B. "Jeff" Jeffries (James Stewart), a photojournalist confined to his apartment because of a broken leg, entertains himself by spying out his rear window, through the telephoto lens of his camera, into the windows of his various neighbors' apartments. Jeff's window-watching becomes an all-engrossing activity for him, especially when he comes to suspect that a murder has occurred across the court yard in the apartment of Lars Thorwald. What Jeff is doing in *Rear Window*, i.e., engaging in engrossing spectatorship of action which is focalized through the lens of a camera and delimited by a rectangular enclosure (the apartment windows, the "aspect ratio" of which is made approximate to that of a movie screen), is what the viewer is doing in watching the film. Although *Rear Window* makes no direct reference to filmmaking, the situation (Jeff witnessing, through a camera lens, events that are occurring with the circumscribed space of the rectangular window) is an analogue to both movie-watching and movie-making. Hitchcock is commenting on these processes in the self-referential, meta-fictional way that characterizes modes of cinematic reflexivity. Movie-making and movie-watching are voyeuristic practices, *Rear Window* reminds us. We are becoming "a race of Peeping Toms," Stella (Thelma Ritter) tells Jeffries. As Robert Stam explains, "Jeffries is our spectacular reflection, our double. We do not merely watch him performing actions; we perform the identical action — looking" (48).

Rear Window is a traditional translation of Cornell Woolrich's short story "It Had to Be Murder," since Hitchcock maintains the overall traits of the short story (its plot, setting, and stylistic conventions) but revamps particular details in those ways that he sees as necessary and fitting. The stylistic conventions that Hitchcock translates are the story's highly visual nature and its limited point of view, the latter of which is restricted to Jeffries's means and ways of seeing. Both works confine the action to a single locale, the apartment of L. B. Jeffries ("Hal Jeffries" in the story), who is immobilized by the cast on his leg. In Woolrich's story, Hal Jeffries is aided by Sam, his "day houseman," a character whose duties in the film are split between the newly-created characters of the visiting nurse, Stella, and Jeffries's girlfriend, Lisa Fremont (Grace Kelly). In Woolrich's story, Hal Jeffries's murder investigation is limited to what he sees. He must work from purely visual clues. He conclusively deduces how the murder was committed and where the body was hidden. Ultimately apprehending what his eye leads him to see, Jeffries remarks toward the end of the story: "The eye is a reliable surveyor" (369). The lesson is that in art, in movies, and in murder, we must *learn* to see. Hitchcock's *Rear Window* successfully translates to film this integral idea from Woolrich's story: the eye as a reliable surveyor of truth to one who has discovered how to see.

Hitchcock has called *Rear Window* his "most cinematic" film (Hitchcock, "*Rear Window*," 40). He further explains:

> I am a purist so far as cinema is concerned.... This film has as its basic structure the purely visual. The story is told only in visual terms.... It's composed largely of Mr. Stewart as a character in one position in one room looking out onto his courtyard. So what he sees is a mental process blown up in his mind from the purely visual. It represents for me the purest form of cinema which is called montage: that is pieces of film put together to make up an idea.... This is one of the reasons why I chose this film. You see, many people think that a little dialogue scene in a movie is motion pictures. It's not ... it's the piecing together of montage which makes what I call a pure film [Hitchcock, "*Rear Window*" 40–41].

The piecing together of film in such a way that the images, not the dialogue, function as the narrating apparatus is what drives another story-based suspense film, director Nicholas Roeg's *Don't Look Now* (1973). Roeg's film, however, challenges the extent to which the eye is a reliable surveyor, reminding us that the human eye is limited to the material world — the empirical — and that the domain of the metaphysical, visionary, or spiritual — if, indeed, a domain, as such, exists — requires a different kind of vision. The movie suggests that the protagonist, John Baxter (Donald Sutherland), may possess the paranormal gift of second sight. Baxter adamantly repudiates such a notion, asserting a rationalist's point of view that nothing exists beyond the scientifically explainable material realm.

Roeg sets images before us in a manner that causes viewers to question Baxter's position. The physical reality of what we see on the screen suggests something other than the rational, material order that John Baxter insists on upholding. It suggests the existence of a spiritual domain, immutable, eternal, and transcendent, distinct from the ever-changing and impermanent visible world that we see. Roeg's film suggests that the vitality of Christine — her soul — exists and lives on, that exchanges between the material and the spiritual domains can and do occur, and that the conduit of exchange — the medium — can be a person endowed with such paranormal power. The film posits these possibilities, offers them as conceivable answers in ways that leave us uncertain over what, exactly, we are seeing as we watch *Don't Look Now*. Thus, the movie creates a complex ambiguity over how we are to understand —*see*— the images reeling before us.

Being a traditional translation of Daphne du Maurier's short story, the film *Don't Look Now* concentrates, as the short story does, on the effect the death of their young daughter, Christine, has on a married couple, John and Laura (Julie Christie) Baxter. In both the film and the story, the Baxters meet two elderly, apparently benign if odd, Scottish sisters in a restaurant in Venice. One of the sisters is blind and is alleged to be clairvoyant. When Laura speaks to them she is told, "Don't be unhappy any more. My sister has seen your little girl. She was sitting between you and your husband, laughing." Laura believes what the two women tell her: that her dead daughter is "still with us," that the blind sister "could see Christine," and that her little girl is happy (du Maurier, "Don't Look Now," 71, 70).

"They are both of them frauds," Laura's husband, John, asserts. "I'm sorry if this hurts you, but the fact is they've found a sucker in you" (du Maurier, "Don't Look Now," 80, 81). Yet, John, curiously, seems to catch glimpses of his daughter in the winding walkways and watery routes of Venice.

In Roeg's film, as in du Maurier's story, there is a constant tension between the authenticity and the fraudulence of the claim to clairvoyance and between the validity and falseness of the notion of a realm beyond the sensible, visible world. In both works, the mystical meets the psychological as the reader/spectator accepts the apparition of the daughter as a mystical reality possible within the actuality of the story/film world, while simultaneously understanding how the desperate and deep psychological need of the parents to see their daughter just one last time could cause them to mistake a similar looking little girl for their child. Both works explore the divergent modes by which a father and a mother handle the tremendous grief suffered on the loss of a child; and both works resolve the mysteries set forth in the narrative by means of a ludicrously flawed ending.

While the film steadily follows the basic twists and turns of du Maurier's suspense tale, Roeg's *Don't Look Now* includes an element not present in the original work: John Baxter as an expert in church restoration. More crucially, Roeg shatters the conventional modes of storytelling that du Maurier's story observes. With his distortions of time and space, his erratic edits, and his innovative crosscuts, Roeg creates a film that is, arguably, much more complex — aesthetically, philosophically, and psychologically — and far more engaging than the original story. The film's Baxters have lost their daughter to drowning, yet they remain in a world where the very streets are made of water — sinuously, ingeniously, and intricately photographed. John Baxter, who angrily dismisses any notions regarding spiritually restorative powers related to his child, works with painstaking faith in his own power to do physical restoration. The Venetian stained glass and the depth of commitment with which he works on it are photographed to show that John is restoring something more than just the visual accuracy of the missing pieces. He is restoring the soul that made the glass alive in its beauty. It is under Roeg's guidance — his mastery — that the camera helps us see this. It is extraordinary.*

Don't Look Now engages a curious dilemma that arises in literature to film translations. In outstripping its parent text, the film can become a translation beyond its parent.

Roeg's directorial sense of how to utilize the camera was honed first in his early capacity as a camera operator (for example, he shots scenes for David Lean's 1965 Dr. Zhivago), who moved on to Director of Photography on such films as Roger Corman's The Masque of the Red Death *(1964), François Truffaut's* Fahrenheit 451 *(1965), and John Schlesinger's* Far from the Madding Crowd *(1967) before directing his first film,* Performance *(1970, starring Mick Jagger) and his second, the critically acclaimed* Walkabout *(1971).*

Screen translations of short stories can emerge as more complex (aesthetically, philosophically, and psychologically), as less dated/more timeless, and as more engaging than the original short story. Examples of this include *Broken Blossoms* (1919, dir. D. W. Griffith; story, "The Chink and the Child," by Thomas Burke); *Sunrise* (1927, dir. F. W. Murnau; story, "A Journey to Tilsit," by Hermann Sudermann); *Stagecoach* (1939, dir. John Ford; story, "Stage to Lordsburg," by Ernest Haycox); and *La Belle et La Bête* (1946, dir. Jean Cocteau, short story of same title by Mme. Leprince de Beaumont).

On occasion, the film will find cinematic ways of creating the equivalent of what the words on the page are accomplishing. *Million Dollar Baby* (2004), directed by Clint Eastwood and based on short stories in F. X. Toole's *Rope Burns*, accomplishes this largely through the performances of Eastwood (as Frankie Dunn), Morgan Freeman (as Eddie "Scrap" Dupris), and Hilary Swank (as Maggie Fitzgerald). Their performances make visual Toole's gritty and pugilistic world, where the only protection against the violence and vice that reign are the rules and regulations that, perforce, keep human conduct in check, and where the only stays against the ever-threatening emotional darkness are commitments of friendship and the reading of poetry.

☞   *Read the poetry of William Butler Yeats, in particular, an early poem, "The Lake Isle of Innisfree," and a later poem, "The Apparitions." Think about what each of these poems is saying. Consider the two poems in relationship to one another, including the idea that one was written by a young and the other by an older Yeats. What are the poems saying to you? Watch* Million Dollar Baby. *Study Eastwood's reading of "The Lake Isle of Innisfree." What does his performance tell us about his character, Frankie Dunn? What does Yeats's poem mean to the ageing Frankie?*

A second strong example of a film that finds cinematic ways of creating the equivalent of what the words on the page are accomplishing is *Memento* (2001), directed by Christopher Nolan from a short story, "Memento Mori," written for *Esquire* magazine by his bother, Jonathan Nolan.* The short story describes a man, Earl, whose wife has been killed in circumstances he witnessed, but cannot recall. The last thing Earl remembers is her death. He is fully unable to construct any new memories from incidents that occur subsequent to the murder. Because Earl's

---

*A full-text copy of "Memento Mori" has been made available by Esquire at: http://www.esquire.com/features/articles/2001/001323_mfr_memento_1.html

conscious knowledge of events fades within minutes of their transpiring, he has lost all capacity to remember even the most immediate or inconsequential of events. Because of his condition, he leaves reminders — mementos — for himself: notes, photographs, even tattoos on his body. Each memento is a reminder of the last thing Earl recalls, his wife's death, so that everything in the story, every memento Earl constructs, is a *memento mori*, a reminder of death.

From its first sentence, the story hurls the reader into immediate confusion. Deliberately disorienting chronology, "Memento Mori" begins at a dislocating and unspecified point in the narration, unseating expectations for the reader who assumes that the story will follow traditional narrative logic and begin at the beginning. We have no expositional or immediate knowledge — no context — with which to make sense of the beginning, and thus we virtually are placed in the same disorienting position as Earl. The story convolutes time, locale, and narrative voice; it dismantles all notions of a stable record of narrative events. It places us in a world of indeterminacy and instability of meaning, and it does so through the disassembling of all traditional modes of storytelling.

"Memento Mori" is narrated in lengthy passages set in standard type and equally lengthy ones set in italics. The standard type indicates narration that is visually explicit, purported to be factual, told from a third person point of view, and delivered in disorienting chronology. The italicized passages are dramatic monologues, commenting on the mental, emotional, and physical condition of Earl (in the movie, renamed "Leonard Shelby" and played by Guy Pearce). The film, *Memento*, replicates this narrative device, utilizing black and white sequences for the story's italicized passages and color sequences for its standard-type ones. The disorienting sequencing of events in the short story is created in the film by placing the color sequences in reverse chronological order. The film does not tell the viewer that it is doing so, but it narrates the events backwards, beginning at the end of the story and moving, by the end, to the beginning. The reverse chronology is a clever cinematic device that allows the audience not only to understand Leonard's disoriented thought process, but also to experience it themselves. Leonard knows what has happened — the narrative past — but not the narrative present. Much as the short story ruptures traditional modes of representation and narration, the movie employs cinematic equivalents to recreate the story's ambiguities. The film's distinctive narrative mode, accomplished largely through its editing of the color and black and white sequences, accomplishes three things integral to Jonathan Nolan's short story:

Memento (2000): Because of his memory loss, Leonard Shelby (Guy Pearce) leaves reminders — mementos — for himself: notes, photographs, even tattoos.

1. It creates convolutions of time, locale, and narrative voice.
2. It dismantles all faith in a stable, reliable narration of events.
3. It fragments any and all information that it presents.

Filmed in Panavision, the movie, curiously, utilizes very few of those shots that are naturally suited to an anamorphic lens which shoots a wide scope of field. Instead of the lens' signature long shots and sweeping establishing shots, the anamorphic lens is often used in *Memento* to focus on the restricted space of Leonard's hotel room, his face, and the contours of his tattooed arms. The effect is strong. The empty space that is left in the wide frame accentuates Leonard's emptiness, and the film's complete absence of establishing shots (in an interview, Christopher Nolan explains that, by design, there was not a single one in the film) and its paucity of long shots create a sense that, as in the story, we cannot quite establish where we are, except that we are restricted to Leonard's world. The use of anamorphic lenses, with their capacity to create a larger expanse of viewing space, underlines the paradoxical theme of both the story and the film:

The more we see, the less we see. The more we find out, the less we know. By the end of both the story and the film, we are not certain of anything that we have seen.

"Memento Mori" has as its epigram a quote from Herman Melville's poem "Shiloh": "What like a bullet can undeceive!"* The story, as well as the film, involves layers and layers of deception, all brought to the surface by the bullet that claimed Earl's/Leonard's wife. Earl/Leonard is "undeceived" into a paradoxical awareness of the unmitigable presence and reality of deception. The world of *Memento* is made up of impenetrable masks and masqueraders, con artists, swindlers and their dupes, all employed in much the same way and to the same end as in Melville's *The Confidence Man*. Melville's world, like Nolan's, is one where mysteries remain impenetrable, humane values are impossible, and holding a full confidence in the attainment of truth is an absurd position.

While both the short story and the film employ non-traditional narrative constructions, the film is a traditional translation of Jonathan Nolan's story, since it maintains the defining traits (the style, narrative structure, characters, and basic story), but revamps particular details of the original work in ways that Christopher Nolan (in consultation with his brother, Jonathan) saw as necessary and fitting for the film. The movie adds characters and incidents that never appear in "Memento Mori," i.e., Teddy (Joe Pantoliano), Natalie (Carrie-Anne Moss), and Sammy Jankis (Stephen Tobolowski) and their corresponding plots. While expanding upon the original story's details, the film maintains (as traditional translations will) what is most integral to the source text. In the specific case of "Memento Mori," this includes the story's elliptical narrative construction, its theme of the indeterminacy of truth, and its melancholic tone, constituted largely through the existential loneliness of Earl.

☞ *Read Jonathan Nolan's short story "Memento Mori." (*Esquire *magazine provides a full-text, on-line copy at: http://www.esquire.com/ features/articles/2001/001323_mfr_memento_1.html.) Study the story's narrative structure, the italicized and the standard-type passages. In the story, these two modes of narrative representation are not fused in a single chain of signification, but, instead, are placed in complex relation to one another. Describe the relationship of the two parallel*

From Battle-Pieces and Aspects of the War (1866), "Shiloh: A Requiem (April, 1862)" is one of Melville's Civil War poem. Told by a narrator looking upon a battle field in the aftermath of a skirmish, he understands how, in a moment's time, the convictions and values of the soldier who has been shot and lies dying can fully change.

structures. Throughout "Memento Mori" indeterminacy and uncertainty reign, not only regarding the facts of all the events, but also regarding who, exactly, is narrating each of the two sequences. Watch the film Memento. *Describe the relationship of the color and black and white sequences. Do they fuse into a single chain of signification? Is the narrative perspective clearly established in the color and the black and white sequences? Both the story and the film posit the unreliability of memory, the propensity of humans to lie, and the unknowability of truth. How do the narrative structures of the story and the film assist in communicating these integral concepts?*

Most short story-based films are traditional translations of their literary work. Exceptions to this include the *American Playhouse* series, which generally maintains a literal approach to film translations of American stories. In doing so, these productions replicate the plot and all its attending details as closely as possible to the letter of the story. One key factor in doing so is having the running time of the film short, under an hour, in keeping with the length of the short story. As literal translations require, these productions do not expand upon the details of the story (as a traditional or radical translation might) by adding layers of characters and incidents that did not appear in the original work. This series includes the films listed in Table 16.

John Huston's film, *The Dead* (1987), is a feature-length example of a literal translation of a short story. "The Dead" is the culminating story of James Joyce's *Dubliners* (1914), a collection of short stories structured to move from childhood through adulthood. The fifteen separate stories that are included in *Dubliners* simultaneously function as an integrated whole (a novel) depicting the soul of Dublin, itself. In the concluding story, "The Dead," Gabriel Conroy experiences an epiphany as he moves from a state of egoism and isolation to one of empathy.

Set in a single evening (the year is 1904 in the film), "The Dead" describes events at a winter party held in the Dublin home of Gabriel's aunts, Kate and Julia Morkan, and their niece, Mary Jane. The social customs (the dancing, singing, toasting, and eating) are done amid congenial chatter and serve to highlight Gabriel's isolation. A university instructor and the writer of a literary column for *The Daily Express*, Gabriel Conroy sees himself as a superior intellect. He often takes "no part in the conversation" of his aunts' guests and he worries if his dinner speech will be "above the heads of his hearers" (179). In the course of the festivities, one of the guests, Mr. D'Arcy, sings a song, "The Lass of Aughrim," which

**Table 16.
Literal Translations of Short Stories:
The *American Playhouse* Series**

Film Title (also short story title)	Author	Running Time (in minutes)
Almos' A Man	Richard Wright	51
Andre's Mother	Terrence McNally	60
Barn Burning	William Faulkner	40
Bernice Bobs Her Hair	F. Scott Fitzgerald	49
The Blue Hotel	Stephen Crane	55
The Golden Honeymoon	Ring Lardner	52
The Greatest Man in the World	James Thurber	51
The Jilting of Granny Weatherall	Katherine Anne Porter	57
The Jolly Corner	Henry James	53
Land of Little Rain	Mary Austin	65
The Man That Corrupted Hadleyburg	Mark Twain	45
I'm a Fool	Sherwood Anderson	38
Paul's Case	Willa Cather	52
Pigeon Feathers	John Updike	45
Rappaccini's Daughter	Nathaniel Hawthorne	57
The Revolt of Mother	Mary E. Wilkins Freeman	60
Soldier's Home	Ernest Hemingway	41
The Sky Is Gray	Ernest Gaines	46

carries Gabriel's wife Gretta back to a memory of her youth in Galway. The festivities come to an end, and Gabriel and Gretta leave for the Gresham Hotel. Alone in their room, Gretta explains to her husband that, years earlier, a young man, Michael Furey, whom she used to "go out walking with," would sing "The Lass of Aughrim" to her and that he died when she had to leave. "I was great with him at the time ... I think he died for me," she reveals (220). Gretta falls asleep in the grief of her memory.

As Gretta sleeps, Gabriel experiences the sudden realization that Gretta's dead lover had a deeper and more passionate connection to his wife than he ever did. He understands that it is better "to pass boldly into that other world, in the full glory of some passion, than fade and wither dismally with age," and that he, Gabriel, has lived in a ring of isolation, even in relation to his wife. In that moment, he sees himself as others do. "A shameful consciousness of his own person assailed him. He saw himself as a ludicrous figure, acting as a pennyboy for his aunts, a nervous well-meaning sentimentalist, orating to vulgarians and idealizing his own clownish lusts, the pitiable fatuous fellow he had caught a glimpse of in the mirror" (219–20).

As he looks out the hotel window, it begins to snow, a "snow faintly falling through the universe and faintly falling, like the descent of their last end, upon all the living and the dead" (224). In that moment, Gabriel has an epiphany. His insight moves him from an arrogance of isolation and a paralysis of soul to a wise understanding of his part in a common humanity and an empathic connection with others.

James Joyce said of *Dubliners*: "My intention was to write a chapter of the moral history of my country and I chose Dublin for the scene because the city seemed to me the center of paralysis" (Joyce, "Letter," *Dubliners*, 269). Gabriel's confrontation with his own moral and spiritual paralysis, with his emotional sterility and his alienation from his wife, delivers him to an expanded awareness, a generosity of heart previously absent, and a deepened consciousness of humanity. His empathic understanding extends first to his wife, then his aunts, through to himself, to Dublin, to "the universe," and, at last, to "all the living and the dead." Within the context of *Dubliners*, with its fourteen previous stories of emotional and spiritual paralysis, "The Dead" offers a final vision of meaning and of redemption. Highly visual, exceptionally musical, and replete with richly suggestive characters, "The Dead" is a short story suited to the screen. Yet only one film translation of it exists to date, and that translation, while rendering the story-facts with great precision, fails to convey the subtle beauty of Joyce's text.

In the film *The Dead*, John Huston recreates the details of the story with a fierce loyalty to the word. The images are there, just as Joyce describes them: the house at 15 Usher's Island where the Morkans hold their annual Christmas dance, the arrivers to the party "scraping the snow from [their] galoshes," the dance of "quadrilles," the "plates of goose and plates of ham and spiced beef" and the "hot floury potatoes wrapped in white napkins," and the exterior shots of the O'Connell Monument, the Liffey, and the Gresham Hotel. Much of the film is given the amber patina that suggests the 1904 past. However, there are some misses. The most egregious criticism leveled against the film's visual recreation of the text is that when Gabriel and Gretta's carriage leaves his aunts' party, it heads, incorrectly, in the direction of Phoenix Park and not, as it should, toward the Gresham Hotel.

Sound is crucial to Joyce's short story, as Huston understands. In the film, we not only hear the song, "The Lass of Aughrim," we also hear James

Joyce, *the poet*, in the cadences of his poetic prose that are taken directly from the story and placed, largely intact, in the film. The film constructs the characters as we see them in Joyce's story, adding only the invention of a Dublin English professor, Mr. Grace, whose argument about politics and Parnell is suppressed by Aunt Kate, because she sees such talk as socially unseemly. But while the film reconstructs the details of Joyce's story, it fails to convey the mastery of symbolic design that Joyce's work displays and it fails to convey the *life* that is there, in the words. The film feels inanimate, lifeless, a dead version of "The Dead."

Even the camera seems dead in this film, unmoving, as emotionally and spiritually paralyzed as the characters that Joyce criticizes throughout *Dubliners*. As literal translations do, this film hovers on the surface of Joyce's work, reverently preserving in celluloid James Joyce's literal descriptions, while missing Joyce's integral depth. *The Dead* is the last movie John Huston made, the last cinematic statement by the great director of *The Maltese Falcon* (1941), *The Treasure of the Sierra Madre* (1948), *The African Queen* (1951) and *The Misfits* (1961). An admiration for John Huston, similar to Huston's admiration for James Joyce, and a reverence for the fact Huston filmed *The Dead* knowing he was dying may prevail upon us to see the emptiness of the film (the flatness of the line readings, the uninspired editing, the artificial patina, the screenplay's superfluities, and the unimaginative camera work) as a dignified and meaningful statement about the emptiness of the lives of the characters.

No doubt James Joyce, who had an acknowledged fascination with film, would have preferred the John Huston who directed *The Maltese Falcon* to have directed *The Dead*. James Joyce was, after all, something of a pioneer in film history. His interest in cinema goes back to the start-up days of movie houses. In 1909, Joyce, then twenty-seven, took his younger sister, Eva, then eighteen, for an extended stay in Trieste, then in Austria-Hungary. Eva grew homesick for Dublin, telling her brother that there was but one thing she liked in Trieste, "its cinema," and remarking "how odd it was that Dublin, a larger city had not even one" (Ellmann, 310). Joyce arranged to work with a small syndicate (four businessmen) who had successfully opened three movie houses, the "Edison" and the "Americano" in Trieste and the "Cinematograph Volta" in Bucharest. Joyce entered into a partnership with them, and on December 20, 1909, they opened the "Volta," the first cinema in Dublin.* *The Evening Telegraph* covered the

The first movies to be shown at the Volta were The First Paris Orphan, La Pourponnière, *and* The Tragic Story of Beatrice Cenci.

event and described the movie house as "admirably equipped for the purpose." It went on to describe that "Mr. James Joyce, who is in charge of the exhibition, has worked indefatigably in its production and deserves to be congratulated on the success of the inaugural exhibition" (Ellmann, 313).

The imprint of cinema appears in Joyce's prose, most notably in his montage edits and dissolving scenes. James Joyce's interest in cinema also includes his meeting with the great filmmaker/theorist Sergei Eisenstein; they discussed the possibilities of making a movie of Joyce's *Ulysses*. James Joyce was also interested in filming his *Finnegans Wake*, in total or in part. *Finnegans Wake* is the record of a dream, where what happens in the book is happening in the mind of its sleeper. The work is composed of strange and intricate language, dream-logic (partly based on Freud), puns (often done in multiple languages), literary and religious allusions, symbols, musical rhythms, verbal distortions, and good-natured wit. To make a film of *Finnegans Wake* would be a ludicrous undertaking if it were attempted, as *The Dead* was, in a literal translation mode.*

The conventions and values of literal film translations find their contrast in radical translations. Akira Kurosawa's *Rashōmon* (1950) is a supremely strong example of a radical film translation of two short stories, "In a Grove" and "Rashōmon" by Ryunosuke Akutagawa, a writer widely read in Japan and highly regarded. The author of poems, essays, and more than one hundred short stories, Akutagawa holds a strong and distinctive position in Japanese letters, "as special as Poe in America or Maupassant in France" (Richie, 70). Like Poe, Akutagawa was a child when his mother died, a situation which left him feeling ever-abandoned. Like Poe, he occupies a prominence among both a popular and academic readership; and like Poe, he has a predilection for the macabre. However, uniquely Akutagawa, he has a distinctive voice which can best be characterized by a coolly detached attitude, a bitter cynicism, an unrelenting intellectual penetration, a feeling of composure even before the most bizarre of events, a clarity of expression, a restraint, and an awe-inspiring elegance. In 1927, at thirty-five, Akutagawa committed suicide, leaving behind his wife and his three young sons.

While no film was made of Finnegans Wake *in Joyce's lifetime, a movie called* Finnegan's Wake *(aka* Passages from Finnegans Wake*) was released in 1965. Initially adapted to the stage by Mary Ellen Bute, the movie* Finnegan's Wake *was directed and edited by Bute from a screenplay she wrote with Romana Javitz. The film tells the story of Finnegan (Martin J. Kelley), a pub owner who, in the state of inebriation, envisions his own death and wake. The film attempts the famous jeweled style of Joyce's book, but does not approximate the mediation on language that Joyce's work conveys.*

His short story "Roshōmon" is set circa 11th century, during the Heian Period, in Kyoto, then capital of Japan. Famine and desperation reign in the city, which has been besieged by a "series of calamities, earthquakes, whirlwinds, and fires," all of which have taken a devastating toll on the once-great city (26). In the opening of the story, a former servant of a samurai, "dismissed by his master, whom he had served many years, because of the effects of this decline," waits beneath the wide Rashōmon gate for a torrential rainfall to stop (27). Rashōmon, the once-grand and momentously imposing southern gateway to Kyoto, is crumbling in great disrepair. It has become a den of "thieves and robbers" and "unclaimed corpses" which are surreptitiously dumped at the gate. The once-eminent gate of Rashōmon stands as a symbol of crumbling ideals and decaying social and political institutions.

As he waits, the servant watches an old woman, defiling a corpse by stripping it of its hair which she plans to sell. The act is deeply profane; the servant feels it to be so. She is a wretched morbidity of bestiality in his eyes. Yet, by the end of the story, reduced by poverty, he assaults the old woman, kicks and robs her, and leaves her groaning and crawling and all alone.

The second of the two stories that are the basis of the film *Rashōmon* is "In a Grove," a work constructed around seven differing accounts of the murder of a samurai, Kanazawa no Takehiko from the province of Wakasa. The story provides the "testimony" of a woodcutter; a Buddhist priest; a policeman; the samurai's mother-in-law; Tajomaru, a robber; Masago, the samurai's wife, and the murdered samurai, Takehiko, himself, speaking through a medium. In their separate testimonies, Tajomaru, Masago, and Takehiko each confesses to having committed the murder (with Takehiko claiming to having committed suicide). Their three testimonies, along with the four others, offer, to varying degrees, contradicting versions of the same, singular event. Throughout the story, not only the point of view shifts, but the narrative context shifts, as well. Four of the testimonies are carried out before the "High Police Commissioner," one (Masago's) in the Shimisu Temple, and two (Tajomaru's and Takehiko's) at undisclosed locales and to an unstated audience. With its varying accounts of the same event, Akutagawa's story undermines our confidence in the strict line between objective and subjective truth, especially as he shows that to whom a story is told (its context) influences what is said. The murder of the samurai seems to have happened "in a grove," but we cannot even be certain of that in a world where truth is fragmentary, unstable, and relativistic. The world of "In a Grove" is void of moral

Rashōmon (1950): Left to right: A priest (Minoru Chiaki), a woodcutter
(Takashi Shimura), and a commoner (Kichijirō Ueda) seek shelter from an
assault of rain by taking refuge beneath the disintegrating Rashōmon gate.
The rain is so forceful that it inhibits the characters' sight, an appropriate
start to a film in which there is no clear perspective from which to see the
truth of the events.

development, so, by the end, we are no closer to the truth than we were
at the start.

The film *Rashōmon* largely recounts events as they occur in Akutagawa's short story "In a Grove." From the short story "Rashōmon," Kurosawa's movie takes only the setting, the mood of desolation and decay, the
situation of characters waiting under the gate for a rainstorm to pass, and
the central symbol of the crumbling gate of Rashōmon. Created as a frame
narrative, the movie tells two stories: the outer frame story, involving characters (including the newly-created character of the "commoner") who are
waiting under the Rashōmon gate for a thunderstorm to pass; and the
central story, a pastiche of the differing accounts of the rape of a noble-
woman (Machiko Kyō) in a bamboo grove, the murder of her samurai hus-

band (Masayuki Mori), and the arrest of a thief (Toshirō Mifune) for the crime.

The movie opens with three men, a priest (Minoru Chiaki), a woodcutter (Takashi Shimura), and a commoner (Kichijirō Ueda) seeking shelter from an assault of rain by taking refuge beneath the disintegrating gate. As they look out from beneath the covering, the rain is so forceful and so unrelenting as to inhibit sight, an appropriate start to a film in which there is no clear perspective from which to see the truth of the events. The three men converse and in the course of their talk the central story emerges.

Rashōmon's central story presents six individuals, each of whom recounts a different version of the same story, with each account casting the speaker in favorable light. Each version is told from a different perspective and reconstructs the details of the event in markedly different ways. It is never made clear the extent to which the discrepancies in the accounts are the result of the fallible nature of memory, the invariable colorings of subjectivity, or the human willingness simply to lie. Kurosawa's film, thus, translates a theme crucial to Akutagawa's work: the unknowability of truth. A distinction must be made, though. For both Akutagawa and Kurosawa, truth, as a stable body of meaning, can and does exist. Both works make it clear, for example, that a samurai *was* killed, that *someone* committed the crime, and that his wife either was or was not raped. Truth exists, but it stands independent and apart from our capacity to apprehend it. For both Akutagawa and Kurosawa, it is the flaws in human nature that render attempts at ever knowing precisely what happened in the grove futile.

Kurosawa translates the nuances of meaning and the integral beauty of Akutagawa's stories by utilizing the language of film like a virtuoso. Throughout *Rashōmon*, the *mise-en-scène* is elegant to the point of rhapsodic. There is a delicacy of skill: in the editing, largely done through the juxtaposition of contrasting shots (*Rashōmon*'s *homage* to Sergei Eisenstein); in the minimal dialogue and the reliance on visual composition to narrate the different versions of the story; in the camera movement, which, while never calling attention to itself, creates the impression of continuous, elegant motion; in the shot-duration, trimmed short and made mosaic in its effect; in the use of cinematic punctuation marks, largely the wipe and the dissolve, to create rhythms and to signal the end of chapters (the dissolve at the end of *Rashōmon* is duly famous); and in the western-style music created by the magnificent Japanese composer, Fumio Hayasaka.

The film maintains the overall traits of the stories (the plot, setting, and stylistic conventions), making only modest alterations in the details of Akutagawa's work (examples: eliminating the mother-in-law's testimony and adding the character of the commoner). As such, *Roshōmon* appears to be a traditional translation of the two stories. However, fundamental to Akutagawa's work is a bleak and darkly pessimistic appraisal of humankind. In "Rashōmon" and "In a Grove," human nature is depicted as stupid, appetitive, dishonest, and self-serving. The Darwinian imperative drives conduct in a species that has failed to evolve in the slightest from the Heian Period through to the present day. Kurosawa, however, dismantles Akutagawa's austerely pessimistic view, replacing it with faith.

Kurosawa's film ends with the cry of an infant abandoned somewhere under the Rashōmon gate. In keeping with Akutagawa's view of humanity, the commoner (the one character created by the film) searches for the baby with the clear intent of stealing her blanket and clothing. However, in a radical departure from Akutagawa's text, the woodcutter, while unrelentingly poor, takes the small baby who has been left to die. "I've six children of my own. Another wouldn't make it any more difficult," he says simply, bundling up the child to bear her to his home. "The woodcutter's capacity for goodness ... is concretely demonstrated when he comes to the infant's defense. By the film's conclusion, his position has evolved from uninvolvement to commitment. As eyewitness to this charitable act, the priest is able to retain faith in humanity" (Goodwin, 138). In the image of the lone woodcutter, the humane benevolence of his act, and its ramifying effect, Kurosawa creates on screen nothing less than the beauty of *mono no aware*, an empathy with the essence of things, an awareness of the bond that links. In its inversion of Akutagawa's dark conclusions, *Roshōmon* arguably is a radical translation, one that reshapes the two stories in the most extreme and revolutionary of ways: by contradicting their fundamental conclusion and making the film a strong, independent statement by Kurosawa.

The image of the solitary man, standing alone for what is right and facing down the wrong — the virulence, greed, and disorder that threatens him and his world — is a recurring one in American westerns, an image that dominates, for example, Fred Zinnemann's film, *High Noon* (1952).

The plot of the film is simple: Will Kane (Gary Cooper), the newly married marshal of Hadleyville, has chosen to hang up his badge and begin a new, simpler life with his bride, Amy (Grace Kelly). As he is about to leave town, he learns that Frank Miller, a ruthless murderer he put into prison, but who has been released because of failures in the judicial system, is arriving in town at high noon. His train will be met by his gang.

Frank is coming to seek revenge and to seize control of the town. Having retired, Kane has no professional obligation to protect the townspeople, and his pacifist, Quaker wife pleads with him to walk away from all the impending violence; but Kane can't. He seeks help from the townspeople, who, cowering before the thought of standing up to Miller and his gang, refuse Kane's entreaties. Only the least able of Hadleyville's citizens offer to stand with him: the town drunk, a young boy, and Kane's mentor, former lawman Martin Howe (Lon Chaney Jr.), grown too arthritic to wield a gun. The three would be liabilities for Kane at the showdown; so, solitary and unfortified, Kane stands alone before the destruction and malevolence that is Frank Miller and his gang.

Based on the short story "The Tin Star" by John M. Cunningham, *High Noon* enlarges upon the literature's details. Most significantly, Cunningham's Sheriff Doane (the film's marshal Will Kane) is a not a newly-wed, with a new life before him and much to risk in staying, but, instead, a widower, arthritic and void of any future plans. Different from Marshal Kane but no less fine, Sheriff Doane illustrates that great strength of character can supercede infirmities of age. The film's newly-created characters, Harvey Pell (Lloyd Bridges), Helen Ramirez (Katy Jurado), and Amy Kane, and corresponding plots involving them, are worthy variations on the story's concern for how people behave before consequential conditions that test them. However, in expanding upon the plot details, the film does not alter the crucial point of the short story: the community's forsaking of a man who stands alone against the evil that threatens them all. The poignancy of the matter is carried through in the film's musical theme, Tex Ritter's simple and deeply straightforward vocals on "Do Not Forsake Me, Oh My Darling."

High Noon is shot in "real time"; its 85-minute length corresponds to the duration (eighty-five minutes) of the events of the story. The movie redefined the American Western hero by presenting him as more realistic, as a flesh and blood man afraid before facing what he must do and what he must risk.* The beauty of the film is considerable and outstrips the effect of the short story's prose. In *High Noon* we see the cinematic achievement, specifically, of classical Hollywood narrative filmmaking, that distinctive kind of beauty that informs such masterful literature-based films as *The Heiress* (1949, dir. William Wyler), *Casablanca* (1942, dir.

John Wayne reportedly was so appalled that an American marshal would appear afraid and seek help in a showdown that he made Rio Bravo *(1959, dir. Howard Hawks) as his retort to* High Noon.

Michael Curtiz), *The Little Foxes* (1941, dir. William Wyler), *The Old Maid* (1939, dir. Edmund Goulding), *The Wizard of Oz* (1939, dir. Victor Fleming), *Gone with the Wind* (1939, dir. Victor Fleming), *Dodsworth* (1936, dir. William Wyler), *The Informer* (1935, dir. John Ford), and *The Bitter Tea of General Yen* (1932, dir. Frank Capra).

Table 17.
Classical Hollywood Narrative

Composition:	The *mise-en-scène* is balanced, elegant, and centered. The human body normally occupies the middle of the frame; and even while the figure moves, s/he will be kept centered by a camera that pans or tilts in accord with the character's movement. Vacancy in the frame is often reserved for characters entering.
Editing:	The film is cut to continuity, aspiring to create editing that is unnoticed, invisible.
Plot:	Narrative construction adheres to traditional modes of storytelling. The *story* is the focus of the film; it drives the audience's attention and manipulates them into remaining focused on *what will happen next?* The story ends in complete closure, resolving (bringing to a close) the issues, large and small, raised by the narrative events.
Camera angles/ Camera Movement:	The camera's angles and movement should not call attention to themselves. All cinematic techniques (camera angles/movement, lighting, editing, composition, sound) should work as indiscernible threads that (in an unseen manner) bind and blend shots/ sound into a harmonious whole.
Sound:	Speech is often dramatic, even melodramatic. Music is emotionally charged, often tonally inflated. Musical motifs introduced in the overture (as the credits roll) recur in the film proper.
Mode of Discourse:	The audience is fully engaged, so caught up in the cinematic *reality* as to lose themselves in the movie. While the audience accepts (comes to believe in) the world of the film, the story itself is not realistic. It is synthetic, dramatic, and emotionally charged, sometimes to the point of melodrama.

☞   *Watch* High Noon. *Analyze it in terms of the qualities of classical
    Hollywood cinema that it specifically demonstrates. Study the* mise-
    en-scène. *Watch for the methods by which the composition is kept
    balanced, elegant, and centered. Try to see the mechanics of the con-
    tinuity editing, how each joint connecting each shot is constructed.
    Study the montage sequence, the two minutes of film that occurs just
    prior to Frank Miller's train arriving at high noon. Hear the rhythm
    that drives the montage editing; see the juxtaposing of images that
    hinges together the separate shots. In short, see that mode of beauty
    that constitutes classical Hollywood narrative filmmaking.*

    The image of the solitary man, standing alone for what is right before
the threatening presence of malevolence, greed, intimidation, and lawlessness, also occurs in a second short-story based American western: *Bad Day
at Black Rock* (1955, dir. John Sturges). The film narrates twenty-four
hours in the life of a guilty town, whose silence over the murder of a Japanese farmer exposes the themes of collective guilt, group conformity, moral
complacency, self-interest, and bigotry. *Bad Day at Black Rock* opens with
a one-armed stranger, John J. Macreedy (Spencer Tracy), arriving in a
small, isolated, never-visited, desert town in southwestern California.
Macreedy's reason for coming to Black Rock is unclear and he is immediately treated with animosity, fear, and suspicion by a town that is apparently keeping something concealed. Macreedy persists against the
escalating warnings of townspeople and the threats of the local thugs,
before whom the citizens of Black Rock cower. Shot in Cinemascope, *Bad
Day at Black Rock* builds tension in unconventional ways: in the vast,
sweeping open space of panoramic view (rather than in closed, constricted
space traditionally used to heighten suspense) and in the full light of day.
    From Howard Breslin's American western short story, "Bad Day at
Honda," the greatness of the film is in what Breslin's literary page cannot
show: acting. Spencer Tracy seems too old, too fragile to be Breslin's "big
man, bulky ... with a long man's stride," but he brings a great moral
strength to Macreedy that belies his (Tracy's) physical fragility, a weight
of ethical authority that ultimately dominates and vanquishes the menacing physicality and malevolence of the thugs. In curing the entire town,
Spencer Tracy's Macreedy demonstrates the moral fortitude that can make
a difference against the organized, malevolent crimes of others.
    Standing antithetical to the noble values of the traditional American
western is the American gangster film, which glamorizes the life of organized crime. Such defining crime dramas as *Little Caesar* (1930), *Public*

Enemy (1931), and *Scarface* (1932) outwardly claim to be admonitions of criminals. (*Scarface* begins with the proclamation, "This picture is an indictment of gang rule in America." *Public Enemy* claims "to honestly depict..., rather than glorify, the hoodlum or criminal.") However, belying their outwardly stated purposes, each film does, in fact, aggrandize its criminal-protagonist, portraying him as infinitely more alluring, provocative, complex, and interesting, even more valorous, than the bland G-men who hunt him. By 1933, however, the Production Code had instituted restrictions affecting gangster films, and movies like *Scarface* and *Public Enemy* could no longer be made. The glamour of the gangster life which was so popular in American films from 1929 through 1933 became replaced by the nobility of the law enforcers who went after the felons and/or by the depiction of a life of crime as perniciously destructive of any and all that is good. Notable among this vintage of American gangster films is *The Killers* (1946, dir. Robert Siodmak) from Ernest Hemingway's short story of the same title.

Hemingway's "The Killers" narrates in fewer than ten pages the premeditated and pre-announced point-blank murder of Ole Andersen. Hemingway's story opens with two strangers, Max and Al, walking in to Henry's local diner ("lunch-room") in Summit, Illinois. Sam, the cook; George, the counterperson; and Nick Adams, a customer are held hostage by the two, who eventually announce that they are in town to kill "a big Swede." In response to the question, "What did he ever do to you?" Max replies, "He never had a chance to do anything to us. He never even seen us.... We're killing him for a friend. Just to oblige a friend" (260). The most that George and Nick can piece together regarding the planned killing is that Ole Andersen was "mixed up in something in Chicago" where he "double-crossed" somebody. When Ole does not arrive for his customary dinner at six o'clock at Henry's, Max and Al go to find him. Nick, the bystander who just happened to be in the diner that night, ignores Sam's advice to "stay out of it," risks the violent response of the two hit men, and acts on principle by going off to warn Ole. Nick finds him before "the killers" do. Ole is alone his room at Hirsch's boarding house, where the "big Swede," fully dressed, is lying on his bed, face turned toward the wall. Without even turning around, he meets Nick's warning with the simple reply "There isn't anything I can do about it" (264).

Escape is impossible. Ole is resigned to that. Worse, Nick's principle-driven behavior, the heroic values that define his decision to help Ole, are useless, provoking an absurd choice similar to choosing the unavailable items on the menu at Henry's. In Hemingway's short story, Nick learns that life does not operate as he (and most readers) have been taught that it does, the way that fiction and film has shown us it works: that one man who stands alone against evil can make a difference. He can't, "The Killers" tells us.

While missing the import of Hemingway's existential view, the Production Code Administration was pleased that Ole Andersen, prizefighter turned gangster, was not glorified, and that his demise, though unfortunate, illustrated the Code's position that movies are responsible for "moral progress, for higher types of social life, and for much correct thinking" ("Production Code," paragraph five). Thus, the PCA gave its approval for the filming of Hemingway's "The Killers."

The film *The Killers* expands upon the plot of Hemingway's short story in several ways: by providing flashbacks that explain Ole Andersen's demise (Burt Lancaster in his film debut); by adding the characters and stories of insurance investigator Jim Reardon (Edmond O'Brien), Lt. Sam Lubinsky (Sam Levene), Big Jim Colfax (Albert Dekker), Lily Harmon Lubinsky (Virginia Christine), and Packy Robinson (Charles D. Brown); and by integrating the wonderfully lethal presence of a *femme fatale*, Kitty Collins (Ava Gardner, then 23, in the break-out performance of her career). The trenchant quality of Hemingway's story is carried over in the style of *film noir* that defines this 1944 film.*

☞   The Killers *is a definitive example of film noir. Study the movie closely and fully in terms of the qualities of this cinematic genre. The opening shots of* The Killers *compose a sequence that is generally regarded as one of the very best in movie history. Why? What do you see when you watch it? Read Hemingway's short story. Study the story and the opening of the film, side by side. See what is extraordinary in each and what is yielded by the interplay of the two. How do the enigmas established by Hemingway's story and rendered in the film's opening sequence beget other enigmas created in the film?*

The characteristics of *film noir*, or any cinematic genre (examples: screwball comedies, classical Hollywood narratives, and westerns), are culled from a group of motion pictures (often from one country) that share defining traits (style, tone, setting, subject matter) so strongly as to give them a collective identity. The cinematic genre of *film noir*, like most

---

The Criterion Collection of The Killers *includes three different film versions of Hemingway's short story: the 1946 feature (dir. Robert Siodmak); the 1964 feature (dir. Don Siegel); and the 1956 short, made by Russian director Andrei Tarkovsky when he was a film student. The collection also includes a 1949 radio version, trailers, and interviews.*

Table 18.
Characteristics of *Film Noir*
(*cinéma noir:* dark or black cinema)

Lighting	dark, shadowy lighting; low key/high contrast illumination that creates strong extremes of light and dark areas in the shot; deep shadows, little fill light; black and white film stock employed to create lighting effects of a brooding, menacing atmosphere; intense darkness punctuated by shafts of harsh bright light, pooling of white light, and fragmented beams of light
Composition	asymmetrical *mise-en-scène* which creates destabilization rather than balance; frequent foreground obstructions; the intrusion of grids (usually created by intersecting shafts of light) and rank and file images (ex.: rows of office desks at night) that underscore the unimportance of an individual or the feeling of entrapment; the menacing obscuring of actors' faces or the threatening presence of dark silhouettes illuminated by a single streetlight
Editing	cut to continuity, with fades to black and dissolves oftentimes employed
Camera Angles/ Camera Movement	frequent use of extreme high, low, and oblique angles; slow tracking shots that feel threatening and predatory
Plot	story is dramatic, specifically centering on hard-boiled detective fiction or crime drama; narrative structure frequently employs voice-over narration and flashbacks; stories reveal the dark side of humanity and society and the dark underpinnings of the American Dream; a dark ideology that matches the dark lighting
Setting	a nocturnal, complicated, corrupt world of secrets and ambiguities, where matters of import happen in the (literal and metaphoric) shadows; action is contained within urban environments that depict the underbelly of life: cheap hotel rooms, dark and dank apartments, dimly-lit and seedy bars, dark alleyways, and shadowy railroad yards
Characters	world-weary, hard-boiled, tough-guy detectives and insurance investigators who abide in an ethical limbo, often working both sides of the law; tough-talking, emotionally-detached males who becomes the dupe of a *femme fatale*; *femme fatales* who are as beautiful, resourceful, and smooth-talking as they are lethally conniving, double-crossing, and murderous

cinematic genres, had a popularity life-cycle. It ushered in something new, flourished, and reached a peak of pure expression (*Double Indemnity* is a peak expression of *film noir*, much as *Casablanca* is a peak expression of classical Hollywood narrative). The defining traits of *film noir* became replicated; its production eventually diminished and then it disappeared, only to reappear in permutation and variation.

Film noir flourished in America from 1941 to 1958 (frequently defined as spanning *The Maltese Falcon* through *Touch of Evil*), a period where the Production Code also flourished and was strictly enforced in American filmmaking. As such, a characteristic of American *film noir* is that the movie's corrupt characters invariably pay for their crimes in the end. Another characteristic that underlies *film noir* is that the majority of these movies are translations of literary texts, principally short stories and novels. The *noir* novels are characteristically short (140–200 pages) page-turners, quick reads capable of being consumed within the time-frame that we associate with long short stories.

Neo-noir films, those post *film noir* movies that demonstrate permutations and variations on the genre, include *Klute* (1971, dir. Alan J. Pakula), *Chinatown* (1974, dir. Roman Polanski), *Body Heat* (1981, dir. Lawrence Kasdan), *Blue Velvet* (1986, dir. David Lynch), *Black Widow* (1987, dir. Bob Rafelson), *The Grifters* (1990, dir. Stephen Frears), *La Femme Nikita* (1990, dir. Luc Besson), *L.A. Confidential* (1997, dir. Kurtis Hanson), *Guncrazy* (1992, Tamra Davis), *Jezebel Kiss* (1990, dir. Harvey Keith), *Delusion* (1991, Harvey Keith), *Femme Fatale* (1991, dir. Andre R. Guttfreund, and 2002, dir. Brian De Palma), and *Mulholland Drive* (2001, David Lynch).

☞ *Film noir and neo-noir are often the subject of feminist criticism, which explores the noir female in terms of her resistance to and destabilization of the male-ordered world, of her power to control events, and of film noir's and neo-noir's willingness to probe "the secrets of female sexuality and male desire within patterns of submission and dominance" (Gedhill in Kaplan, 15). Choose any noir or neo-noir movie. Try to see why film noir is of special interest to contemporary feminism.*

Certain contemporary short story writers prove so popular with audiences that several of their works become translated to film. A myriad of Stephen King horror novels and tales have been made into movies, as have two more socially conscious short stories, "The Body" and "Rita Hayworth and the Shawshank Redemption," which were made into the films *Stand*

Table 19.
Literature-Based *Films Noirs*

Film Title	Director	Literary Title	Author
The Maltese Falcon (1941)	John Huston	same (novel)	Dashiell Hammett
Out of the Past (1941)	Jacques Tourneur	*Build My Gallows High* (novel)	Geoffrey Homes
This Gun for Hire (1942)	Frank Tuttle	*A Gun for Sale* (novel)	Graham Greene
The Woman in the Window (1944)	Fritz Lang	*Once Off Guard* (novel)	J. H. Wallis
Laura (1944)	Otto Preminger	same title (novel)	Vera Caspary
Farewell, My Lovely (a.k.a. Murder, My Sweet, 1944)	Edward Dmytryk	same title (novel)	Raymond Chandler
Phantom Lady (1944)	Robert Siodmak	same title (novel)	Cornell Woolrich (under the name: "William Irish")
Double Indemnity (1944)	Billy Wilder	same title (novel)	Raymond Chandler
Lady in the Lake (1946)	Robert Montgomery	same title (novel)	Raymond Chandler
Gilda (1946)	Charles Vidor	same title (short story)	E. A. Ellington
The Big Sleep (1946)	Howard Hawks	same title (novel)	Raymond Chandler
The Killers (1946)	Robert Siodmak	same title (short story)	Ernest Hemingway
The Big Clock (1947)	John Farrow	same title (novel)	Kenneth Fearing
The Lady from Shanghai (1948)	Orson Welles	*If I Die Before I Wake*(novel)	Sherwood King
Criss Cross (1948)	Robert Siodmak	same title (novel)	Don Tracy
The Night Has a Thousand Eyes (1948)	John Farrow	same title (novel)	Cornell Woolrich (under the name: "George Hopley")
Gun Crazy (a.k.a. *Deadly Is the Female*, (1950)	Joseph H. Lewis	"Gun Crazy" (short story)	MacKinlay Kantor

Film Title	Director	Literary Title	Author
Where Danger Lives (1950)	John Farrow	unpublished short story	Leo Rosten
On Dangerous Ground (1951)	Nicholas Ray	*Mad With Much Heart* (novel)	Gerald Butler
The Blue Gardenia (1953)	Fritz Lang	same title (short story)	Vera Caspary
The Sweet Smell of Success (1957)	Alexander Mackendrick	same title (novel)	Ernest Lehman
Touch of Evil (1958)	Orson Welles	*Badge of Evil* (novel)	Whit Masterson

by Me (1986, dir. Rob Reiner) and *The Shawshank Redemption* (1994, dir. Frank Darabont). Cult science fiction writer Philip K. Dick wrote the short stories "We Can Remember It for You Wholesale," "Second Variety," "The Impostor," and "Minority Report" which were made into the mainstream films *Total Recall* (1990, dir. Paul Verhoeven), *Screamers* (1996, dir. Christian Duguay), *The Impostor* (2002, dir. Gary Fleder), and *Minority Report* (2002, dir. Steven Spielberg) respectively. As an indication of Dick's more mainstream acceptance, the documentary feature of him, *The Gospel According to Philip K. Dick* (2002, dir. Mark Steensland and Andy Massagli), was given a wider release than documentaries normally receive. Television scenarist, telecommunications expert, and science fiction writer Arthur C. Clarke's short stories "Breaking Strain" and "The Sentinel" were made into the films *Trapped in Space* (1994, dir. Arthur Allan Seidenman) and *2001: A Space Odyssey* (1968, dir. Stanley Kubrick)

Case Study: "The Sentinel" and 2001: A Space Odyssey

What makes *2001: A Space Odyssey* especially interesting as a film translation of a literary work is that it demonstrates why a filmmaker would want to take up the particular challenge of turning a short story into a movie: to develop integral ideas that the story raises and to cultivate complexities of story and character that the initial story seeded. "The Sentinel" posed provocative issues to Kubrick, who used the expanse that a feature film allows to expound upon them. In extending the information provided by Arthur C. Clarke's short story, Stanley Kubrick's film

creates a meditation on the large concepts ushered in by, but left unde-
veloped in, "The Sentinel."

Clarke's short story narrates a single episode involving human contact with a more fully evolved, extraterrestrial intelligence. The contact
holds consequential intimations regarding humankind's role in the cosmos, our position in the evolutionary order of the universe, the nature of
extraterrestrial beings, the disposition of a direct exchange between our
Earth civilization and an alien one, and the place of God (if God even
exists) in all these inter-workings. The short story, with its ramifying concerns, is wonderfully succinct; the movie that takes up those concerns is
sprawling, absolutely spatial.

Arthur C. Clarke's Short Story: "The Sentinel" (1948)

*Sometimes I think we are alone in the universe and sometimes I think
we are not; either way, the thought is staggering.*
                                                —Arthur C. Clarke

In 1948 Arthur C. Clarke, then thirty-one, submitted his short story
"The Sentinel" to a writing competition sponsored by the BBC. His story
did not even get an honorable mention.* While the work that won the
competition is long forgotten, "The Sentinel" continues to be read by subsequent generations who see staggering thoughts about our place in the
universe in the wonderful compression of Clarke's prose.

"The Sentinel" is narrated in first person recent retrospect by the
geologist leader of a team of research scientists who have established a
space station on the moon in 1996. Their lunar work (the study of the
"southern region" of the "great walled plain" within the *Mare Crisium* or
"Sea of Crises") overlaps with their domestic chores (such Earth practices
as cooking the breakfast sausage). The narrator finds the lunar work is as
pleasantly uneventful and quotidian as the domestic work is, with "nothing hazardous or even particularly exciting about lunar exploration" (136).

One morning, the narrator notices out the window of the galley
kitchen of their pressurized lunar home, "a metallic glitter high on the
ridge of a great promontory" (137). The geologist ("selenologist") in him
is "curious to know what kind of rock could be shining so brightly up
there," so in search of its source, he and a colleague complete the gruel-

In 1951 "The Sentinel" was published in the Avon Science Fiction and Fantasy Reader.

ing ascent of the lunar mountain (138). At the top, the narrator discovers a very curious object, a "roughly pyramidal structure, twice as high as a man, that was set in the rock like a gigantic, many-faceted jewel" (140). The pyramid had been left by a civilization far more advanced than the narrator's own. The story ends with him speculating that the artifact may be a sentinel which, when discovered, would transmit a signal to its makers that humans had developed to that point that proves their "fitness to survive — by crossing space and escaping from the Earth, our cradle." The last sentence states his conclusion: "I do not think we will have to wait for long" (144). In its straightforward, analytical tone, "The Sentinel" credibly and respectfully places large questions before us.

In 1964, sixteen years after writing "The Sentinel," Arthur C. Clarke met with Stanley Kubrick in New York City to discuss the possibility of turning a few of Clarke's stories into a screenplay. Both men agreed that it would be easier to write the script from an integrated prose piece, which would be longer and more fully developed than a short story. Clarke moved into the infamous New York Chelsea Hotel (where he came into contact with Andy Warhol, Allen Ginsberg, Arthur Miller, and Norman Mailer). There and then, in conjunction with Kubrick, he began expanding "The Sentinel" into the 130-page prose treatment that became the basis for the Clarke-Kubrick script of *2001: A Space Odyssey*. Subsequent to the shooting of the film, the story treatment was further refined and released as the novel *2001: A Space Odyssey*.

Clarke further expanded *2001* into *The Odyssey Saga*, consisting of three subsequent works: *2010: Odyssey Two* (1982), *2061: Odyssey Three* (1988), and *3002: The Final Odyssey* (1996).

Stanley Kubrick's Film
2001: A Space Odyssey (1968)

The film *2001: A Space Odyssey* opens in silence and to a completely dark screen. Indistinct sounds emerge, that grow subtly louder, but never loud. They seem, at first, primordial, then like the sound of vast emptiness. The darkness persists, over two minutes, and we feel confused, dislocated by our own expectations of how movies begin. The meditative music and the black screen are suddenly interrupted by a hard cut to the unmistakable logo of MGM (it's funny, a comment on what commercial presentations — interruptions — do to our engagement with the screen). The image of the logo is followed by the trumpeting, pounding, dramatic power of the musical strains of Richard Strauss's *Thus Spake Zarathustra*

(Opus 30, 1896). As Strauss's music thunders, an image of the dark side of the moon yields to an image of the moon and the Earth in darkness which yields to the Earth's gradual illumination by the sun — a dawning. At that moment, the moon, Earth, and sun are in perfect alignment. The musical and visual themes of the film's opening, the visual cycle of darkness into dawning light and the musical exultation that accompanies the dawning, is a self-contained, miniature narrative film unto itself.

☞ *Watch* 2001: A Space Odyssey. *Try to see and hear how the visual and musical themes established in the opening sequence (described above) recur in the film. See how the metaphoric cycle of darkness into dawning occurs four subsequent times in the movie. Think about the music. Strauss has said of his work, "I did not intend to write philosophical music or portray Nietzsche's great work musically. I meant to convey by means of music an idea of the development of the human race from its origin, through various phases of evolution, religious as well as scientific, up to Nietzsche's idea of the Superman" (Cross, 89). Think about Strauss's comment in the context of the film. Read and research Nietzsche's* Thus Spake Zarathustra *(Parts I–III, 1883–84, Part IV, 1891). Watch the opening sequence again. In what ways is that opening a narrative film unto itself?*

In the movie, Clarke's metallically glittering artifact of "roughly pyramidal" shape is changed into a towering and imposing black monolith of elegant and precise form. The movie enlarges on the single-event appearance of the pyramid in "The Sentinel" by having the monolith appear four different times, at four different crucial moments in the evolutionary life of humankind.

The monolith first appears in "The Dawn of Intelligence," a fully non-verbal segment, approximately twenty minutes in length. In that first section, a large group of apes becomes agitated by the sudden intrusion of the monolith that has appeared near their watering hole. With plucky trepidation, one of them approaches and touches the imposing black structure; the others follow, eventually doing the same. Shortly after, the same ape notices that a bone in his hand can be used as a weapon (ironically, humankind's first tool). In the sheer exultation that he feels in his discovery, he tosses the bone overhead. The pronounced significance of the incident is conveyed through Kubrick's effective use of slow motion and through the recurrence of Strauss's *Zarathustra* theme which heralds the momentous dawning of intelligence. The evolutionary moment (ape to ape-man) is indicated not only by the discovery, itself, but also by the ape's triumphant response to it. Not only cognitive development has occurred, we clearly see, but emotional and psychological development, as well.

The bone spins and twists in the air, and before our eyes its elongated image transforms into a spacecraft, of similar shape. Four million years have past. It is 1999. Humans have evolved sufficiently to travel "From Earth to the Moon," the movie's second section, which will signal another momentous event in human evolution. The spacecraft glides along elegantly, in peaceful accord with the strains of Johann Strauss Jr.'s waltz, "The Blue Danube." Dr. Heywood Floyd, a puffed-with-importance space official, is the single passenger (he must be important) aboard this spacecraft. His stop at the space station near the moon is followed by his transport via a smaller craft to the lunar surface, where an excavation has *unearthed* the monolith, its second appearance in the film. (Floyd, the bureaucrat's, reason for being at the momentous site or the work he actually will do there is never made clear.) Heywood Floyd and other scientists pose for photographs in front of the structure, activating, or so it appears, the harsh, piercing tone that issues from the imposing structure. We later learn that the monolith — the sentinel that watches over humankind — has transmitted a signal back to Jupiter that communicates its discovery by humans to the intelligent extraterrestrials who had placed the structure on Earth. Their nature, their motive, or the part they play in humankind's evolution is left ambiguous, as it was in the "Dawn" segment.

This episode is followed by the film's longest and best remembered section: "Jupiter Mission, 18 Months Later," the story involving Mission Commander Dave Bowman (Keir Dullea) and HAL-9000 (voice of Douglas Rain), the supercomputer that maintains spaceship *Discovery One*'s functions in the year 2001. Their mission is to go to Jupiter and attempt to "discover" the objective and meaning of the monolith's signaling and the nature of the extraterrestrial recipients of it. The crew's efforts are sabotaged by the deranged, puffed-with-importance HAL, a highly evolved computer, whose evolution, like that of the ape to ape-man, is not only cognitive, but psychological and emotional, as well. *What qualities individuate a human being from other material beings?* the film asks, positing through the events narrated in this section, that HAL may very well be yet another link in the great evolutionary Chain of Being.

The monolith is seen a third time, in the final section of the film entitled "Jupiter and Beyond the Infinite." In a spectacular view of Jupiter and the planetary constituents of it neighborhood, Dave Bowman, in a small space pod, vulnerable before the immensities and mysteries of space,

2001: A Space Odyssey (1968): As Mission Commander Dave Bowman (Keir Dullea, left) and Major Frank Poole (Gary Lockwood) discuss a significant computer malfunction, they are unaware that the computer, HAL-9000 (voice of Douglas Rain), is reading their lips. Throughout the film, as in this still, director Stanley Kubrick uses the movie screen (Super-Panavision) like a telescope or a science-fiction peep-hole through which we view immensities.

enters the monolith, where he plunges, ever-faster, toward the infinite unknown. He finds himself in a room, which looks like a familiar domicile on Earth, yet eerily somehow not. Standing outside of himself and in the presence of the monolith, Dave watches "Dave Bowman" age, die, and be reborn ... a star-child, a consequential evolutionary moment, like the ape-man, another link in the great Chain of Being. The meaning of the star-child is kept appropriately ambiguous because it is a stage in the hierarchy of the cosmos that we cannot know now, one that we simply cannot understand as humans in our current evolutionary state.

The natures of the monolith and its maker(s) are also kept undefined. Kubrick understands that to define is to limit; and he knows that the individual imagination of each viewer, once stirred to thought, can conjure ideas far greater than that which cinema can show or explain.

Kubrick's film was and remains a revolution in the way that it used cinema to articulate science fiction, never once showing us any aliens and using very few words to narrate its "fiction." It simultaneously transcends its genre, as it moves beyond the boundaries of science fiction into more spatial modes of aesthetics and metaphysics. The movie is made as a logical and a poetic extension of the integral and ponderous questions that Clarke's short story raises (Clarke claims that it is Kubrick's film, and that he only acted as "the first stage booster"). *2001: A Space Odyssey* is Stanley Kubrick's meditation on the stars and beyond. As such, it becomes ours, as well. As poetry, it connotes rather than denotes, intimates rather than delineates, and abides in the realm of figurative language rather than literal usage. As logic, the movie asserts certain reasonable notions: that there is intelligent life out there, that it monitors human development, that evolution implies an ever-expanding Chain of Being, and that humans occupy a shifting, ever-developing place in what Kubrick calls "the hierarchy of the universe."

The film is a phenomenon of cinematic collaboration. Kubrick's screen, large as it is (the film was shot in Metrocolor and Super-Panavision) feels like a telescope or a science-fiction peep-hole through which we view immensities. His intent, according to Clarke, was to create a movie that conveyed "the wonder and the beauty and above all the promise of space exploration."* With the help of his crew, Kubrick achieves his mission. His cinematographers,' Geoffrey Unsworth and John Alcott, employment of a fluid camera technique creates a lovely, spacey, slowness of tempo and lilt of touch (traceable to Max Ophuls). It also creates a visual realism necessary if the audience is to accept the events of the story as credible. The production design of Tony Masters and Harry Lange, in conjunction with John Hoesli's art design, creates a visually witty, yet plausible, near-future, far enough away in time that it should and does look different, but close enough that it does not look alien.

The special effects were "entirely unlike anything seen before — and in many respects [have] never been surpassed" (Howard, 107). Kubrick designed and directed these pre-digital effects[†]; and their charm and power simply do not diminish with time. Most noteworthy are: the film's overall feel of airlessness and weightlessness; the beauty of the spacecraft's and the space station's unhampered-by-gravity glides beside the moon in what Kubrick calls a "machine ballet"; the single-shot phenomenon of the stewardess aboard the zero-gravity space shuttle taking dinner trays into the cockpit by walking 180° to an upside down position; the credible recreation of the lunar surface; the pensive solitude of Major Frank Poole (Gary Lockwood) jogging alone and full-circle around the *Discovery* as his crew is seen hibernating; and the boggling beauty and suggestiveness of Dave

---

From the interview with Arthur C. Clarke archived on the DVD: 2001: A Space Odyssey: The Stanley Kubrick Collection. In that interview Clarke also states that it is "taken for granted" among scientists that "life and intelligence is common throughout the universe."

[†]*The special effects were executed largely by Douglas Trumbull, Wally Veevers, Con Pederson, and Tom Howard. In designing them, Kubrick had what Clarke describes as "the great co-operation of the aerospace industry," scores of experts who gladly consulted on details.*

Bowman's propulsion through the Star Gate. And, through the whole movie, there abides the uncanny appropriateness of its sound, the effects and the music.

Kubrick integrates wicked humor in the film's visual lampooning of cultural icons and rituals. We see this in the spacecraft TV dinners, the suited space-age bureaucrats, the zero-gravity toilets (with a long list of instructions), and the spaceport lounges. The humor is even more pointed in the film's depictions of the corporate executives less interested in work than in photo-opportunities (in front of the monolith) and the ease with which they justify lying to the press (Heywood Floyd's response to the false story that these is an epidemic at the lunar base station). The humor extends to the notion that not only biological organisms evolve, corporate ones must, also, as Kubrick shows in the pernicious persistency — the sheer Darwinian adaptability — of IBM, AT&T, the BBC, Howard Johnson's, and Pan American (ironically, now defunct). In each and all of these instances, Kubrick illustrates that the more cultural codes change, the more they simply stay the same.

2001: A Space Odyssey reminds us that the best films are like the best literature. We can return them again and again, and each time that we do, our understanding of them and our pleasure in them deepens. They do not age. A great film, like a great literary work, rewards our subsequent return by allowing us to see things, hear sounds, delight in a variety of subtle wonders that were so incidental before as to go unnoticed. As Shakespeare understood in *Antony and Cleopatra*: "Age cannot wither her, nor custom stale/Her infinite variety."

CHAPTER VII

Writing about Film

Every film has its own DNA. The job of the writer who takes up the study of a film is to understand that movie's particular complex structure. In a general way, we can get a sense of just how complex the structure of a feature film is by watching closing credits and seeing the rolling multitude of names of people who worked on the movie. A film is composed of intricacies of involvement and complex orchestration of tasks that result in the unique structure of the particular movie. All movies share a common anatomy, much like humans do, but they also maintain individuating qualities, their distinct, metaphoric DNA.

The writer on film needs an understanding of the common, constituent codes of cinematic structure (discussed in Chapter II). However, the writer also needs a strong, well-trained eye that discerns the distinctive elements of a given movie. Without these two qualities, the writer's analysis of a film is, at best, arbitrary, and any assessment of the film becomes a perfunctory judgment, a subjective response where nothing in particular, except perhaps the writer's personal preference, informs the appraisal.

The writer on film needs an educated and discerning eye, a mastery of sight combining knowledge and aesthetic awareness. Such mastery is developed over time and through perseverance. Students of film-writing can begin to expand their capacities to see by watching all nature of movies and by maintaining a journal in which they consistently write on each and every film that they watch. Over time, it is revealing for writers to reread their journals and see the development of their film eye.

☞ *Get in the habit of keeping a film journal. Immediately after watching a movie, write a minimum of three pages in reaction to what you just saw. While your tendency may be to be subjective (recording the impression that movie made on you and describing how you felt as you watched it), try to remain objective and critical, instead. Write about what you saw on the screen. React to the cinematic methods that you observed: the camera work and editing techniques; the specific ways in which the movie organizes its narrative information, including its temporal organization (chronological? fractured chronology? multiple flash-backs?); the defining qualities of the director that are apparent in the movie; the ways in which the film negotiates its cinematic genre; the point(s) of view (the perspective(s) through which the information is focalized); the use of sound, music, effects, and spoken language; the effectiveness of the acting; and, most crucially, any particular features you saw that are unique to that film.*

What film-writers see and hear informs their writing, and, in turn, the act of writing clarifies what they have seen and what they come to understand. Writing, thus, is not only a mode of expression, it is a mode of discovery and refinement of thought. Film students, of all degrees, will find that writing serious-mindedly about movies will not only further enhance their expressive, communicative, and critical skills, but also will refine their capacities to see more fully and to discern more satisfyingly.

When writing about film, the general principle to follow is that a minimum amount of attention should be devoted to writing about the story (the plot, the sequence of the events, the character's actions). The greater part of the writing should be focused on some aspect of the film's discourse, in the sense of the signifying practices, the particular modes by which the narrative information is organized and communicated. When writing about literature-based movies, it becomes especially crucial to remain mindful of this general principle, as any review or analysis of literature into film should, as this book has detailed, be much more than an explanation of how the movie tampered with the literature's story and characters.

In writing in response to the particular situation of literature-based films, the writer needs to be aware of the inherent nature of each medium. While, overall, literature's form and the form of narrative film share many commonalities, they also are clearly different media, with different inherent traits. The writer needs to be aware that cinema can do things that literature either simply cannot do or must work harder at accomplishing, and vice versa.

A movie, for example, is able to have us hear the grain of a voice, its inflections and intonations. While a novel, a printed play, or a short story can describe a character's voice and can create a context in which we can imagine the intonations, it cannot have us literally hear the speaker. Films can employ the sound of the actor's voice so effectively that, at times, the voice the creates an imprint on us so affecting that the memory of the character speaking malingers hours, days, or years after we have seen the movie. We quote lines from these films, imitate the intonations, inflections, and vocal grains. We are seized by the power and depth of the voice, not only by what is says, but also by the quality and mode of expression — by its capacity to move us and to have us understand layers of character and emotions. The films listed in Table 20 are examples of literature-based films known for an actor's memorably effective use of voice.

Sound in film is built up of layers or multiple tracks which allow a variety of sounds to occur in simultaneity. These sounds can be amplified, muted, stretched, and bent — mechanically altered in any number of ways. In a movie, we are able to hear an intricacy of spoken words, music, and effects, all occurring at the exact same time. Literature cannot do this, except, perhaps, in emerging, multimedia forms where the text is digitized and links are embedded that enable us to click and hear the sounds and songs referenced in the text. However, the nature of non-digitized reading makes it impossible for us to experience the intricacy of simultaneous sound that we can experience through a film.

Literature has the extraordinary capacity to have us imagine the complex of noises that are happening as events are unfolding, but a written text cannot actually replicate the intricacy of *concurrent*, literal sounds — those multiple soundtracks which convey the variety of noises occurring at the exact same moment. The work of the reader's imagination constructs any intricate concurrence of sound that is experienced in course of reading. Literature's inherent structure and material are different from those of a film. Sound in writing is structurally sequential rather than concurrent. One word or one cluster of words follows another; sounds follow sounds in a successive order.

☞ *Film is such a visually dominant medium that, in responding to it, writers tend to stress what they see. Here you are asked to hear more fully and to write about what you discover in the layers of a movie's sound track. Select one of the following activities:*

    1. Choose a movie that is known for its sound. Examples include Ryan's Daughter *(1970),* Tchaikovsky *(USSR, 1971),* The Conversation *(1974),* Dersu Uzala *(USSR, 1975),* Star Wars *(1977),* Close Encounters of the Third Kind *(1977),* Raging

Table 20.
Examples of Effective Use of Actor's Voice in Literature-based Films

Movie	Actor	Role	Literary Title, Author
Emperor Jones (1933)	Paul Robeson	Brutus Jones	play: *The Emperor Jones*, Eugene O'Neill
Showboat (1936)	Paul Robeson	Joe	novel: same title, Edna Ferber
Angels with Dirty Faces (1938)	James Cagney	William "Rocky" Sullivan	short story: same title, Rowland Brown
The Hunchback of Notre Dame (1939)	Charles Laughton	Quasimodo	novel: same title, Victor Hugo
Gone with the Wind (1939)	Clark Gable Vivien Leigh	Rhett Butler Scarlett O'Hara	novel: same title, Margaret Mitchell
The Wizard of Oz (1939)	Judy Garland	Dorothy Gale	novella: same title, L. Frank Baum
	Margaret Hamilton	Miss Almira Gulch/The Wicked Witch of the West	
	Billie Burke	Glinda, the Good Witch of the North	
Casablanca (1942)	Humphrey Bogart	Rick Blaine	play: *Everybody Comes to Rick's*, Murray Burnett and Joan Alison
To Have and Have Not (1944)	Lauren Bacall	Marie "Slim" Browning	novel: same title, Ernest Hemingway
The Third Man (1949)	Orson Welles	Harry Lime	novel: same title, Graham Greene
All About Eve (1950)	Bette Davis	Margo Channing	short story: "The Wisdom of Eve," Mary Orr
A Streetcar Named Desire (1951)	Marlon Brando	Stanley Kowalski	play: same title, Tennessee Williams

Movie	Actor	Role	Literary Title, Author
Forbidden Games (*Jeux interdits*) (1952)	Georges Poujouly	Michel Dolle	novel: *Jeux interdits*, François Boyer
	Brigitte Fossey	Paulette	
On the Waterfront (1954)	Marlon Brando	Terry Malloy	novel: same title, Budd Schulberg
The Searchers (1956)	John Wayne	Ethan Edwards	novel: same title, Alan LeMay
Whatever Happened to Baby Jane? (1962)	Bette Davis	Jane Hudson	novel: same title, Henry Farrell
	Joan Crawford	Blanche Hudson	
To Kill a Mockingbird (1962)	Mary Badham	Jean Louise "Scout" Finch	novel: same title, Harper Lee
2001: A Space Odyssey (1968)	HAL-9000	Douglas Rain	short story: "The Sentinel," Arthur C. Clarke
Patton (1970)	George C. Scott	Gen. George S. Patton Jr.	novelized biography: *Patton: Ordeal and Triumph*, Ladislas Farago
The Godfather (1972)	Marlon Brando	Vito Corleone	novel: same title, Mario Puzo
One Flew Over the Cuckoo's Nest (1975)	Jack Nicholson	Randle Patrick MacMurphy	novel: same title, Ken Kesey
Apocalypse Now (1979)	Robert Duvall	Lt. Col. William "Bill" Kilgore	novella: *Heart of Darkness*, Joseph Conrad
The Shining (1980)	Jack Nicholson	Jack Torrance	novel: same title, Stephen King
Prizzi's Honor (1985)	Anjelica Huston	Maerose Prizzi	novel: same title, Richard Condon
	Kathleen Turner	Irene Walker	
Silence of the Lambs (1991)	Anthony Hopkins	Dr. Hannibal Lecter	novel: same title, Thomas Harris
Shrek (2001)	Mike Myers	Shrek	short story: same title, William Steig

Bull *(1980)*, Amadeus *(1984)*, Blue Velvet *(1986)*, Babette's
Feast *(Denmark, 1987)*, The Music Teacher *(Belgium, 1988)*,
Salaam Bombay! *(India, 1988)*, The Abyss *(1989)*, Ju Dou
(People's Republic of China, 1990), Unforgiven *(1992)*, The
Scent of Green Papaya *(Vietnam, 1993)*, Pulp Fiction *(1994)*,
L.A. Confidential *(1997)*, and Chicago *(2002)*. *Watch the
entire movie. Select one sequence of shots that strikes you as particularly interesting because of its use of sound. Write down
everything that you hear, all intricacies of spoken words, music,
and sound effects . Write an analysis of the sound that explains
how all the intricacies work together to produce the specific effects
of the sequence.*

2. *Read Joseph Conrad's novella* Heart of Darkness. *Reread the
opening frame of the story, i.e., the unnamed narrator's account
of the evening spent aboard the yawl* Nellie. *Watch* Apocalypse
Now *(1979). Rewatch the film's opening frame, i.e., Captain
Benjamin L. Willard (Martin Sheen) alone in his hotel room.
Focus on how sound is used in the film sequence to replicate the
tumultuous chaos stirred by the memories that Willard, like
Marlowe in Conrad's work, will narrate. Explain how the intricacies of sound effects, monologue, and music all contribute to
the effect of the sequence.**

While both literature and film have a sympathetic relationship to
other art forms, film is capable of literally incorporating other arts within
its medium. For example, a film can integrate dance, music, and painting in its own cinematic composite. The medium of movie-making allows
for the filming of a painting or even the hand-painting of individual frames
and the incorporation of music in its soundtrack and dance in its sequence
of images. Digitized texts of literature that include links to referenced
paintings, music, or dance, or even a traditional paper text that includes
a reproduced painting, a packaged CD of sounds, or a DVD of dance in
with the paper book are possible to produce, but accessing the referenced
work in either the digitized or paper format creates a break in the words,
a disruption in the text. Movies, in contrast, are able to integrate other
arts through the very mechanics and material of their own, singular
medium.

**For a further explanation of the relationship of the novella and the film see: Cahir, "Narra-
tological Parallels in Joseph Conrad's Heart of Darkness and Francis Ford Coppola's Apocalypse Now."*

Ghost World (2000): Rebecca (Scarlett Johansson, left) and Enid (Thora Birch, right) from Terry Zwigoff's film of Daniel Clowes' underground comic book *Ghost World.*

   Film can incorporate the medium of animation in with its live-action images (*The Piano, Crumb*). It can also turn to cartoon books and magazines as rich sources for stories, characters, and plots (*Superman, Spider-Man*), with the film often expanding the complexities and capabilities of the cartoon text.* *Ghost World* (2000) is a particularly strong example of this trans-media process. Based on co-screenwriter Daniel Clowes's underground comic book of the same name, the film expands and transforms the original material, making Clowes's angst-filled teenagers, Enid and Rebecca, far more complex. The two dimensions of his comic book pages are given depth in this Terry Zwigoff film,† as Enid (Thora Birch) and her friend Rebecca (Scarlett Johansson), speaking with droll wit and cynical

Film does not always expand on the comic book text. Many argue that Batman, *for example, is much more complex in its thirty years of comic book treatment than in the feature films based on his character.*

   †*Terry Zwigoff also directed the film* Crumb *(1995), a documentary of the underground comics artist R. Crumb. In the film* Ghost World, *the drawings in Enid's sketchbook diary were done by Crumb's daughter, Sophie.*

voice, outgrow their cartoonized selves, and emerge as fully realized — intelligent, confused, and socially disenfranchised — young women in the film. The two outsiders find affirmation of sorts in one another and in the record collector Seymour (Steve Buscemi), whose eccentricity, authenticity, honesty, and aloneness help Enid understand herself. The three face the complexities of attempting to find a spot in a culture whose values they largely do not share. The film expands on the Clowes cartoon, most obviously by adding the characters of Seymour and Roberta (Illeana Douglas), Enid's pretentious summer school art teacher, but more subtly through the dialogue (spoken by the major to the most minor characters) and witty visual details that so enrich this film. Reading Daniel Clowes's cartoon book, *Ghost World*, and scrutinizing the means by which the film enlarges upon and vivifies the original written text shows the capacity of film to develop literary characters and their idiosyncrasies.

In writing about literature-based films, we need to remain mindful of the inherent qualities of each medium so that we do not expect from it something that, by nature of its form, the medium cannot deliver. Literature can approximate, but cannot replicate, film's capacity to provide an abundance of visual information in a flash. Literature is not nearly as efficient in having us see the intricacies of detail that a single frame of film provides. But arguably, movies cannot create the profundity of visual effects that our reading imagination can, and movies have far greater difficulty translating the ambiguity, internal conflict, and sub-text that is inherent in great literature. Still, in each medium there are works that come as close to magic as we may ever know. Literature can conjure in a single word, like film can conjure in a single frame, worlds and worlds of meaning, ponderous greatness that lingers, and beauty that approaches the supernal.

The study of a film translation of a literary work is intricate, as there are many facets to the literature-based movie. Writers must establish the particular focus of their work, the specific approach that their writing will undertake. (Several approaches are discussed below and initially noted in bold type.) Whatever the approach, the writing needs to be informed by a suitable knowledge. While everyone, certainly, may be entitled to an opinion, writing that opinion so that reading it is worth a reader's time is another matter entirely, the simple reason why, while everyone who sees a movie can be a critic of it, not everyone can be a professional critic.

Not all professional film critics and scholars are equal. What distinguishes one from another is what distinguishes all professionals: the quality of their work. Students of film-writing profit from reading professional film-writers not just for what they are saying, but for how they are framing their ideas. To this end it is important for students of film-writing to read not just for *what* the professionals are saying, but also for *how* they are saying it.

☞ *Start to read like a writer. Choose five or more essays (both popular film reviews and scholarly articles) all written on the same movie. This can be done by taking a random sampling from the internet. For example, "Rotten Tomatoes" and "The Movie Review Query Engine" archive full-text popular reviews;* The New York Times *makes its own film criticism available even to non-subscribers; and full-text academic data bases provide a gateway to juried journal articles written on film. Excellent sources for scholarly journal articles include* Literature/Film Quarterly; Cinema Journal; Media, Culture, and Society; *and* Historical Journal of Film, Radio, and Television, *as well as most literary journals, which frequently now carry related articles on film.*

Think about each separate work that you have read. Note any seminal points that are made. Analyze the specific ways that the writers make their points. Try to see how each work is organized and what the focus of the work is. Are any of the essays relatively empty of ideas and style? Trivial? Think about the five essays comparatively. Where do you see the strongest writing? Can you define what makes that writing strong?

The focus, the point, of the writing defines the approach the writer will take. If, for example, the focus is an overall appraisal of the movie written for a general readership with an interest in film, but only a rudimentary knowledge of it, the suitable writing approach is the **film review**.

Film reviews do not, as a rule, engage in a thorough lengthy analysis of the movie. They are brief, usually 500–1,500 words long. Written immediately after the critic has seen the movie, the film review does not have the benefit of repeated viewings, of the close-reading scrutiny that such repetition allows, or even of the space of time needed to think about and process the intricacies that occurred on the screen. Film reviews are typically subjective, as much about the critic and his or her own response to the film as about the film, itself. Their principal value is commercial, first and foremost, because merely writing about the movie, positively or negatively, gets the film publicized.

Film reviews are commercial products (the reviewer is paid, the publication sells copies/get viewers) written for popular consumption. Generally, they reach a wider audience than scholarly writing does and, as such, they are the vehicle that gets a movie known. In remarking on movie reviews, independent filmmaker, novelist, and theorist Marguerite Duras wrote: "I have the feeling that established film critics pay no attention to movies unless they've cost a lot. Even if they say that film is not very good, if it's expensive they say so in three full columns. You can tell how expensive a film was by the length of the article" (98).

☞   *Go to the library or go on-line and survey newspapers and popular magazines for what movies they reviewed in the past month. Were they large-budget, studio-backed films or small, independent movies? How many of the films reviewed were produced in foreign countries? Does your survey lead you to agree or disagree with Duras's comment?*

The film review is commercial in a second way. Beyond getting the movie known, the critics' views help shape the financial success of a movie, the draw of its ticket purchases and DVD rentals. The film review helps readers determine if the movie discussed is worth seeing, if it is worth their time and money, thus giving rise to a cliché: *There are two things in life vital to find: a restaurant and a critic that you can always depend upon.* Whether it is that singular, specific critic at *The New York Times* whose views one comes to rely upon or the clerk at the video store whose opinions one trusts, the critic of worth is that individual whose work gains reliance, whose reviews are consistently credible, accurate, knowledgeable, and well-argued.

While film reviews benefit from research, research is not a requisite for writing film reviews, and, in fact, in practice, any information that the professional critic may need is handily provided by the press kit available normally at the film's press screening. Press screenings are generally held five to seven days prior to the movie's opening date. Depending on the advertising budget, press kits include anything from simple production notes through an elaborate packaging of slides, stills, and promotional gadgets. While the information contained in the production notes (a summary of the movie's plot and characters, a production history, information about the cast and filmmakers, details regarding the soundtrack, and the full credits) appears to be merely facts, objectively presented, these notes are written by the publicity department of the film's distribution company. Thus, those film critics who base the information that they cite in their reviews solely on the information contained in the production notes are limiting their fact-finding search to that one source least likely to be objective.

Press screenings of films are often accompanied by junkets in which the reviewers are invited to nearby hotels where they interview the film's principal contributors: the writer, director, producer, and principal cast. Legendary film critic Pauline Kael avoided junkets and declined offers of private interviews, asserting that direct contact with the filmmakers (the press's rubbing elbows with the stars) would invariably affect the content of the film critic's reviews.

Film reviews are most often constructed to be quick reads — plot-driven and simple in their critical assessments (thumbs up, thumbs down). The prose style is straightforward, sometimes incorporating clever turns of phrase, which, again, serve to reveal more about the reviewer than about the film. The great film reviewers (such as James Agee, *The Nation*; Pauline Kael, *The New Yorker*; and Andrew Sarris, *The Village Voice*) avoid simplistic evaluative critical tools (thumbs or awards of stars). Instead, they use their subjective response to the movie as an entry point for under-standing — for informing — their analysis of the merits of the film.

☞ *Think of a movie that provoked a strong (subjective) response in you (one that excited, scared, saddened, uplifted, or rattled you). Watch it again, remaining fully attentive to the things that the film is doing to structure that response. Write an analysis of the specific factors (the plot? camera placement? sound? lighting? editing? acting?) that con-spired to create the effect you experienced.*

Great film reviews, like those written by Agee, Kael, and Sarris, are extended analyses so insightful that they teach ways of seeing that the readers of the reviews may not have discovered on their own. The best film reviewers are simultaneously teachers, whose prose mentors the open-minded reader to greater understanding of the nuances of the movie. Film reviews have a traditional structure. The first paragraph introduces the film, establishes the tone of the review, and provides a brief summary of the basic story, without giving away crucial plot information. The best plot summaries are exquisitely succinct. Peter M. Nichols, writing for *The New York Times*, provides a worthy example of this traditional structure in the opening two sentences of his film review of the literature to screen work *The Cat in the Hat* (2003). Nichols writes, "Extraneous plotting complicates Dr. Seuss's classic. As Seuss had it, two children and a top-hatted cat wreck the house on a rainy day and put it back in order just as mom returns" (28 Nov. 2003, E13). Nichols's writing immediately estab-lishes the tone of his review and his position on the movie as a transla-tion of Seuss's book; it provides a summary of the basic plot; and it does all three in an admirable succinctness of prose.

In the traditionally-structured film review, each subsequent paragraph should provide close examination of the key features of the movie that were successful or flawed. The review should always explain those features sufficiently and should support the general, critical claims with specific examples. The review should end with a clear articulation of the critic's appraisal of the film.

☞   *After reading several examples of film reviews, write one yourself that follows the traditional structure of the film review as described above.*

Another approach to writing about film is the **aesthetic analysis**. Much more thorough in its investigation of the film than a movie review is, the aesthetic analysis focuses on the ways in which the film is or is not "beautiful." The aesthetic analysis requires that the writer establish a definition of beauty and, in doing so, understand how intimately that definition is tied to form and to genre. (The aesthetics of *film noir* may be very different from the aesthetics of horror or humor.) An aesthetic analysis usually requires that the writer establish a criterion, much like the aesthetic rubric for literature-based films that is introduced in Chapter IV, expanded upon throughout this book, and provided again in Appendix A.

The study of aesthetics yields a heightened appreciation of form and an awareness that aesthetic values are influenced by psychology, sociology, history, and ethnology. An aesthetic approach to writing about film requires an understanding of and receptivity to these variables in aesthetic values, as well as an appreciation of the universal, essential qualities that constitute beauty of cinematic form. Under an aesthetic film analysis, the movie is exhaustively assessed in relationship to the complex aesthetic standards that have been established by the writer, instead of through the arbitrary thumbs up or down standard that constitutes a popular film review's assessment of whether or not the movie was "good."

☞   *Reread the four points of the aesthetic rubric in this book (Appendix A). That rubric is specifically designed for literature-based films. Write an aesthetic analysis of a film, either by applying the rubric established in this book or by creating your own aesthetic criteria, those standards you establish in making judgments about the artistic merit of a movie. In writing your aesthetic analysis, you may want to choose a film that has a solid reputation. For example, in 2002, the critics writing for the highly regarded British journal,* Sight & Sound, *concurred on a list of the ten greatest movies ever made. That list, in ranking order, is:*

1. *Citizen Kane*
   (1941, dir. Orson Welles)
2. *Vertigo*
   (1958, dir. Alfred Hitchcock)
3. *La Règle du jeu/The Rules of the Game*
   (1939, dir. Jean Renoir)
4. *The Godfather* and *The Godfather, Part II*
   (1972, 1974, dir. Francis Ford Coppola; novel, *The Godfather*, by Mario Puzo)
5. *Tokyo monogatari* (*Tokyo Story*)
   (1953, dir. Yasujiro Ozu)
6. *2001: A Space Odyssey*
   (1968, dir. Stanley Kubrick; story, "The Sentinel," by
   Arthur C. Clarke*)*
7. *Sunrise*
   (1927, dir. F. W. Murnau; story, "A Journey to Tilsit,"
   by Hermann Sudermann)
8. *Battleship Potemkin*
   (1925, dir. Sergei Eisenstein)
9. *8½*
   (1963, dir. Federico Fellini; story by Ennio Flaiano)
10. *Singin' in the Rain*
    (1952, dirs. Gene Kelly and Stanley Donen)

Under an aesthetic analysis, it is possible for the film to be tremendously flawed, yet worth seeing and worth writing about because some
aspect of it works so very beautifully. One example is Alfred Hitchcock's
movie *Frenzy* (1972), from playwright Anthony Shaffer's screenplay based
upon the novel *Goodbye Picadilly, Farewell Leicester* by Arthur Labern. A
suspense thriller about an infamous necktie killer, *Frenzy* centers an outwardly genial Covent Garden fruit seller, Bob Rusk (Barry Foster), who
turns out to be a "mama's boy" and a sadistic murderer of women. The
film incorporates some of Hitchcock's favorite tropes: fetishism, voyeurism,
and dark humor. While *Frenzy* ranks among Hitchcock's weaker films, it
includes some individual shots that are the best in his career, most memorably the film's early sequence (36 minutes in) where, with mobility and
fluidity, the camera follows the murderer up the steps of an apartment
building, backs out, then waits sorrowfully outside, poised on the exterior of the building while the murder takes place. This brief sequence in
Frenzy is a study in cinematic aesthetics, in and of itself.

Fires on the Plain (1959): Kon Ichikawa's traditional translation of Shohei Ooka's anti-war novel of the same title. The film, like Ooka's book, memorably and hauntingly depicts the unthinkable depths to which men, degraded by circumstances of war, can plunge.

An aesthetic analysis may incorporate aspects of **formal analysis** (see Table 21). A formal analysis examines the movie's "form" in terms of its components and discusses how the components contribute to the entire film. Formal analysis can be understood as seeing the integrated complexity of the whole by scrutinizing the construction of the separate, constituent parts and their interrelated functions. A formal analysis may be written on the entire movie or on a representative section of it. It may be written as an examination of all the constituent elements that make up the film or as an analysis of just one, specific element among the film's constituent parts. The opening sequence of the film *Fires on the Plain* (1959), for example, provides abundant material for a formal analysis.

Fires on the Plain, directed by Kon Ichikawa, opens with a partial close-up and with the unexpected sound of a slap in the face. (We feel the slap.) It begins with an act of violence and humiliation by one man against another. The opening sequence is a formal antithesis of the norm of cinematic exposition, i.e., opening with an establishing shot, often panoramic in scope. A traditional translation of Shohei Ooka's great post World War II novel of the same title, Ichikawa's film shares with the Ooka's book the horror of how fully war can degrade men, compelling them, in the name of personal survival, to the most vile acts against others. Through its indelible images of fear and deprivation, and the acts of violence and taboo that such hardships engender, *Fires on the Plain* counterposes the instinct for survival against the struggle to retain human dignity amid the madness of war. The movie is a masterpiece of form, distinctive in its beautifully modulated photography, elegant in its narrative structure, and dignified in its articulation of theme. As Pauline Kael explains, the theme of *Fires on the Plain* is that "when survival is the only driving force, when men live only to live, then survival comes to seem irrelevant" (Kael, *I Lost It*, 204).

☞ *Watch* Fires on the Plain. *Go back and rewatch the opening sequence (the first six minutes/nineteen shots) and attempt to understand it within the context of the entire film. Study the basic* mise-en-scène *of each of the nineteen shots. Note the composition, the lighting. Study the shots in relationship to one another for the editing practices and for the beautifully modulated photography. Listen to the various sounds occurring. Note what stylistic qualities and what themes are introduced in the opening sequence and are expanded upon in the film.*

The formal analysis requires the writer to see, to hear, and to describe, as specifically as possible, the properties of any one or all of the film's components (the lighting, the editing, the sound, etc.). The art of the analysis comes from what the writer can apprehend and how expertly that writer can construe formal, causal relationships. In preparing a formal analysis, the writer needs to determine (think through) the ways that each constituent element that is being analyzed affects three things in the film:

1. its narrative structure (examples: traditional, non-linear, and elliptical)
2. its style (examples: realism, *film noir*, expressionism, *avant-garde*, minimalism, and fantasy)
3. its theme

In writing a formal analysis, it would be helpful to review the information contained in Chapter I: "The Language of Film" and in the glossary of this text and to use the grid below as an outline for structuring the formal analysis.

☞ *Write a formal analysis of a film of your choice. The formal analysis may be written on the entire movie or on a representative section from it, as an examination of all the constituent elements that make up the film or as an analysis of just one, specific element among the film's constituent parts (example: an analysis of sound, or even, more specifically, of music throughout a film or in a given sequence within the film). In preparation for writing the formal analysis, as you watch the movie, fill in as much information as possible on the grid below. Use the information you accumulate to focus the specific thesis of your formal analysis and to structure the details of your writing.*

A formal analysis could also be structured around a specific technique pioneered in or made famous by a specific film: the multi-plane camera in Disney's *Pinocchio* (1940), deep focus in *Citizen Kane* (1941), *noir* lighting in *Double Indemnity* (1944), shot duration in *Rope* (1948), music and silence in *Ikiru* (1952), slasher-editing in the shower scene of *Psycho* (1960), montage editing in *Koyaanisqatsi* (1983), "image-based rendering" (IBR) in *The Matrix* (1999), or "the Fluid Animation System" (FLU) in *Shrek* (2001).

A formal analysis that examines a specific technique pioneered in a particular movie is also a method of **historical analysis**, yet another approach to writing about film. An historical analysis examines film in the larger context of history or film history. A film analysis conducted through the larger context of history would explore any of the following areas:

1. The historical and/or political issues that affected the construction and outcome of a particular film

2. The role of government in overall film production, with topics to include financial support, censorship, and/or propaganda

3. The initial reviews of a film and what the reviews, themselves, reveal about the historical context in which they were written

4. The effect that shifts in social values and/or linguistic and visual meanings have had on a particular film's reception

5. The ways in which a particular film was advertised and what those promotional strategies tell us about the film's historical context

6. The various responses (popular and/or academic) that a particular film has had in different historical times

7. The effect that a literature-based film's release has on subsequent sales of the book which it translates

8. The means by which the film changed the literary text in order to accommodate the time in which the movie was made

9. The liberties that the literature or film took with historical fact.

Table 21.
Formal Analysis of a Film:

Constituent Element:	*Properties:* (describe as specifically as possible)	*The Effect:* (describe effect on the narrative structure, the style, and the theme)
Mise en scène	:: the compositional style within the frame: balance? asymmetrical?	
	:: the placement of actors and objects? how free space is used within the frame?	
	:: the decor? the costumes?	
Camera Placement	:: when and how the camera moves?	
	:: the angles?	
Lighting	:: the key: high or low?	
	:: the contrast?	
Editing	:: overall editing method: continuity? montage?	
	:: specific methods, if any, of transitioning between shots and/or sequences? (examples: fades? dissolves? jump cuts? cross-cuts?)	
	:: the duration of shots	
Sound	:: the quality and nature of the sound effects, the music, and the spoken words	
Screenplay	:: the dialogue: how, when, and why dialogue is used?	
	:: the images: how, when, and where images are used to narrate story?	
	:: the plausibility of the story and characters within the world of the narrative?	
Acting	:: the effectiveness of the actor's use of voice? body? facial expressions?	

   Girl with a Pearl Earring (2003), a traditional translation of Tracy
Chevalier's 2001 novel of the same name, speculates on the chain of events
that may have occurred during the composition of the famous painting
by 17th-century Dutch artist Johannes Vermeer. While the film, like the
novel, is largely fictional in its creation of plot, the film is adroit, accurate, and absorbing in its visual re-creation of Vermeer's work. The daily
life of the Vermeer household goes on, and scenes that we already are
familiar with from Vermeer's paintings appear in a moment, on which the
camera lingers, and, just as quickly, the film moves forward in the story.
Director Peter Webber, in conjunction with cinematographer Eduardo
Serra and production designer Ben van Os, create momentary *tableaux
vivants* showing how life becomes reconstituted into art. They recreate Vermeer's paintings with the color, ethereal light, serene tones, textures, and
composition that define his work.* Rather than focus on the historical
accuracies of details of plot, an historical analysis of a literature-based film
could explore the visual accuracy of the film world, as *Girl with a Pearl
Earring* illustrates.

☞   *An historical analysis employs research from outside of the work being
      analyzed as a means of exploring or assessing it within an historical
      context. Write an historical analysis that uses the general focus of any
      one of the topics above and that integrates sufficient research in its
      findings.*

   Each and every film is an historical document of sorts, a record of
the cultural, technological, aesthetic, and linguistic expressions of the
time. Even the most mediocre of movies archive a complex of fundamental historical information. Each and every movie, thus, is a document
which preserves the ideas, standards, customs, and values of the age and
culture that produced it. In the specific case of such literature-based movies
as *The Birth of a Nation* (1915) and *Gone with the Wind* (1939), the films
appear to narrate a story occurring at a particular point in history (the
American South prior to, during, and immediately after the Civil War),
but with far greater historical accuracy, they are documenting the fundamental values, ideas, and practices (ethical practices as well as technological ones) of the historical moment that produced them. Thus, as an
approach to writing about film, an historical analysis is, at heart, a sys-

---

**The paintings that are integrated into the film's story, often showing from where Vermeer took
the subjects of his work, include* View of Delft, Woman with a Pearl Necklace, The Milk-
maid, The Concert, The Girl with the Wineglass, Woman with a Water Jug, *and* Girl with
a Pearl Earring.

tematic attempt to learn about and verify the complexities of the past as either related to or constructed by the movies.

An historical film analysis conducted through the more specific context of *film* history is a systematic attempt at understanding issues specifically related to film production and the film industry. General topics would include:

1. Historical innovations that a given film introduced
2. A trend in film that a particular film ushered in
3. An analysis of a film's production costs posed against its profits or losses
4. The historical evolution of a particular film technology
5. The historical cycle of a film genre: its peak of pure expression, its subsequent replications in other films, its periods of diminished production, and its reappearance in permutation and variation
6. The specific special effects technology that made the filming of fantastic and imaginary literature possible
7. The specific production history of a given film

All films have production histories which involve the details of why, when, how, and by whom a particular movie was made. The path to and through production affects the final outcome of a film, and, interestingly, that production path frequently begins in a literary work. The movie *A.I.: Artificial Intelligence* (2001) is an example of a film whose origins are in a literary work and whose distinctive production path affected, in distinguishable ways, the final form of the film.

A traditional translation of Brian Aldiss's 1969 short story "Super Toys Last All Summer Long," *A.I.* adds layers of plot and character that did not appear in the short story. Overall, however, it maintains the integral traits of Aldiss's work: its futuristic setting; its plot involving the "super toy" David, his toy "Teddy," and his love for his adoptive mother, Monica; and the story's theme of what makes a boy "real" and alive, what constitutes Being?* The movie improves upon the literature by wisely deciding not to employ the story's gimmick of withholding the fact that David is a robot until the very end.

Both the story and film center on David, a highly evolved, sentient, "synthetic life-form," who looks just like a real boy and who has been programmed to have all the feelings a real boy would. David (Haley Joel

*A full-text copy of "Super Toys Last All Summer Long" is available at: http://www.wired. com/wired/archive/5.01/ffsupertoys_pr.html

Osment) deeply loves his human mother, Monica (Frances O'Connor), who, in the film, abandons him. We are led to conclude that Monica, in Aldiss' story, will also abandon David. The story ends with Monica's and Henry's (her husband) vast excitement in learning that they are to have a human baby and, in contrast, their emotional detachment before their decision to send David "back to the factory again," indefinitely.

The movie *A.I.* is a composite of the work of two very high-profile filmmakers: Stanley Kubrick and Steven Spielberg. While the movie was released in 2001, plans for its production were undertaken as early as the mid–1980s when Stanley Kubrick began developing Aldiss' story for a feature film. Throughout the development, Kubrick worked with various writers in producing a story treatment: Arthur C. Clarke, Bob Shaw, Sara Maitland, and Brian Aldiss, himself. The major obstacle to Kubrick's launching the project was that the special effects technology needed to complete the film as he envisioned it simply did not exist yet, so Kubrick put "Super Toys" aside for other projects.

Subsequently, Kubrick saw Spielberg's *Jurassic Park* (1993) and, intrigued by the sophistication of CGI technology (computer generated images), he approached Spielberg about making "Super Toys." (The two had met earlier, in London, 1979, when Kubrick was working on *The Shining* and Spielberg on *Raiders of the Lost Ark*.) Sometime after their discussions of Aldiss' story, Spielberg and Warner Bros. announced that *Artificial Intelligence* would be Spielberg's next film. Two years later, however, the same studio announced that after completing *Eyes Wide Shut*, Kubrick would direct *A.I.*

On March 7, 1999, Stanley Kubrick died; *Eyes Wide Shut* opened posthumously on July 16, 1999; and Steven Spielberg went on to make *A.I.*, dedicating the film to Kubrick and writing the screenplay himself (an unfortunate decision, as the film's major flaws can be traced back to the screenplay). The movie retains the dark, thematic tones that Kubrick and Spielberg had discussed in the early 1990s, as well as the visual designs (the storyboards, sketches, and notes) that Kubrick had left to him. What results is a strange hybrid of styles: a film driven both by the warm, feel-good, emotional superfluities that have come to be Spielberg's signature and by the icy, conceptual, high-tech, analytical approach of Kubrick. Kubrick's work is most noticeable in the visual designs (certain sets, props, camera angles and movement, lighting, and color), that are, at points, unsettling beautiful. Throughout *A.I.*, to one extreme we see the rich, strange, and imaginative visual textures that Spielberg has long admired in Kubrick's work and, to the other, we see the no-stops, no-shame, full-out manipulation of audience sentiment that mars even the best of Spielberg's movies. The film is worth seeing as an outcome of its production history: its obvious divide in style between the warm sentiment that is Spielberg and the dark ethos that is Kubrick. If *A.I.* were examined in terms of the distinctive directorial imprints of Spielberg and of Kubrick that we see on the film, the writing approach (an historical analysis, focused through production history) would overlap with another approach to writing about film, ***auteur* analysis**.

The *auteur* analysis presumes that certain films are the product of one person, most often the director. Under *auteur* analysis, the film is examined in terms of the distinctive imprint that the "author" (the producer, actor, cinematographer, etc.) has left on the film. However, a work of *auteur* analysis can fail if based on a mistaken assumption that movies are like novels, short stories, and plays in that they are composed by just one person. (See Chapter II for a discussion of *auteur* theory.)

An *auteur* analysis explores particular patterns traceable throughout the work of one director (or producer or actor, etc.). As such, an *auteur* approach to writing about film integrates other modes of analysis (history, film history, aesthetics, and formalism). An *auteur* analysis can be focused in any number of ways. Among these are:

1. Defining the stylistic traits of one film *auteur* and tracing those traits either through his/her *oeuvre* or through one specific film of his/hers

2. Tracing a particular genre favored by one film *auteur* through several of his/her films

3. Tracing a particular theme favored by one film *auteur* through several of his/her films

4. Tracing the influences (historical, literary, filmic, and personal) that shaped the work of one film *auteur*

An *auteur* analysis requires that writers watch as much as is accessible of the film work attributed to the *auteur* and that the writers complete the research necessary to illuminate the topic. The easy availability of movies in DVD and VHS formats makes an *auteur* approach much more feasible than such work was in the past for the writer whose access to large film libraries was limited or non-existent. The writer of a director-based *auteur* analysis may want to pursue the study of a director whose work is legendary (examples: Charles Chaplin, Fritz Lang, D. W. Griffith, John Ford, Orson Welles) or those contemporary directors whose work holds a particular interest (examples: Jim Jarmusch, Gus Van Sant, Kevin Smith, or Quentin Tarantino). See Table 22 for more names.

Again, with the emergence of movies on DVD and VHS, the world of film is more widely open to us all, and the writer of a director-based *auteur* analysis may even want to explore the work of other national cinemas.

Table 22.
Representative Multi-national Directors Whose Work Can Be Studied by *Auteur* Standards

Director	Country		
Hector Babenco	Argentina	Win Wender	Germany
Peter Weir	Australia	Satyjait Ray	India
Gillian Armstrong	Australia	Ritwik Ghatak	India
Jane Campion	Australia	Mrinal Sen	India
Baz Luhrmann	Australia	Shyam Benegal	India
Carlos Diegues	Brazil	Luchino Visconti	Italy
Glauber Rocha	Brazil	Federico Fellini	Italy
Pereira dos Santos	Brazil	Michaelangelo Antonioni	Italy
Raùl Ruiz	Chile		
Xie Jin	China	Piero Paolo Pasolini	Italy
Chen Kaige	China	Bernardo Bertolucci	Italy
King Hu	China	Giuseppe Tornatore	Italy
Zhang Zimou	China	Akira Kurosawa	Japan
Ang Lee	China	Nagisa Oshima	Japan
Miloš Forman	Czechoslovakia	Kon Ichikawa	Japan
Jiří Menzel	Czechoslovakia	Kenji Mizoguchi	Japan
Robert Bresson	France	Masahiro Shinoda	Japan
François Truffaut	France	Souleymane Cissé	Mali
Jean-Luc Godard	France	Andrzej Wajda	Poland
Agnes Varda	France	Andrei Tarkovsky	Russia
Alain Resnais	France	Elem Klimov	Russia
Leos Carax	France	Ingmar Bergman	Sweden
Werner Herzog	Germany	Ousmane Sembène	Senegal
Rainer Werner Fassbinder	Germany		

An *auteur* analysis may, in fact, intersect with another approach to writing about film, the **national cinema** or **cultural studies** analysis. Under this approach, films are studied for what they reflect and display regarding a nation's culture; values; religious, political, and gender practices; even its modes of humor. The cultural studies or national cinema approach asks that the writer be attentive to the fact that, perhaps, the single most accessible and most global way that we can understand and appreciate cultural diversity is through film. Multi-national films are making their way to American screens. No longer the domain of small art houses, movies from India, China, Mexico, Argentina, Viet Nam, Nigeria, and Iran have become more mainstream. They are screened in multiplexes and available at the local Blockbuster on video and DVD. Because they are essentially visual, these movies help us see, in all the ramifying meanings of the term, foreign worlds, cultures, and values. We witness, in the minutiae of detail uniquely possible in film, the physical properties of ethnicity: the faces, the clothes, the terrain, the food, the religious practices, the operation of government, and the everyday routines.

Through film, we can hear the different music of other languages, without losing the necessary translation into English (via subtitles) that film uniquely allows. Film guides us through an understanding of the sublime diversity of this planet, as well as the fundamental commonality inherent in all apparent human diversity.

☞ *Watch a movie from a country with a culture foreign to your own. The movie could be a more current film (Examples include:* Osama *[2003, Afghanistan],* Y tu mama también *[2002, Mexico],* Late Marriage *[2002, Israel],* Bloody Sunday *[2002, U.K./Ireland],* Spirited Away *[2002, Japan],* Devdas *[2002, India],* 100 Days *[2001, Rwanda],* Breaking the Waves *[1996, Denmark],* The White Balloon *[Iran, 1995],* or Before the Rain *[1994, Macedonia]) or an established one [Examples include:* Pather Panchali *[1956, India],* Wild Strawberries *[1957, Sweden],* La Dolce Vita *[1960 , Italy],* The Last Wave *[1977, Australia],* The Gods Must Be Crazy *[1980, Botswana], and* Yellow Earth *[1984, China]). Write about what in the film is unique to the country in which it was made, what in the film is common to human experience, and what contrasts can you draw between your culture and the culture portrayed in the film?*

A cultural or national film analysis could lead to another approach to writing about film, the **ideological analysis**. A classic example of this is Sergei Eisenstein's *Battleship Potemkin*. The movie can be appreciated and understood within its national, cultural, and historical context, as it dramatizes the 1905 uprising of Russian sailors against conditions aboard the battleship, the supportive reaction of their rebellion by the citizens of Odessa, and the harsh retribution of the Czarist militia against its own Odessa citizens. The film, however, is also clearly ideological, glorifying and promoting then emerging Soviet Marxist values. A worthy approach to writing about it, thus, would be to engage in an analysis of the specific ways in which *Battleship Potemkin* uses the devices of cinema to promote Eisenstein's ideology.

An ideological analysis explores doctrinaire aspects of a film, the collective, concretized beliefs or attitudes operating throughout the movie. An ideological analysis also could be implemented through the perspective of the writer, who analyzes the film through a particular ideological framework that she/he has assumed. Thus, an ideological approach to writing about film either explores the set of beliefs that the film, itself, is promoting (the film's ideology) or looks at the film through a set of beliefs held by the writer (the writer's ideology).

☞ *Write an ideological analysis that examines an ideological position and the specific ways that a particular ideological film frames the set of beliefs that it is promoting. Film examples include:* The Grapes of Wrath *(1940),* Harlan County U.S.A. *(1976),* Days of Heaven *(1978),* Norma Rae *(1979),* Reds *(1981)* Matewan *(1987),* Running on Empty *(1988),* Roger and Me *(1989),* Europa, Europa *(1990),* Dances with Wolves *(1990),* Thelma and Louise *(1991), and* The Incredibly True Adventure of Two Girls in Love *(1995).*

☞ *Watch a film that is not ideological in intent. Write an analysis of it from an ideological perspective. Examples include a feminist, Marxist, nationalist, religious, humanist, queer theory, politically conservative or politically liberal perspective.*

The word "ideology" can carry something of a negative connotation, as an ideology is a belief held with or *without* criteria of objectivity and is assumed, by the holder, to be obviously true and universally applicable. An ideological film, like the ideological writer of a film analysis, promotes an agenda. The work can and often is, therefore, manipulative, even propagandistic, in its attempt to attain the desired end, conversion of the reader or spectator to the ideology. The most radical ideologues maintain that all films carry either overt or inscribed ideologies.

Whatever focus — ideological or otherwise — that the writer on film assumes, new and emerging technologies are expanding the possibilities of how one could and will write about movies. One final approach to writing about film is a **multi-media analysis**. Under this approach, the writer integrates other media in with the written analysis. For example, if the writing is done in a computer format rather than a paper format, it could integrate digitized clips from the film that correspond to the passage being described in the analysis; or layers of sound could be separated, analyzed by the writing, and integrated into the digitized "paper." Writing in a multi-media approach could, perhaps, be collaborative, like film production, itself, with the modes of collaboration limited only by the ingenuity of the multi-media writers, themselves.

Writers on film can integrate a multi-media approach within a print (literal paper copy) of a film analysis. As film is so highly visual, the writers may want their words to be attended by sketches, for any number of reasons. A single sketch can communicate "the feel" of the total film or provide a representation of the ideas that the writer is describing in words. For example, the writer completing an aesthetic analysis of the literature to film translation of *The Wizard of Oz* (1939) may want to detail how the film expands upon the book's more two-dimensional depiction of Dorothy. The film's Dorothy is replete with youthful complexities, a fragmented sense of identity, and a determination to follow the path to self-understanding to the very end. These qualities could be suggested in a sketch that complements the analysis (see page 260).

In writing about film one final aspect needs mentioning. While much of this text was focused on literature as a parent text for film, the *child*, film, has proved *father to the man,* influencing literary composition in significant ways, as John Dos Passos and Gertrude Stein predicted that it would. Film has permeated writers' sensibilities, in subconscious and in very conscious ways. William Burroughs consciously employs the "cut-up technique" of film's montage editing throughout his novels *Naked Lunch* (1959), *The Soft Machine* (1961), and *The Ticket That Exploded* (1962). Marguerite Duras uses "alternating long shot and close-up that establish the basic rhythm of [her 1958 novel] *Moderato cantabile*" (Cohen, 91); and Manuel Puig describes how his ambition to be a screenwriter led him to be a novelist. "I began to write a script that inevitably became a novel" (273).

Lately, within the very pages of their fiction, writers are making unabashed, unapologetic appeals to premier movie actors to notice, and hopefully star in, film versions of their books, which they hope will be developed by a major film studio into the next blockbuster. Smack within their novels, these writers overtly stroke the machinery of film production and the egos of the very movie stars who, they hope, will agree to act in the actual films of their novels. They do this by name-dropping, by introducing (by name) a real actor, described in very complimentary tones, into the fictional world of their stories.

In *The Hours* (published in 1998), author Michael Cunningham has

The film *The Wizard of Oz* (1939) expands upon the book's more two-dimensional depiction of Dorothy. Judith Hernandez's sketch, which would be integrated as part of a written analysis, illustrates the film's Dorothy as a character of youthful complexities, a fragmented sense of identity, and a determination to follow the road to self-understanding to the very end.

his sophisticated, intelligent, artistic character, Clarissa Vaughan, notice a movie star quickly exiting a film trailer on a street in Greenwich Village. Clarissa is fascinated by the woman, whose "aura of regal assurance" is matched only by the second impression that the woman creates: it is "as if an angel had briefly touched the surface of the world with one sandaled foot." Sure of the wondrous impression the actress had made, Clarissa is unsure, though, if this angel is "Meryl Streep?" or "Vanessa Redgrave?" (27). The film, *The Hours,* opened in 2002, starring Meryl Streep as Clarissa Vaughan.

In 2003, Dan Brown's *The Da Vinci Code* was published. The protagonist, Robert Langdon, is a full professor of Religious Symbology at Harvard University. With an impressive *curriculum vitae* that matches his "sharp blue eyes," his "strong jaw," his "thicket of coarse black hair," his "dimpled chin," and his voice which "his female students describe as 'chocolate for the ears,'" Langdon has been named by *Boston Magazine* as "one of that city's top ten most intriguing people" (8, 9). Brown goes on to describe his perfect male character as "Harrison Ford in Harrison Tweed" (9). As we read, we may have wondered how long it would be before *Variety* described "Harrison Ford in *The Da Vinci Code.*" (As it happens, the role went to Tom Hanks.)

The gardens of earthly delight that we know of as literature and film, cross-fertilize and produce all nature of hybrids — exotic and glorious, pedestrian and predictable. We can only hope that the new generation of gardeners, writers and filmmakers, recognize how rich a cross-fertilizing source literature and film are for one another.

The Aesthetic Rubric

1. The film must communicate definite ideas concerning the *integral* meaning and value of the literary text, as the filmmakers interpret it.

2. The film must exhibit a collaboration of filmmaking skills (the details of which are provided in Chapter II).

3. The film must demonstrate an audacity to create a work that stands as a world apart, that exploits the literature in such a way that a self-reliant, but related, aesthetic offspring is born.

4. The film cannot be so self-governing as to be completely independent of or antithetical to the source material.

APPENDIX B

Shot Sequences: Decoupage and Storyboard

Decoupage

Film Title: *Lord of the Rings: The Fellowship of the Ring*
DVD Location of Shot Sequence
   Title 1; Chapter 19; beginning at 1:15:58
Group Members: Heather Strout

Images	Spoken Words	Music	Sound Effects
Quarter shot, high angle of Gandalf; segues into dolly which ends withquarter shot, low angle of Lord Elrond 9 secs. Shot 1.	Gandalf: *You're beginning to mend.* Lord Elrond: *Welcome to Rivendell, Frodo Baggins*	Dreamy music	Birds chirping
Quarter shot, high angle of Frodo Baggins in bed; camera stationary 2 secs. Shot 2.		↓	↓

Long shot, high angle of Rivendell; camera zooms-in 12 secs. Shot 3.				Horse trotting
Full-shot, high angle of Frodo Baggins walking -> long shot of Rivendell; camera tracks 11 secs. Shot 4.				Birds chirping Frodo walking Waterfall cascading
Quarter shot, slight high angle of Frodo and Sam; camera tracks 3 secs. Shot 5.				
Three quarter shot -> mid-shot, high angle of Frodo, Sam, Merry, and Pip; camera tracks 14 secs. Shot 6.	Sounds of general cheer of the four friends reuniting			Birds chirping
Long shot, straight-on of Bilbo Baggins writing; camera tracks 2 secs. Shot 7.		↓	↓	

Mid-shot, straight-on of Frodo, Sam, Merry, and Pip -> Frodo exiting frame; camera stationary 2 secs. Shot 8.	Frodo: *Bilbo!*			
Mid-shot, high angle of Bilbo -> quarter shot, straight-on of Bilbo and Frodo embracing; camera dollies-up slightly 2 secs. Shot 9.	Bilbo: *Hello, Frodo, my lad! Oh...*			Birds chirping Bilbo clapping Frodo on the back
Close-up, high angle, slightly oblique of page from Bilbo's book: *there and back again, a hobbit's tale, by Bilbo Baggins* 4 secs. Shot 10.	Frodo: *There and back again...*			Birds chirping

Storyboard

Film Title: *Lord of the Rings: The Fellowship of the Ring*
DVD Location of Shot Sequence: Title 1; Chapter 19; beginning at 1:15:58
Drawn by: Heather Strout

Shot 1

Shot 2

Shot 3

Shot 4

Shot 5

Shot 6

Shot 7

Shot 8

Shot 9   Shot 10

Shot Sequence: Decoupage
(Sample grid)

Film Title:

Group Members:

(Number the first shot in your *decoupage* "number 1," no matter where the shot sequence appears in the film. Continue the numeration sequentially. Numbers should correspond to the same shots depicted in your storyboard.)

Images	Spoken Words	Music	Sound Effects
Shot 1.			
2.			
3.			
4.			
5.			

Shot Sequence: Storyboard
(Sample grid)

Film Title:

Group Members:

(Number the first shot in your storyboard "number 1," no matter where the shot sequence appears in the film. Continue the numeration sequentially. Numbers should correspond to the same shots depicted in the *decoupage*.)

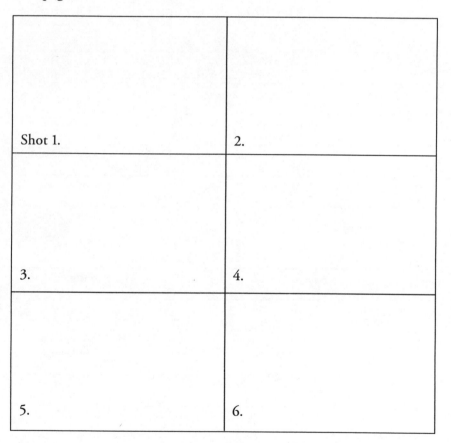

Shakespeare Plays on Film

Play Title	Film Title	Year Released (Country)	Director
Antony and Cleopatra (1608)			
	Antony and Cleopatra	1972 (U.K./Spain)	Charlton Heston
As You Like It (1599)			
	As You Like It (silent)	1908 (U.S.A.)	Kenean Buel
	As You Like It (silent)	1912 (U.S.A.)	Charles Kent
	As You Like It	1936 (U.K.)	Paul Czinner
	As You Like It	1978 (U.K.)	Basil Coleman
	As You Like It	1985 (Canada)	Herb Roland
	As You Like It	1992 (U.K.)	Christine Edzard
The Comedy of Errors (1593)			
	The Boys from Syracuse (musical)	1940 (Germany)	A. Edward Sutherland
Coriolanus (1608)			
	Coriolanus	1979 (U.S.A.)	Wilford Leach
Cymbeline (1611)			

Play Title	Film Title	Year Released (Country)	Director
	Cymbeline (silent)	1913 (U.S.A.)	Frederick Sullivan
	Cymbeline (silent)	1925 (Germany)	Ludwig Berger
	Cymbeline (silent)	1981 (U.S.A.)	Patrick Tucker
	Cymbeline	1982 (U.K.)	Elijah Moshinsky
Hamlet (1601)	(There are, at least, forty-five film versions of *Hamlet*. Random samplings include:)		
	Le Duel de Hamlet (silent)	1900 (France)	Clement Maurice
	Amleto (silent)	1917 (Italy)	Eleuterio Rodolfi
	The Mystery of Hamlet (silent)	1921 (Germany)	Sven Gade, Heinz Schall
	Khoon Ka Khoon	1935 (India)	Sohrab Modi
	Hamlet	1948 (U.K.)	Laurence Olivier
	Hamlet	1953 (U.S.A.)	George Schaefer
	Der Rest ist Schweigen (The Rest is Silence)	1960 (Germany)	Helmut Kautner
	Hamlet	1960 (Germany)	Franz Peter Wirth
	The Bad Sleep Well	1960 (Japan)	Akira Kurosawa
	Hamlet	1964 (U.S.S.R.)	Grigori Kozintsev (from Boris Pasternak's Russian translation of the play)
	Hamlet	1964 (U.S.A.)	John Gielgud
	Hamlet	1969 (U.K.)	Tony Richardson
	Hamlet	1970 (U.K./U.S.A.)	Peter Wood

Play Title	Film Title	Year Released (Country)	Director
	Hamlet, Prince of Denmark	1989 (India)	S. Nathan
	Hamlet	1990 (U.S.A.)	Franco Zeffirelli
	Hamlet	1990 (U.S.A.)	Kevin Kline and Kirk Browning
	Hamlet	1996 (U.S.A./U.K.)	Kenneth Branagh
	Hamlet	2000 (U.S.A.)	Michael Almereyda
	Hamlet X	2003 (Germany)	Herbert Fritsch
Henry IV, Part I (1597)			
Henry IV, Part II (1598)			
	Chimes at Midnight	1967 (Spain/ Switzerland)	Orson Welles
	My Own Private Idaho	1991 (U.S.A.)	Gus Van Sant
Henry V (1599)			
	Henry V	1944 (U.K.)	Laurence Olivier
	Henry V	1989 (U.K.)	Kenneth Branagh
	Henry V	2003 (U.S.A.)	Neal J. Gauger
Henry VIII (1613)			
	Henry VIII (silent)	1911 (U.K.)	William G. Barker
Julius Caesar (1599)			
	Julius Caesar (silent)	1908 (U.S.A.)	J. Stuart Blackton and William V. Ranous
	Julius Caesar (silent)	1911 (U.K./Portugal)	Frank R. Benson
	Cajus Julius Caesar (silent)	1914 (Italy)	Enrico Guazzoni

Play Title	Film Title	Year Released (Country)	Director
	Julius Caesar	1950 (U.S.A.)	David Bradley
	Julius Caesar	1970 (U.K.)	Stuart Burge
	Julius Caesar	1953 (U.S.A.)	Joseph L. Mankiewicz
King John (1591)			
	King John (3 minutes, early silent)	1899 (U.K.)	Sir Herbert Beerbohm Tree
King Lear (1606)			
	King Lear (silent)	1909 (U.S.A.)	J. Stuart Blackton and William V. Ranous
	King Lear (silent)	1916 (U.S.A.)	Ernest C. Warde
	The Yiddish King Lear	1934 (U.S.A.)	Harry Thomashefsky
	King Lear	1948 (U.K.)	Royston Morley
	King Lear	1953 (U.S.A.)	Andrew McCullough and Peter Brook
	Karol Lir	1970 (U.S.S.R.)	Grigori Kozintsev
	King Lear	1971 (U.K.)	Peter Brook
	King Lear	1975 (U.K.)	Jonathan Miller
	King Lear	1976 (U.K.)	Steve Rumbelow
	King Lear	1977 (U.S.A.)	Edwin Sherin
	King Lear	1982 (U.K./U.S.A.)	Jonathan Miller
	King Lear	1983 (U.K.)	Michael Elliott
	Ran	1985 (Japan)	Akira Kurosawa
	King Lear	1987 (France)	Jean-Luc Godard
	King Lear	1997 (U.K.)	Richard Eyre

Play Title	Film Title	Year Released (Country)	Director
	A Thousand Acres	1997 (U.S.A.)	Jocelyn Moorhouse
Love's Labour's Lost (1595)			
	Love's Labours Lost	2000 (U.K.)	Kenneth Branagh
Macbeth (1606)			
	Macbeth (silent)	1916 (U.S.A.)	John Emerson
	Macbeth	1948 (U.S.A.)	Orson Welles
	Joe MacBeth	1955 (U.K.)	Ken Hughes
	Throne of Blood/ The Castle of the Spider's Web	1957 (Japan)	Akira Kurosawa
	Macbeth	1972 (U.K.)	Roman Polanski
	Men of Respect	1990 (U.S.A.)	William Reilly
	Macbeth-Sangrador	1999 (Venezuala)	Leonardo Henriquez
	Rave Macbeth	2001 (Germany)	Klaus Knoesel
	Scotland Pa	2002 (USA)	Billy Morrissette
Measure For Measure (1604)			
	Dente per Dente	1943 (Italy)	Marco Elter
The Merchant of Venice (1598)			
	The Merchant of Venice (silent)	1908 (U.S.A.)	J. Stuart Blackton
	The Merchant of Venice (silent)	1912 (U.S.A.)	Barry O'Neill
	The Merchant of Venice (silent)	1914 (U.S.A.)	Phillip Smalley and Lois Weber

Play Title	Film Title	Year Released (Country)	Director
	The Merchant of Venice (silent)	1916 (U.K.)	Walter West
	The Merchant of Venice (silent)	1922 (U.K.)	Challis Sanderson
	Zalim Saudagar	1941 (India)	J. J. Madan
	Le Marchand de Venise	1953 (Italy)	Pierre Billon
	The Maori Merchant of Venice	2002 (New Zealand)	Don Selwyn
	The Merchant of Venice	2004 (USA)	Michael Radford
The Merry Wives of Windsor (1597)			
	The Merry Wives of Windsor (silent)	1910 (U.S.A.)	Francis Boggs
	Die Lustigen Weiber von Windsor (musical)	1950 (East Germany)	Georg Wildhagen
	The Merry Wives of Windsor (opera)	1952 (Germany)	Georg Wildhagen
	Die Lustigen Weiber von Windsor (musical)	1965 (Austria)	Georg Tressler
A Midsummer Night's Dream (1596)			
	A Midsummer Night's Dream (silent, 12 mins.)	1909 (U.S.A.)	J. Stuart Blackton and Charles Kent
	Ein Sommernachtstraum (silent)	1924 (Germany)	Hans Neumann
	A Midsummer Night's Dream	1935 (U.S.A.)	Max Reinhardt and William Dieterle
	Sen Noci Svatojanske (animation)	1959 (Czechoslovakia)	Jiri Trnka
	A Midsummer Night's Dream (ballet)	1967 (U.S.A.)	George Balanchine and Dan Erikson

Play Title	Film Title	Year Released (Country)	Director
	A Midsummer Night's Dream	1968 (U.K.)	Peter Hall
	A Midsummer Night's Dream	1996 (U.K.)	Adrian Noble
	William Shakespeare's A Midsummer Night's Dream	1999 (U.K./Italy)	Michael Hoffman
	Midsummer	1999 (U.S.A.)	James Kerwin
	The Children's Midsummer Night's Dream	2001 (U.K.)	Christine Edzard
Much Ado About Nothing (1598)			
	Much Ado About Nothing	1973 (U.S.A.)	A. J. Antoon
	Much Ado About Nothing	1984 (U.K.)	Stuart Burge
	Much Ado About Nothing	1993 (U.K./U.S.A.)	Kenneth Branagh
Othello (1604)			
	Othello (silent)	1907 (Germany)	Franz Porten
	Othello (silent)	1908 (U.S.A.)	William V. Ranous
	Othello (silent)	1922 (Germany)	Dimitri Buchowetzki
	Men Are Not Gods	1937 (U.K.)	Walter Reisch
	Othello	1946 (U.K.)	David MacKane
	A Double Life	1947 (U.S.A.)	George Cukor
	Othello	1952 (Morocco/Italy)	Orson Welles
	Il Peccato di Anna (Anna's Sin)	1953 (Italy)	Camillo Mastrocinque
	Othello	1955 (U.S.S.R.)	Sergei Yutkevich
	Othello (ballet)	1960 (U.S.S.R.)	Vakhtang Chabukiani

Play Title	Film Title	Year Released (Country)	Director
	All Night Long	1962 (U.K.)	Basil Dearden
	Othello	1965 (U.K.)	Stuart Burge
	Catch My Soul (rock opera)	1973 (U.S.A.)	Patrick McGoohan
	Othello (U.S.A.)	1980	Liz White
	Othello, el comando negro	1982 (Spain/France)	Max H. Boulois
	Othello	1995 (U.K.)	Oliver Parker
	O	2001 (U.S.A.)	Tim Blake Nelson
Pericles, Prince of Tyre (1608)			
	Pericles, Prince of Tyre	1984 (U.K.)	David Hugh Jones
Richard II (1595)			
	Richard II	2001 (U.S.A.)	John Farrell
Richard III (1592)			
	Richard III (silent)	1908 (U.S.A.)	J. Stuart Blackton and William V. Ranous
	Richard III (silent)	1911 (U.K.)	Frank R. Benson
	Richard III (silent)	1912 (U.S.A./ France)	James Keane and Andre Calmettes
	Tower of London	1939 (U.S.A.)	Rowland V. Lee
	Richard III	1955 (U.K.)	Laurence Olivier
	Tower of London	1962 (U.S.A.)	Roger Corman
	Richard III	1986 (France)	Raoul Ruiz
	Richard III	1995 (U.S.A.)	Richard Loncraine

Play Title	Film Title	Year Released (Country)	Director
	Looking for Richard	1996 (U.S.A.)	Al Pacino
Romeo and Juliet (1596)			
	Romeo and Juliet (silent)	1900 (France)	Clement Maurice
	Romeo and Juliet (silent)	1908 (U.S.A.)	J. Stuart Blackton
	Romeo and Juliet (silent)	1911 (U.S.A.)	Barry O'Neill
	Romeo and Juliet (silent)	1916 (U.S.A.)	J. Gordon Edwards and Maxwell Karger
	Romeo and Juliet (silent)	1916 (U.S.A.)	Francis X. Bushman and John W. Noble
	Romeo and Juliet	1936 (U.S.A.)	George Cukor
	Romeo and Juliet	1944 (Mexico)	Miguel Delgado
	Giuliete e Romeo/ Romeo and Juliet	1954 (Italy/U.K.)	Renato Castellani
	Carry On Teacher	1959 (U.K.)	Peter Rogers
	Romeo, Julie a tma (Sweet Light in a Dark Room)	1960 (Czechoslovakia)	Moris Ergas
	West Side Story	1961 (U.S.A.)	Robert Wise and Jerome Robbins
	Romanoff and Juliet	1961 (U.S.A.)	Peter Ustinov
	Panic Button	1964 (U.S.A.)	George Sherman
	Los Tarantos	1964 (Spain)	Rovira-Beleta
	Romeo and Juliet (ballet)	1966 (U.K.)	Paul Czinner
	Giulietta e Romeo	1968 (Italy)	Riccardo Freda
	Romeo and Juliet	1968 (U.K./Italy)	Franco Zeffirelli
	Romeo and Juliet	1978 (U.K.)	Alvin Rakoff
	Romeo and Juliet	1982 (U.S.A.)	William Woodman

Play Title	Film Title	Year Released (Country)	Director
	China Girl	1987 (U.S.A.)	Abel Ferrara
	Romeo and Juliet	1988 (U.K.)	Joan Kemp-Welch
	Romeo–Juliet	1990 (Belgium)	Armando Acosta
	Zebrahead	1992 (U.S.A.)	Anthony Drazan
	Romeo and Juliet	1993 (Canada)	Norman Campbell
	Romeo and Juliet	1994 (U.K.)	Alan Horrox
	William Shakespeare's Romeo + Juliet	1996 (U.S.A.)	Baz Luhrmann
	Shakespeare in Love	1998 (U.S.A.)	John Madden
The Taming of the Shrew (1604)			
	The Taming of the Shrew	1929 (U.S.A.)	Sam Taylor
	Kiss Me Kate	1953 (U.S.A.)	George Sidney
	The Taming of the Shrew	1966 (U.S.A./Italy)	Franco Zeffirelli
	10 Things I Hate about You	1999 (U.S.A.)	Gil Junger
The Tempest (1611)			
	The Tempest (silent)	1908 (U.K.)	Percy Stow
	Tempest	1939 (U.K.)	Dallas Bower
	Forbidden Planet	1956 (U.S.A.)	Fred McLeod
	The Tempest	1956 (U.K.)	Robert Atkins and Ian Atkins
	The Tempest	1960 (U.S.A.)	George Shaefer
	The Tempest	1968 (U.K.)	Basil Coleman
	The Tempest	1979 (U.K.)	John Gorrie

Play Title	Film Title	Year Released (Country)	Director
	The Tempest: by William Shakespeare, as seen through the eyes of Derek Jarman	1980 (U.K.)	Derek Jarman
	Tempest	1982 (U.S.A.)	Paul Mazursky
	Prospero's Books	1991 (U.K./France)	Peter Greenaway
	The Tempest	1999 (U.S.A.)	Jack Bender
Titus Andronicus (1594)			
	Titus Andronicus	1999 (U.S.A.)	Christopher Dunne
	Titus	1999 (U.S.A./Italy)	Julie Taymor
	Titus Andronicus	2000 (U.S.A.)	Richard Griffin
Twelfth Night (1602)			
	Twelfth Night (silent)	1910 (U.S.A.)	Charles Kent and Eugene Mullin
	Dvenadsataya Noch	1956 (Russia)	Yan Frid
	Eros Perversion	1979 (Italy)	Ron Wertheim
	Twelfth Night	1987 (Argentina)	Neil Armfield
	Dvenadsataya Noch	1992 (Russia)	Mariya Muat
	Twelfth Night	1996 (U.K.)	Trevor Nunn
The Two Gentlemen of Verona (1594)			
	Zwei Herren aus Verona	1963 (West Germany)	Hans-Dieter Schwarze
The Winter's Tale (1611)			
	The Winter's Tale (silent)	1910 (U.S.A.)	Theodore Marston and Barry O'Neil
	The Winter's Tale	1968 (U.K.)	Frank Dunlop

Glossary of Film
and Literary Terms

Accelerated Motion *see* **Fast Motion**

Aerial Shot (Bird's Eye): A shot filmed by a camera, placed at a great height, as attached to a helicopter or a plane.

Allegory: A narrative that employs extended metaphors in such a way as to have characters, actions, and objects assume abstract meanings and values.

Allusion: A brief reference to a person, event, character, or artistic work; allusions are effective to the extent that the audience shares the common body of knowledge being referenced.

Ambiguity: The intentional or unintentional expression of an idea in language that yields more than one meaning and leaves uncertainty as to the intended significance of the statement.

Analytic Editing: The technique of editing together film sequences or literary passages in such a way that an emphatic meaning is constructed; editing tightly constructed on reasoning with the intention of leading the reader or viewer to specific percepts.

Analytical Criticism: A mode of criticism that holds that a work of art is an autonomous whole, whose meaning is stable and can be discerned through application of rigorous and logical systems of analysis.

Anamorphic Lens: A camera lens that produces a widescreen image.

Answer Print (Trial Print/Trial Composite): The first draft of the complete film, including editing, synchronized sound, and light and color adjustments. Further changes are usually made in this print before **release prints** are made.

Anti-hero: The protagonist of a film or literary work who has attributes opposite of those a traditional **hero.**

Apostrophe: A figure of speech in which a personified object or an absent person is directly addressed.

Art Director *see* **Production Designer**

Aspect Ratio: The height-to-width ratio of the image projected on the screen. The aspect ratios are: Standard Wide: 1::1.85; widescreen/CinemaScope: 1::2.35.

Asynchronous Sound: Any sound whose source is not visible on screen; also referred to as "off screen sound."

Auteur **Theory:** Derived from French term for "author"; first advanced by the film journal *Cahiers du cinéma,* the theory asserts that a movie, though a collaborative art form, has a dominant influence, usually seen as the director. *Auteur* theory further developed into sustained studies of the formal characteristics and recurring themes of individual directors.

Avant-garde: Art that exhibits striking, self-aware innovations in style, form, and subject matter, often constructed in conscious assault against the prevailing values, forms, and traditions of its age.

Back Lighting: Lighting from directly behind the subject, placing it in silhouette.

Best Boy: First assistant to the **gaffer** who is the chief electrician during film production.

Bid: An exhibitor's written request to a distribution company for the right to show a particular film. The request includes all terms relating to finances, advertising, and length of exhibition.

Biographical Film (Biopic): A film that narrates, to varying degrees of authenticity, the life of a real and well-known person.

Bird's Eye Shot *see* **Aerial Shot**

Blacklist: The roster of known and suspected members of the American Communist Party compiled by the House Un-American Activities Committee, headed by Senator Joseph McCarthy. This list resulted in the annihilation of reputations and ruination of lives of many writers and filmmakers working in America.

B-picture: A film made more quickly, more cheaply, and less ambitiously than, for example, a large Hollywood feature; on occasion, these films reach a high degree of artistry and popularity.

Burlesque: A form of comic art characterized by exaggerated, heightened ridicule.

Burn-in: The sudden shift from an image to an all-white screen.

Burn-out: The sudden shift from an all-white screen to an image.

Camera Angle: The position of the camera in relation to the subject being photographed. The most basic camera angles are: high, low, aerial, eye-level, and oblique.

Catharsis: From the Greek word for "purging" (*katharsis*), Aristotle's term for the effect of tragedy on the spectator's emotions. Through an "imaginative participation" with the suffering of the characters, the audience experiences a purging, a sense of emotional release that results in a certain serenity.

Chiaroscuro: From the Italian "chiaro" meaning "clear" and "oscuro" meaning "dark," the technique of placing very dark and very light portions of a work in opposition; a term used to describe a painting, print, photograph, or motion picture with strong, particularly dramatic contrasts of light and dark In painting, some finest examples of this technique are found in the work of Caravaggio and Rembrandt.

Cinema Verite: A style of filmmaking that attempts to replicate real-life; shots are constructed in ways that de-emphasize the technical means of production (camera placement and movement, script, lighting, etc.) and emphasize the reality of the screen world.

CinemaScope (Scope): The trade name (created by 20th Century–Fox) for the widescreen process that utilizes an aspect ratio of 1::2.35.

Cinematographer (Director of Photography/DP): The individual in charge of filming the shots. The cinematographer is responsible for choice of cameras, film stock, lenses, and filters; lighting; general composition; camera placement and movement; and maintenance of a consistency of style throughout the film. As such, the cinematographer often leaves the actual operation of the camera(s) to other camera operators.

Classic (Classicism, Classical):
1. Any work of art that has achieved a long-recognized status for its superior qualities.
2. Any work of art that demonstrates the values and traditions of ancient Greek and Roman culture: restraint, clarity, balance, dominance of reason, logical organization, decorum, elegance, and a harmony of form.

Close-Up: A shot in which the human face or an object fills the frame.

Comedy: Any work that is humorous in its treatment of characters and theme.

Composition: The arrangement of all the elements within the screen image: the objects, lighting, shadows, and color.

Composition in Depth *see* **Deep Focus**

Conflict: The struggle which emerges from an interplay of opposing forces.

Continuity Editing: A style of editing that maintains a continuous and seemingly uninterrupted flow of action between shots.

Continuity Mistake: An error resulting among shots from mismatches in dialogue, direction of movement, props, or costumes.

Contrast: the relationship between both the extremes of lighting in a frame and the intermediate gray scales between light and dark.

Copy Text: The specific text of a literary work that forms the basis against which other versions (editions, impressions, and issues) are compared.

Copyright: The exclusive legal right to use, publish, or reproduce works of literature and art.

Crane Shot: A moving shot taken from a high perspective by a camera mounted in a crane specially constructed for that purpose.

Critic: One who estimates, evaluates, and explores the quality of the work of others. The best critics are knowledgeable in their field, possess a sophisticated aesthetic appreciation, and function much as great teachers do, helping to illuminate matters we may not have seen on our own.

Cross-Cutting (Parallel Editing): Editing that jumps back and forth between two or more locations, causing the audience to see a relationship between two or more events.

Cut:
1. Verb: To edit a film by selecting shots and splicing them together.
2. Noun: A transition made by editing two pieces of film together.

Cutaway: A shot or sequence of shots inserted in such a way as to create a break in continuity, which is usually achieved by creating a jump in time, locale, or action.

Dailies (Rushes): The film prints, generally including the sound recorded while filming, that are processed the same day and sent to the production team for immediate viewing and are used as an indicator of how the film is progressing.

Decelerated Motion *see* **Slow Motion**

Deep Focus: A technique in which objects in the foreground, the mid-ground, and the distant background appear in equally sharp focus.

Depth of Field: Distance between the nearest and furthest points at which the screen image is in focus.

Deus ex machina: From the Latin for "god from the machine," any sudden, unexpected incident in a narrative that restores order and makes the events turn out well.

Diptych: Two separate, independent, similarly shaped canvases or panels, depicting antithetical states of the same basic theme (example: spring and winter) that are hinged together in an attempt to have the viewer meditate on the relation between the opposing conditions.

Director of Photography/DP *see* **Cinematographer**

Dissolve: An editing technique by which one shot gradually merges into the next through the superimposition of a fade-out or fade-in.

Documentary: A film that attempts to convey the reality of actual people, places, and events and focuses on the facts instead of a fictional account of the subject.

Documentary Novel: A term created by literary critic F. O. Matthiessen, for a work of fiction that integrates elaborate and profuse factual detail and cultural information, including newspaper accounts, trial transcripts, and real cultural occurrences.

Dolly Shot *see* **Tracking Shot**

Dub/Dubbing: Dialogue or sound that is recorded and matched to action in shots already filmed.

Edit: The splicing together of separate shots; the two basic styles of editing are **continuity** and **montage editing**. Also, to prepare a work for a wider audience by revising it.

Establishing Shot: A shot or sequence of shots showing the setting (time and place) of a movie or a specific scene; often the opening shot of a film.

Expressionism:
1. An early twentieth century mode of artistic expression that followed and enlarged upon **impressionism** through its effort to objectify inner experience. It rejects realistic methods of verisimilitude because of its belief that objects in art are not representational but transmitters of impressions and moods. Expressionism employs distortion and exaggeration as a means of transforming the physical world into an expression of the inner self.
2. In film, expressionism is characterized by a nightmarish quality, unreal atmosphere, distortion of images, dislocation of time, and rupture of space and logic. It flourished in the 1920s, in part as a response to the mechanization of society, with its tendency to devalue people and art.

Extreme Close-up: A shot which shows a portion of the human face, a small portion of an entirety, or the entirety of a small object.

Extreme Long Shot: A shot filmed from a considerable distance, often a quarter of a mile or farther.

Eye-Level Shot (Straight-on Shot): A shot taken from the height of normal vision or 5' to 6' from the ground.

Eye-line Match: Shots which cut from a character to what that character is seeing.

Fade: A visual transition placed between shots in such as way that the image on screen gradually goes to black (fade-out) or emerges from black (fade-in).

Fast Motion (Accelerated Motion): Mechanical distortion of a shot which causes it to occur at a faster speed than it did in reality.

Figurative Language: Writing that incorporates any of the various figures of speech, such as: **metaphor, simile, personification, hyperbole, irony, apostrophe, metonymy,** and **synecdoche.**

Fill-light: A soft light, normally placed near the camera on the side opposite the **key-light**; it fills in areas left inadequately lit by the key-light or it softens shadows, thereby reducing the **contrast**.

Film Noir: French for "black film"; a style that emerged in Hollywood in the late 1940s through 1950s; characterized by a brutal, violent urban world of crime and corrupt characters; filmed in a manner that emphasizes dark shadows, pools of light, **low-key**/high contrast illumination; the frequent use of extreme high, low, and oblique angles; and slow tracking shots that feel threatening and predatory.

Fin de siècle: The "end of the century"; a term often applied to the transitional period marking the last ten years of a century.

Flash-Forward: A shot or sequence of shots that transports the action of the story into the future.

Flash Pan (Swish Pan): A shot in which the camera pans so rapidly that the images are blurred as they "flash" by; normally used as transition between shots to indicate the passage of time.

Flashback: A shot or shot sequence that transports the narrative action of the story into the past.

Flat Lighting: The distribution of light within the image so that bright and dark tones are not in high contrast.

Foreshortening: The compressing into a single sentence or a single shot sequence any event that recurs multiple times.

Frame:
1. Noun: One single cell from a piece of motion picture film; the boundaries that contain the screen image.
2. Verb: To compose a shot.

Freeze-Frame: A mechanical distortion in which the action appears to come to a dead stop; achieved by reprinting a single frame and splicing it into a sequence many times in succession.

Full Shot: A shot which contains the human body, head to toe, or the visual equivalent of another object.

Gaffer: Chief electrician during film production responsible for supplying, placing, operating, and maintaining the power sources and the required lighting equipment both on a set and on location.

Gauge: The width of a filmstrip as measured in millimeters (mm); 8mm or Super 8mm is the width originally shot for home movies; 16mm for student filmmaking, schools, and museums; 35mm for commercial movie theaters; and 70mm very large-screen theaters.

Genre: The types or categories into which films or literary works are grouped;

from the French (*genre*) for type or kind. Used to indicate a medium, manner, or style of art.

Ghost Writer: Someone whose writing is published under the name of another person.

Grip: A general handyworker who may rig the electrical equipment, construct the lighting scaffolding, lay dolly tracks, push the dolly during shooting, or help build the sets in accord with where and how the camera will move to film the scenes. The name is derived from the fact that this worker must have a "firm grip" on matters.

Hand-Held Shot: A shot made with the camera held in hand; the resulting image lacks the visual stability achieved from mounting the camera on a tripod or other stabilizing fixture.

Hero: The protagonist of a story; the principal character who embodies those superior qualities of a given culture.

High-Angle: A shot in which the camera is positioned above and looks down at the subject, with the resulting effect of diminishing the subject or making it appear vulnerable.

High-Key Lighting: A distribution of light within the frame so that the bright tones predominate.

Humanism: Any expression in art or philosophy that values, exalts, or penetrates into human endeavors, as opposed to divine or supernatural elements.

Hyperbole: A figure of speech marked by exaggeration.

Impressionism: A highly personal mode of artistic expression in which the subject is presented as it appears to the artist's individual temperament rather than as it appears in actuality.

Intertextuality: The relationship between two or more texts that quote from one another, allude to one another, or in any other manner create connections.

Iris: A transitional device used between shots in which the image seems to disappear (iris in) or grow larger (iris out) within the confines of a circle that expands or contracts, much as the iris in a human eye does.

Irony: A figure of speech in which the actual intent is expressed in words or images that carry the opposite meaning.

Jump Cut: A cut that abruptly jumps forward within a single action and creates a sense of discontinuity or dislocation.

Key-Light: The major source of illumination for a shot; the key light is normally positioned above, in front of, and to the side of the visual subject.

Literal: Accurate to the letter, without embellishment or interpretation.

Long Shot: A shot taken with the camera at a distance approximately equal to an orchestra seat from a proscenium stage in a live theater.

Low Angle: A shot in which the camera is positioned below and looks up at the subject, with the resulting effect of empowering the subject.

Low-Key: A distribution of light within the frame so that the **key-light** does not dominate; instead, the scene is underlit, grayer and darker, with shadows and pools of bright light that often contrast with the darkness. Low-key lighting is employed in horror films and **film noir**.

Match on Action/Match on Movement: The editing together of shots to create a continuation of a dramatic action or a particular physical movement across a cut to the subsequent shot.

Match on an Object: The editing together of shots to carry an image of a person, place, or thing across a cut to the subsequent shot.

Matte Shot (Mask Shot): A partial covering placed over a portion of the camera lens to reduce or change the shape of the frame or to allow another image to be inserted later.

Medium (Mid) Shot: An intermediate shot between a close-up and a long shot; refers to a shot of the human body from the waist up.

Melodrama: An unrealistic, pathos-filled tale of romance or domestic situations with stereotypical characters that often include a much-put upon central female character. Melodrama is a combination of drama and *melos*, the Greek for "to play with music," and this genre incorporates music to heighten the emotions of the story.

Metaphor: A figure of speech in which an object is used to refer to something that it does not literally denote in order to suggest a similarity.

Metatext: A text that comments upon, describes, or explains another text; a text in which a writer, artist, or filmmaker analyzes his or her own previous work.

Metonymy: A figure of speech in which a word, phrase, or attribute is substituted for the whole (example: a "crown" for the king).

***Mise-en-Scène*:** A term originally used in the theater to describe the staging of a scene: the set, the placement of the actors, and the lighting. In film, it describes the arrangement of all the compositional elements within the frame of a single shot.

Modernism: An early twentieth century movement characterized by a rejection of tradition and authority in favor of an emphasis on novelty, on the exploration of possibilities, on experiments in structure, and on the ongoing search for uniqueness. Modernist works of literary or visual art value abstract thought and complex reasoning; exhibit an eclectic approach; often collapse together high art and low; blur distinctions between genres; incorporate **ambiguity** and discontinuity; utilize fragmented forms, discontinuous narratives, and seemingly random collages of various materials; reject elaborate formal aesthetics in favor of minimalist designs; and express interest in the individual (the unique self), the subjective perspective, and the inner life, and, consequently, often incorporate psychological elements.

Montage: A form of editing in which shots are joined together in accord with their visual value rather than in accord with narrative continuity. There are two basic methods of montage editing:

Russian: The rapid succession of shots edited in accord with dialectical principles; editing in which images are joined together in a rhythmic pattern that displays a collision of ideas and cinematographic conflicts.

American: The rapid succession of shots edited together, usually by means of super-impositions, swish pans, or dissolves, to convey a visual effect, such as the passing of time.

Narration: A composition that recounts a story, an event, or a series of events.

New Wave: A film style developed in France in 1959–1966, initially by directors Claude Chabrol, François Trauffaut, Jean-Luc Godard, and Alain Resnais. Characteristics of this style include:
1. Realistic, loosely structured plots
2. Nontraditional, unheroic, and unsentimental approach to character
3. Hand-held cameras that create a sense of realism or verisimilitude
4. Experimentation with time and with film space
5. Employment of location and outdoor filming
6. Editing that is elliptical or calls attention to the relationship of the images to one another
7. Existential themes and tones that reinforce that idea that life is absurd
8. Allusions to other films as a means of creating continuity in the film tradition, of paying homage to the work other directors, and of engaging in **self-reflexivity**.

Noh (No) Theater: A classical Japanese performance form, with its origins in the fourteenth century. Noh combines elements of dance, drama, music and poetry into one aesthetic, highly stylized stage art. The actors of Noh plays wear masks (or highly stylized make-up made to look like a mask), speak, or sing monotonally, and are often accompanied by a chorus and traditional Japanese musical instruments The Noh stage traditionally includes a roof or canopy supported by four columns and is usually located outdoors.

Oblique Angle (Tilt Shot): A shot which creates a sense of disequilibrium, created by tilting the camera so that the images recorded appear to lean diagonally; this shot is used to imply that a character is inebriated, hallucinating, or in a foreboding situation.

Off-camera: Any portion of a movie that does not actually appear on screen and in view, but is known to be part of the film's overall information.

One-shot: A shot with a single person in the frame.

Option: The legal right to make an agreement within a specified amount of time; normally books or screenplays are "optioned." Under such an agreement, the party interested in producing the work pays a fee to the writer (normally 10% or less of the agreed purchase price). This fee secures the exclusive production rights to the material within the agreed-upon time. Options provide producers the necessary time to assemble the film's **package** and secure necessary financial backing for the project.

Over-the-shoulder Shot: A shot in which the camera is positioned over the shoulder of one character, who is usually in dialogue with another.

Package: The various major elements needed for the production of a film: the property (book, screenplay), the director, the screenwriter, and the actors. The package is normally assembled by the producer.

Painted Matte Shot: A special-effects shot in which a painted image is combined with a live-action one.

Panning (Pan) Shot: A shot in which the camera remains in place but moves horizontally on its axis; the term comes from "panorama" as the shot often follows movement across a landscape or a field of action.

Parallel Action: Action that is related, but takes place at two or more different locations often at the same time; through the use of **cross cutting**, the film shifts back and forth between the separate, but related, actions.

Parallel Editing *see* **Cross Cutting**

Parallelism: A structural arrangement by which coordinating ideas or actions have coordinating presentation.

Parody: A work that humorously or satirically imitates another work of a more serious nature.

Period Film: Any movie that attempts to recreate or evoke the reality of another time.

Persistence of Vision: The capacity of the eye to retain an image for a brief moment after it has disappeared. Persistence of vision allows the human brain to perceive the separate frames of projected film as coherent, moving images.

Personification: A figure of speech in which animals, objects, ideas, or abstractions are endowed with human qualities.

Pixel: The smallest dots that make up the image on a video screen; the greater the number of pixels the greater the image's resolution. "Pixel" is a shortened version of "picture element."

Plot: The particular structure of a **narration**; the arrangement of events that form a **story**.

Point of View: The position, perspective, or vantage from which something is observed; the source and scope of the narrative voice of a work of literature or film.

Postmodernism: Follows the basic ideas of **modernism** by emphasizing novelty; by rejecting formal aesthetic standards; by incorporating **ambiguity** and discontinuity; and by collapsing the boundaries between genres and between high and low forms of art. Postmodernism, however, places greater stress on reflexivity, self-consciousness, and the decentered, dehumanized subject. While postmodernism is a close relative of modernism, it has a different philosophical underpinning. Modernism recognizes and laments a meaningless universe, and modernist works believe that art can provide the unity, coherence, and meaning which has been lost in modern life; art can do what other human institutions fail to do. Postmodernism, in contrast, accepts the unrelenting absurdity of all existence, including the existence of art. Consequently, postmodernism often involves constructions of nonsense as comments on the belief that even art cannot make meaning where there is none.

Post-structuralism: A response to structuralism, most clearly in its expansion upon structuralism's central claim that texts are the product of complex systems and must be approached through any number of reductivist methodologies (studying patterns, binary systems, and structures). Post-structuralists further the structuralists' arguments by claiming that an infinite interplay of signifiers exist within a given text and that one should not impose or privilege one reading of a text over another. There are many post-structuralist theories, but few stand in agreement. Central post-structuralists include: Jacques Derrida, Michel Foucault, Roland Barthes, and Jean Baudrillard.

Production Designer (Art Director): The person in charge of the design, construction, and overall physical appearance of the various settings (locations and sound stages) and costumes of a film.

Protagonist: The principal character in a story, who may be heroic, non-heroic, or anti-heroic.

Psychological Novel: Prose fiction which emphasizes characterization (characters' motivations and internal actions) over external dramatic development.

Pure Cinema: The aesthetic standard that asserts that a film is most successful when it uses, manipulates, and exploits the *image*, alone, unaided by extraneous devices of sound.

Reaction Shot: A shot of a person responding to something or someone in the preceding shot

Realism: A method that attempts a truthful treatment of its material through a fidelity to the actuality of its representation, untouched by romantic or impressionistic coloring.

Reading: An audition for a part during which the actor reads from the script.

Read-through: A preliminary rehearsal in which the actors read the script aloud, in order to acquaint the cast with one another and to begin discussions among the director and them.

Record Film: The filming of a specific event (example: a baseball game) or series of events (example: the World Series) in a straightforward manner, without artistic input.

Release: The initial exhibition and distribution of a film. If the budget is large enough, this initial exhibition is preceded by previews and advertising campaigns.

Release Print: That particular form of the film that is the composite print distributed for exhibition. These are made from the **sample print** and in large numbers for commercial distribution.

Remake: A newer version of a film that had already been made.

Reverse-angle: A shot taken by a camera placed opposite from where the previous shot was taken.

Roman Noir: French for "black novel"; used to refer to the English gothic novel of the nineteenth century, a genre in which mystery, the supernatural, horror, villainous forces, dark shadows and eerie passageways abound.

Romance: Any narrative work that emphasizes a love relationship at the expense of all other story elements.

Romantic (Romanticism):
1. Any work of art from the eighteenth and nineteenth centuries that functions as a reaction to neo-classicism.
2. Any work of art that demonstrates the Romantic era's values and traditions: the significance of nature to inspire and to heal; the primacy of imagination and intuition over reason and logic; the interest in and celebration of ordinary people and language; the belief in limitless potential and perfectibility; a fascination with the supernatural, strange, unusual, aberrant, distant, mystical, exotic or bizarre; the eminence of the individual; and a melancholic tone.

Rough Cut: An early edited version of the composite film that assembles the general structure of the movie, but lacks the proficient, crafted work of the final cutting.

Running Time: The duration of a projected film.

Rushes see **Dailies**

Sample Print: That final print of a film that is intended for distribution. It is the composite of choices made regarding selection of specific **takes**, editing, sound mixing, and special effects. The sample print is the master copy, used for duplicating the **release prints**.

Satire: Any work which blends criticism with wit and humor in an attempt to bring about reform.

Score: Music composed for a film; the musical background of any movie.

Screenplay: The movie script which is comprised of dialogue, scenes, and descriptions of action and may also include camera placement and movement.

Second Unit: A small group of technicians that shoot those scenes that do not require the presence of the director, the principal cinematographer, or the central actors (example: location shots, establishing shots, and scenes involving extras). A second unit is normally employed on larger productions.

Self-reflexivity: A work of art that meditates upon its own status as art.

Semiotics: From the Greek word for "sign" (*semeion*); the study of signs as developed by the Swiss linguist, Ferdinand de Saussure; the French anthropologist, Claude Lévi-Strauss; and the American linguist, C. S. Pierce.

Sequence: A series of related film shots, edited together, to form a coherent dramatic or visual unit.

Serial: A single story divided and presented in a sequential series of individual units: literary chapters or short films.

Set: An artificially constructed environment in which a movie's action is photographed.

Sharp Focus: A shot in which the edges are clearly defined and the details are markedly visible.

Shock Editing: Any editing practice that is so unexpected or discordant as to startle the spectator. The effect of shock editing only works if it is used sparingly.

Shot:
1. The amount of visual information contained within a frame. The basic shots are: extreme close up (ecu), close up (cu), quarter (qs), medium (ms), full (fs), long (ls), and extreme long (els).
2. A sustained point of view recorded by the camera; the continuous recording of the camera from start to stop. Films are traditionally composed of **sequences** of shots edited together.

Simile: A figure of speech, usually introduced by "like" or "as," that expresses a resemblance between things of different kinds.

Slow Motion (Decelerated Motion): Mechanical distortion of a shot which causes it to occur at a slower speed than it did in reality.

Sneak Preview: The exhibition of a film, prior to its release, in order to furnish important information regarding audience reaction and promotion/distribution strategies.

Soft Focus: A shot in which an image is created to appear hazy, not sharply defined, often evoking a romantic effect.

Sound Track:
1. The sound portion of a film which includes spoken words, sound effects, and music.
2. The narrow band along one side of a print of film upon which the sound is set down.

Split Screen: The dividing of film frames into two or more sections, each featuring a separate image, working as a composite.

Star System: A system in Hollywood in the 1920s through the early 1950s by which a film studio would discover young actors, sign them, and cultivate their image into that of a star through heavy publicity and script development. The star worked exclusively for one studio, which, in turn, managed and publicized the on-screen and off-screen life of the performer and constructed an image of the star that appealed to the public in simplistic or complex ways.

Steadicam: A trade name that has become synonymous with any camera that allows the cinematographer to maintain a steady image during hand-held filming in situations where it is not possible to use a **tracking shot**. The camera operator wears the Steadicam, made up of a vest-like apparatus with an articulated arm which holds the camera.

Stereotype: Any character or story derived from other works and so familiar to the audience as to lack any originality.

Story: A narration of dramatic events occurring within a particular time-sequence.

Story Treatment: A brief explanation, written in simple prose, of a story, including the action, characters, and scenes. Story treatments seldom contain dialogue or shots and are anywhere from one to forty pages long. The treatment forms the basis for a future script.

Storyboard: A series of sketches placed in sequence, much like a comic strip, that provide a visual map for the entire film.

Straight-on Shot *see* **Eye-Level Shot**

Stream of Consciousness Novel: Prose fiction in which the inner thoughts and feelings of a character are presented as they occur; a record of the conscious experiences of a character as a continuous, flowing series of images and ideas running through the mind and functioning as a variation on the **psychological novel**.

Style: The specific manner in which something is composed, expressed, or performed; the particular way in which the ideas expressed in any work find form in the individuality of the author's mode of expression.

Subjective Shot: A shot that presents visual information from the point of view of a particular character; a shot in which the camera is placed in such a way that it replicates what a character would be viewing

Subplot: A subordinate story or complication that runs through and contributes to the principal plot.

Superimposition: A shot in which one or more images are placed on top of one another.

Swish Pan *see* **Flash Pan**

Symbol/Symbolism: A significance given to inanimate objects, by which philosophical, spiritual, religious, or social abstractions are concretized; an object that indicates something beyond itself.

Synecdoche: A figure of speech in which an part is substituted for the whole (example: using "Hollywood" for the entire American film industry).

Take: The single, uninterrupted filming of a shot. Several takes are normally filmed and numbered for one shot, and the best take is edited into the movie. The number assigned to the shot always remains the same, but each take is given a different number. For example: Shot 341, Take 1; Shot 341, Take 2.... As filming is going on, the production team keeps a running track of what takes appear most successful.

Tale: A simple narrative, in prose or verse, that lacks complications of plot.

Telephoto Lens: A camera lens that operates much like a telescope, bringing into focus a subject in the distance, while flattening or blurring other planes of action in the frame.

Theater of the Absurd: An avant-garde genre of drama that presents the absurdity of the human condition created by discarding rational narrative and theatrical devices and realistic forms.

Theme: The central or dominating idea in a work; an abstract concept that is made concrete through the repetition of words, images, or music.

Theme Music/Theme Song: The recurring musical melody or musical passage that runs throughout the film and comes to be associated with a principal character, a theme, or a dominant emotion.

Three-Shot: A shot encompassing three actors.

Tie-in: A book that is based on and written subsequent to a specific film; often, it is a novelized version of the screenplay.

Tilt Shot *see* **Oblique Angle**

Tone: The mood of a work; the author's implied attitude toward the subject.

Tracking Shot (Dolly Shot): A shot in which the camera is moved by means of wheeled support and is generally positioned parallel to its moving subject.

Tragedy: A dramatic form in which the principal character is ruined or suffers extreme hardship and sorrow, especially as a consequence of a tragic flaw, a moral weakness, or an inability to overcome opposing circumstances.

Trailer: A short film of one to three minutes produced to advertise a soon-to-be-released or newly-released film.

Treatment: A short, written account of a film done prior to the drafting of the screenplay; it includes a detailed description of the story, but does not include dialogue or shots.

Trial Print/Trial Composite *see* **Answer Print**

Two-shot: A shot with two people in the frame.

Unit: The individual crew(s) working on a film; larger film productions have both a first unit, which is responsible for filming the principal shots, and a second unit, that works on ancillary shots.

Unreliable Narrator: An narrator whose account of events is built upon errors, faulty understanding, or misjudgments; a narrator who intentionally misleads in the reporting of events.

Voice-over: Commentary by an unseen character or narrator.

Westerns: Literary or film works set in the western United States and centered on the adventurous lives of settlers, cowboys, scouts, and native Americans in the newly emerging frontier.

Wide-Angle Shot: A shot in which a camera lens of shorter-than-normal focal length is employed to photograph images that appear in a longer horizontal plane of action and in a greater depth of field.

Wide-screen: Any **aspect ratio** wider than 1:1.33; commercial leaders in wide-screen film include: CinemaScope, Techniscope, VistaVision, and Panavision.

Wipe: A transition from one shot to another in which one shot replaces another, horizontally or vertically.

Writers Guild of America (WGA): The professional union for screenwriters. The guild also represents writers for television and radio.

Zoom: The simulation of camera movement toward or away from the subject by means of the movement of a lens of variable focal length.

Bibliography

Akutagawa, Ryunosuke. *Rashōmon and Other Stories.* Trans. Takashi Kojima. Tokyo, Japan: Charles E. Tuttle Company, 1996.

Andrew, J. Dudley. *Concepts in Film Theory.* New York: Oxford University Press, 1984.

Arnheim, Rudolph. *Film as Art.* Berkeley: University of California Press, 1971.

_____. "Visual Thinking." In *Education of Vision*, ed. Gyorgy Kepes, 1–15. New York: Braziller, 1965.

Bachelard, Gaston. *The Poetics of Space.* Trans. Maria Jolas. Boston, MA: Beacon Press, 1969.

Balazs, Bela. *Theory of Film, Character and Growth of a New Art.* Trans. Edith Bone. New York: Dover Publications, 1970.

Ball, Robert Hamilton. *Shakespeare on Silent Film.* New York: Theater Arts Books, 1968.

Barthes, Roland. "The Death of the Author." In *Theories of Authorship*, ed. John Caughie. London: Routeledge and Kegan Paul, 1981.

_____. "Diderot, Brecht, Eisenstein." Trans. Stephen Heath. *Screen* 15:2 (1974): 33–39.

Baudry, Jean Louis. "The Apparatus: Metapsychological Approaches to the Impression of Reality in Cinema." In *Narrative, Apparatus, Ideology*, ed. Philip Rosen. New York: Columbia University Press, 1986.

Bazin, André. "On the *Politique des Auteurs.*" In *Cahiers du Cinema*, ed. Jim Hillier. London: British Film Institute, 1985.

Beauchamp, Gorman. "Henry V: Myth, Movie, Play." *College Literature* 5 (1978): 228–38.

Benjamin, Walter. "The Work of Art in the Age of Mechanical Reproduction." In *Illuminations*, trans. Harry Zohn, ed. Hannah Arendt. New York: Schocken Books, 1969.

Booth, Wayne C. *The Rhetoric of Fiction.* Chicago: The University of Chicago Press, 1961.

Brecht, Bertolt. *Brecht on Theater.* Ed. and trans. John Willett. New York: Hill and Wang, 1964.

Brown, Dan. *The Da Vinci Code.* New York: Doubleday, 2003.

Buchman, Lorne M. *Still in Movement: Shakespeare on Screen.* New York: Oxford University Press, 1991.

Cahir, Linda Costanzo. "Narratological Parallels in Joseph Conrad's *Heart of Darkness* and Francis Ford Coppola's *Apocalypse Now.*" *Literature/Film Quarterly* 20.3 (1992): 181–187.

Cahir, Stephen. *"The Unbearable Lightness of Being." Novels into Film.* Eds. John C. Tibbetts and James M. Welsh. New York: Facts on File, 1998.

Cain, James. *Mildred Pierce.* New York: Vintage Books, 1989.

Callenbach, Ernest. "The *Auteur* Policy." *Film Quarterly* 17.1 (1963): 57.

Cameron, Ian A., *et al.* "*Movie* Vs. Kael." *Film Quarterly* 17.1 (1963): 57–62.

Canby, Vincent. "*Ran* Weathers the Seasons." *The New York Times*. http://movies2.nytimes.
      com/gst/movies/review.html?title1=&title2=RAN%20%28MOVIE%29&reviewer=
      Vincent%20Canby&v_id=40236. 18 September 2003.
Chandler, Raymond. *The Simple Art of Murder*. Boston, MA: Houghton Mifflin, 1972.
Clarke, Arthur C. "The Sentinel." In *The Mirror of Infinity*, ed. Robert Silverberg, 135–144.
      New York: Harper & Row Publishers, 1970.
Cohen, Keith, ed. *Writing in a Film Age: Essays by Contemporary Novelists*. Ed. Keith Cohen.
      Niwot: University of Colorado, 1991.
Corman, Roger. *How I Made a Hundred Movies in Hollywood and Never Lost a Dime*. Bal-
      timore, MD: Midnight Marquee Press, Inc., 2000.
Cross, Milton, and David Ewen. *New Encyclopedia of the Great Composers and Their Music*.
      Revised and expanded edition. Vol. 2. Garden City, New York: Doubleday, 1969.
Cunningham, Michael. *The Hours*. New York: Farrar, Straus and Giroux, 1998.
Davies, Anthony. *Filming Shakespeare's Plays*. Cambridge: Cambridge University Press, 1991.
Davis, Paul, *et al.*, eds. *The Bedford Anthology of World Literature: The Middle Period, 100
      C.E.–1450*. New York: Bedford/St. Martin's, 2004.
Dean, Anne. *David Mamet: Language as Dramatic Action*. Rutherford, NJ: Fairleigh Dick-
      inson University Press, 1990.
Diether, Anton. *Moby Dick: Screenplay*. Moby Dick Productions Pty. Ltd. 13 March 1997.
_____. Personal interview. 10 December 2002.
Donaldson, Peter S. *Shakespearean Films/Shakespearean Directors*. Boston: Unwin Hyman,
      1990.
Du Maurier, Daphne. "The Birds." In *The Birds and Other Stories*. London: Pan Books,
      Ltd., 1977.
_____. "Don't Look Now." In *No, But I Saw the Movie: The Best Short Stories Ever Made
      into Film*, ed. David Wheeler. New York: Penguin Books, 1989.
Duras, Marguerite. "Green Eyes (*Les Yeux verts*): Selections." In *Writing in a Film Age:
      Essays by Contemporary Novelists*, ed. Keith Cohen, 96–103. Niwot: University of
      Colorado, 1991.
Ebb, Fred, and Bob Fosse. *Chicago: A Musical Vaudeville*. New York: Samuel French, 1976.
Ellmann, Richard. *James Joyce*. New York: Oxford University Press, 1959.
Erskine, Thomas L., and James M. Welsh, eds. *Film Adaptations of Plays on Video*. West-
      port, CT.: Greenwood Press, 2000.
Farley, Walter. *The Black Stallion*. New York: Random House, 1969.
Fitzgerald, F. Scott. *The Great Gatsby*. New York: Charles Scribner's Sons, 1953.
Frank, Alan. *The Films of Roger Corman*. London: B.T. Batsford Ltd, 1998.
Goodwin, James. *Akira Kurosawa and Intertextual Cinema*. Baltimore, MD: The Johns
      Hopkins University Press, 1994.
Gottlieb, Sidney, ed. *Hitchcock on Hitchcock: Selected Writings and Interviews*. Berkeley:
      University of California Press, 1995.
Halliwell, Leslie, ed. *Halliwell's Film Guide*. 7th edition. New York: Collins Publishing
      Group, 1987.
Harbage, Alfred. "*King Lear*: Introduction." In *William Shakespeare: The Complete Works*,
      ed. Alfred Harbage, 1060–1064. New York: The Viking Press, 1971.
Hemingway, Ernest. "The Killers." *The Short Stories*, 256–265. New York, Scribner Clas-
      sics, 1997.
Hitchcock, Alfred. "*Rear Window*" *Focus on Hitchcock*. Ed. Albert J. LaValley. Englewood
      Cliffs, N.J.: Prentice-Hall, 1972.
Hoffman, Daniel. *Poe, Poe, Poe, Poe, Poe, Poe, Poe*. New York: Doubleday, 1972.
Howard, James. *Stanley Kubrick Companion*. London: B. T. Batsford Ltd, 1999.
Joyce, James. *Dubliners: Text Criticism, and Notes*. Eds. Robert Scholes and A. Walton Litz.
      New York: The Viking Press, 1971.

Jung, Carl. "Approaching the Unconscious." In *Man and His Symbols*. New York: Dell, 1964.

Kael, Pauline. "Circles and Squares." *Film Quarterly* 16.3 (1963): 12–26.

_____. "Criticism and Kids' Games." *Film Quarterly* 17.1 (1963): 62 64.

_____. *For Keeps*. New York: Dutton, 1994.

_____. *I Lost It at the Movies*. New York: Bantam Books, 1965.

Kaplan, E. Ann. *Women in Film Noir*. London: British Film Institute, 1980.

Leitch, Thomas. *The Encyclopedia of Alfred Hitchcock*. New York: Checkmark Books, 2002.

Levine, Stuart. *Edgar Poe: Seer and Craftsman*. Deland, FL.: Everett/Edwards, 1972.

Manvell, Roger. *Shakespeare and the Film*. London: J. M. Dent, 1971.

Nichols, Peter M. "Dr. Seuss' *The Cat in the Hat*." *The New York Times* 28 November 2003, late ed.: E13.

Olivier, Laurence. *Confessions of an Actor*. London: Weidenfeld and Nicholson, 1982.

Ooka, Shohei. *Fires on the Plain*. Trans. Ivan Morris. Tokyo, Japan: Charles E. Tuttle Company, 2001.

Oumano, Ellen. *Movies for a Desert Island*. New York: St. Martin's Press, 1986.

Parker, Barry, ed. *The Folger Shakespeare Filmography*. Washington, D.C.: The Folger Shakespeare Library, 1979.

Perry, Dennis R. "Imps of the Perverse: Discovering the Poe/Hitchcock Connection." *Literature/Film Quarterly* 24.4 (1996): 393–399.

Pickett, Rex. *Sideways: A Novel*. New York: St. Martin's Griffin, 2004.

Plato. "Symposium." In *The Portable Plato*, ed. Scott Buchanan, 121–190. New York: The Viking Press, 1968.

Poe, Edgar Allan. *Eureka*. Boston: Dana Estes, 1884.

_____. "The Philosophy of Composition." In *Essays and Reviews*, 13–25. New York: The Library of America, 1984.

_____. *The Works of Edgar Allan Poe*. 10 vols. New York: John Hovendon, 1959.

Prince, Stephen. *The Warrior's Camera: The Cinema of Akira Kurosawa*. Princeton, NJ: Princeton University Press, 1991.

"Production Notes for *The Age of Innocence*." Columbia Pictures Industries, 1993.

Puig, Manuel. "How the Provincial Argentine Left Literature for the Movies, Thereby Discovering the Immense Potentials of the Novel." In *Writing in a Film Age: Essays by Contemporary Novelists*, ed. Keith Cohen, 271–276. Niwot: University of Colorado, 1991.

Quinn, Patrick. *The French Face of Edgar Poe*. Carbondale and Edwardsville: Southern Illinois University Press, 1971.

Richie, Donald. *The Films of Akira Kurosawa*. Revised edition. Berkeley: University of California Press, 1984.

Rohmer, Eric. "Renoir Américain." *Cahiers du Cinema* 8.1 (1952).

Rosak, Theodore. *Flicker*. New York: Summit Books, 1991.

Sarris, Andrew. "The *Auteur* Theory and the Perils of Pauline." *Film Quarterly*. 16.4 (1963): 26–33.

_____. "Notes on the *Auteur* Theory in 1962." In *Film Theory and Criticism*, eds. Gerald Mast and Marshall Cohen. New York: Oxford University Press, 1974.

Shakespeare, William. *William Shakespeare: The Complete Works*. Ed. Alfred Harbage. New York: The Viking Press, 1971.

Spoto, Donald. *The Dark Side of Genius: The Life of Alfred Hitchcock*. Boston: Little, Brown, 1983.

Stam, Robert. *Reflexivity in Film and Literature*. New York: Columbia University Press, 1992.

Sterritt, David. *The Films of Alfred Hitchcock*. Cambridge: Cambridge University Press, 1993.

Tibbetts, John. *The American Theatrical Film*. Bowling Green, Ohio: Bowling Green State University, 1985.

Tibbetts, John C., and James M. Welsh. *The Encyclopedia of Stage Plays into Film*. New York: Facts On File, Inc., 2001.

Trauffaut, François. *Hitchcock*. Revised edition. New York: Simon and Schuster, 1985.

Triwush, Ken. personal interview. 17 September 2003.

Van Ness, Elizabeth. "Is a Cinema Studies Degree the New MBA?" *New York Times*. 6 March 2005, late ed., sec. 2:1, 15.

Vardac, A. Nicholas. *Stage to Screen: Theatrical Origins of Early Film: David Garrick to D. W. Griffith*. New York: Da Capo Press, 1949.

Watkins, Maurine. *Chicago*. New York: Alfred A. Knopf, 1928.

Welsh, James M., Richard Vela, and John C. Tibbetts. *Shakespeare into Film*. New York: Checkmark Books, 2002.

Welsh, James M., and Thomas L. Erskine, eds. *Literature/Film Quarterly*. Shakespeare Issues: 1:4 (1973), 4:2 (1976), 5:4 (1977), 11:3 (1983), 14:4 (1986), 20:4 (1992), 22:2 (1994), 25:2 (1997), 28:2 (2000), 29:2 (2001), 30:3 (2002).

Wharton, Edith. *The Age of Innocence*. New York: Collier Books, 1992.

_____. "Permanent Values in American Fiction." *Saturday Review of Literature* 10 (7 April 1934): 603–604.

Wilbur, Richard. "Edgar Allan Poe." In *Major Writers of America,* eds. Perry Miller, *et al.* New York: Harcourt, Brace & World, 1962.

Woolrich, Cornell. "Rear Window." In *No, But I Saw the Movie: The Best Short Stories Ever Made into Film*, ed. David Wheeler. New York: Penguin Books, 1989.

Yates, James N. *"King Lear."* In *The Encyclopedia of Stage Plays into Film*. Eds. John C. Tibbetts and James M. Welsh. New York: Facts On File, 2001.

Index